Houghton Mifflin

English

Shirley Haley-James   John Warren Stewig

Marcus T. Ballenger   June Grant Shane

Jacqueline L. Chaparro   C. Ann Terry

Nancy C. Millett

Houghton Mifflin Company   Boston

Atlanta   Dallas   Geneva, Illinois   Lawrenceville, New Jersey   Palo Alto   Toronto

Acknowledgments

"Action," from *The Zoo That Grew* by Ilo Orleans. Copyright © 1960 by Ilo Orleans. Reprinted by permission of Karen S. Solomon.

"Always Wondering," from *I Wonder How, I Wonder Why* by Aileen Fisher. Copyright © 1962 by Aileen Fisher. Reprinted by permission of the author.

"The Ant and the Dove," from *Aesop's Fables,* retold by Anne Terry White. Copyright © 1964 by Anne Terry White. Reprinted by permission of Random House, Inc.

"Ants," adapted from *Ants* by Charles A. Schoenknecht; additional excerpt on p. 370. Copyright © 1961 by Follett Publishing Co., reprinted by permission of Modern Curriculum Press, Inc.

"Arthur's Thanksgiving," from *Arthur's Thanksgiving: An Arthur Adventure* by Marc Brown; additional excerpt on p. 177. Copyright © 1983 by Marc Brown. By permission of Little, Brown and Company, in association with The Atlantic Monthly Press.

"The Best Town in the World," adapted from *The Best Town in the World* by Byrd Baylor; additional excerpt on p. 240. Text copyright © 1982 Byrd Baylor. Reprinted with the permission of Charles Scribner's Sons.

"The Fourth," from *Where the Sidewalk Ends: The Poems & Drawings of Shel Silverstein.*

Copyright © 1974 by Snake Eye Music, Inc. Reprinted by permission of Harper & Row, Publishers, Inc., and Jonathan Cape Ltd.

"The Geese" ("Los Gansos") by José Juan Tablada, from *Haiku of a Day: Anthology of Mexican Poetry,* translated by Samuel Beckett and compiled by Octavio Paz. Reprinted by permission of Indiana University Press. Further use is prohibited by law.

"The Grasshopper," from *One at a Time* by David McCord. Copyright 1952 by David McCord. By permission of Little, Brown and Company, and Harrap Limited.

"The Horses" by Elizabeth Coatsworth reprinted by permission of Grosset & Dunlap from *The Sparrow Bush* by Elizabeth Coatsworth, copyright © 1966 by Grosset & Dunlap, Inc.

"How to Dig a Hole to the Other Side of the World," excerpted from *How to Dig a Hole to the Other Side of the World* by Faith McNulty; additional excerpt on p. 106. Text copyright © 1979 by Faith McNulty. Reprinted by permission of Harper & Row, Publishers, Inc.

"A Letter from the Author," from "Meet Your Author: Clyde Robert Bulla" by Clyde Robert Bulla. Reprinted by permission of *Cricket Magazine,* © 1980 by Open Court Publishing Company.

"The Meal," from *Dogs & Dragons, Trees & Dreams: A Collection of Poems* by Karla Kuskin. Copyright © 1962 by Karla Kuskin. Reprinted by permission of Harper & Row, Publishers, Inc.

"My Friend Jacob," adapted from *My Friend Jacob* by Lucille Clifton; additional excerpts on pp. 36, 39, and 41. Text copyright © 1980 by Lucille Clifton. Reprinted by permission of the publisher, E. P. Dutton, a division of New American Library, and Curtis Brown, Ltd.

"Oasis of the Stars," adapted from *Oasis of the Stars* by Olga Economakis; additional excerpt on p. 107. Copyright © 1965 by Olga Economakis, reprinted by permission of Coward-McCann.

(Acknowledgments continued on page 437.)

Table of Contents

Unit 1 1

Grammar: The Sentence

Unit 2 28

Reading and Writing: A Story About Yourself

Unit 3 · 56

Grammar: Nouns

Unit 4 · 92

Reading and Writing: Instructions

Unit 5 128

Grammar: Verbs

Unit 6 168

Reading and Writing: Story

Unit 9 260

Mechanics: Capitalization and Punctuation

Unit 10 294

Reading and Writing: Letters

Grammar

Where
Have you been dear?
What
Have you seen dear?
What
Did you do there?

Karla Kuskin
from "Where Have You Been Dear?"

The Sentence

Getting Ready When we speak, we usually speak in sentences. Most of the time, we are telling or asking something. In this unit, you will learn more about the different kinds of sentences we use.

Activities

Listening Listen as the sentences on the opposite page are read. Do the sentences tell or ask? How do you know? Who do you think is speaking?

Speaking Look at the picture. What do you see? Suppose the girl in the picture goes home and is asked the questions in the poem. How do you think she would answer each one? Answer in sentences. Have someone write the sentences on the board.

A **sentence** is a group of words that tells a complete thought. It tells who or what, and it tells what happens.

NOT SENTENCES
My best friend.
Barks all night.

My best friend tells who or what. It does not tell what happens. *Barks all night* tells what happens. It does not tell who or what.

SENTENCES
My best friend found a dog.
The dog barks all night.

These groups of words are sentences. They tell who or what, and they tell what happens.

Guided Practice Which groups of words are sentences? Which groups are not sentences? Why?

Example: Buddy does many tricks.   *sentence*

1. A furry tail.
2. Buddy barks.
3. Big paws and floppy ears.
4. He sleeps all day.
5. His favorite rubber ball.
6. He plays with the cat.
7. They never fight.

lives here.

Buddy

More Practice Read the two groups of words after each number. Write the group of words that is a sentence.

Example: Live in the water.
Beavers live in ponds.   *Beavers live in ponds.*

8. Good swimmers.
Beavers swim fast.

9. They have flat tails.
Look like paddles.

10. Beavers steer with their tails.
Can swim under the water.

11. Together in small groups.
Beaver families work together.

12. They cut down trees with their teeth.
Very strong front teeth.

13. Beavers make houses out of sticks.
Made of big sticks and small stones.

14. Mud from the river.
Mud holds the sticks together.

15. Young beavers stay warm.
Dry all winter long.

Writing Application: Sentences
Imagine you are in a pet store. Pick your favorite animal. Write five sentences about the animal.

2 | Statements and Questions

Every sentence begins with a capital letter. There are four kinds of sentences. Statements and questions are two kinds.

1. A sentence that tells something is a **statement**. It ends with a period.

STATEMENTS: Kirk runs every morning.
He jogs around the lake.

2. A sentence that asks something is a **question**. It ends with a question mark.

QUESTIONS: How far does Kirk run?
Can he run a mile?

Guided Practice Which sentences are statements? Which sentences are questions? What mark should end each sentence?

Example: Is Peg nine years old   *question*   ?

1. Peg is my neighbor
2. What is her best sport
3. It is softball

4. She can play with us
5. Can she pitch
6. Peg can catch

Summing up

▶ All sentences begin with a capital letter.
▶ A **statement** is a sentence that tells something. It ends with a period.
▶ A **question** is a sentence that asks something. It ends with a question mark.

More Practice

A. Write *statement* if the sentence tells something.
Write *question* if the sentence asks something.

Example: Carlos is my best friend. *statement*

   7. Where is Carlos?
   8. We like to play soccer.
   9. Would you like to play?
 10. How far can you kick the ball?
 11. Will you come to the game?
 12. You can meet us at the school later.
 13. I will find Carlos.

B. Write each sentence. Start with a capital letter.
End with the correct mark.

Example: do you like the zoo
Do you like the zoo?

 14. what is your favorite animal
 15. monkeys are my favorite
 16. what kind of food do monkeys
      like to eat
 17. monkeys love bananas
 18. can monkeys climb trees
 19. they never fall
 20. they swing with their tails
 21. do you see the baby monkeys
 22. they stay near their mother

Writing Application: Creative Writing

Imagine that you have your own zoo. What kind of
animals do you have? Write five sentences about your
zoo animals. Make sure that at least two of your
sentences are questions.

3 | Commands and Exclamations

You have learned about two kinds of sentences, statements and questions. Two other kinds of sentences are commands and exclamations.

1. A **command** is a sentence that tells someone to do something. It ends with a period.

   COMMANDS: Please hold my bat.
   Watch the ball.

Start the game.

2. An **exclamation** is a sentence that shows strong feeling, such as excitement, surprise, or fear. It ends with an **exclamation point** (!).

   EXCLAMATIONS: She hit a home run!
   Our team won the game!

Guided Practice Which of the following sentences are commands? Which sentences are exclamations?

Example: Baseball is great! *exclamation*

1. Please play with us.
2. Pick up the bat.
3. Look at the pitcher.
4. Here comes the ball!
5. Hit the ball hard.
6. It is over the fence!

Summing up

▶ A **command** is a sentence that tells someone to do something. It ends with a period.
▶ An **exclamation** is a sentence that shows strong feeling. It ends with an **exclamation point** (!).

More Practice

A. Write each command correctly.

Example: come to the game   *Come to the game.*

7. get the bat
8. sit here with me
9. watch our team
10. pick the best player
11. please bring the juice for our team
12. hit the ball past the pitcher
13. throw the ball to first base
14. help me find my glove
15. listen for the score
16. have a good time at the game

B. Write each exclamation correctly.

Example: paul is a great hitter
         Paul is a great hitter!

17. i caught the ball
18. paul struck out
19. i hit the first home run of the game
20. the crowd cheered for me
21. my team won the game
22. it was a wonderful game
23. we are in first place
24. we will get the gold medal
25. i cannot wait until the next game
26. baseball is a great sport

HOME 5   VISITORS 4

It's a home run!

Writing Application: Creative Writing

Pretend that you are in a baseball game. You are the
baseball. Write about the game. Write three
exclamations and three commands.

4 | The Subject of a Sentence

You know that a sentence is a group of words that tells a complete thought. The **subject** is the part of a sentence that tells whom or what the sentence is about. The subject usually comes at the beginning of the sentence.

The subject of the first sentence below is *Sam*. What are the subjects of the other sentences?

Sam walked to the beach.

He brought a towel.

The rocky beach looked crowded.

Some people sat under umbrellas.

The subject can be one word or more than one word. You can always find the subject of a sentence by asking, Whom or what is the sentence about?

Guided Practice What is the subject of each sentence?

Example: The children walked along the shore.
The children

1. The water looked blue.
2. Some strong waves splashed.
3. Ana played in the sand.
4. She made a castle.
5. Beautiful shells lay on the sand.

The shells are pink and purple.

▶ The **subject** tells whom or what the sentence is about.

More Practice Write each sentence. Underline the subject.

Example: My family went on a trip.
My family went on a trip.

6. Our neighbors came along with us.
7. We stayed in cabins.
8. The cabins were in the woods.
9. My brothers explored the woods.
10. Joey saw a baby rabbit.
11. The rabbit had big ears.
12. Tim heard an owl.
13. It hooted loudly.
14. A gray squirrel ran up a tree.
15. My little sister walked to the lake.
16. The lake was near the cabins.
17. Frogs jumped into the water.
18. They made funny noises.
19. We fished in the lake.
20. My new pole was heavy.
21. Mom caught three fish.
22. One big fish got away.
23. My father cooked the fish.
24. The dinner tasted great.

Writing Application: Sentences

Pretend that you and some friends are going on a trip.
Write five statements about your trip. Make sure that
each sentence has a subject.

5 | The Predicate of a Sentence

Every sentence has two parts. The subject is one part of a sentence. The other part of a sentence is the predicate. The **predicate** tells what the subject does or is. The predicate can be one word or more than one word.

SUBJECT	PREDICATE
Jenny	won a prize .
The crowd	clapped .
She	is happy .
Her brother	rode on the rides .
He	had fun .

Guided Practice What is the predicate of each sentence?

Example: Music floats through the fair.
floats through the fair

1. A man sells balloons.
2. The clowns are funny.
3. Roberto laughs.
4. The young children pet the animals.
5. We bought a ticket for a ride.

Summing up

▶ The **predicate** is the part of a sentence that tells what the subject does or is.

More Practice

A. Write each sentence. Underline the predicate.

Example: Emily takes swimming lessons.
Emily <u>*takes swimming lessons.*</u>

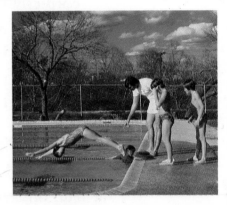

6. Sam goes with her.
7. They take lessons together.
8. Each lesson lasts an hour.
9. The two children listen.
10. A coach teaches Emily.
11. Another coach watches Sam.
12. Sam dives from a board.
13. He dives well.
14. Everyone follows the safety rules.

B. Write each sentence. Draw a line between the subject and the predicate.

Example: Emily swims on the school team.
Emily|swims on the school team.

15. The team practices after school.
16. Emily is the team captain.
17. Her team swims against another school.
18. The first race begins.
19. Each team dives into the water.
20. It is a close race.
21. The crowd cheers.
22. Emily won!

Writing Application: Sentences

Pretend that you are swimming. You find a treasure chest. Write five statements about what you find. Make sure that each sentence has a subject and a predicate.

6 | Correcting Run-on Sentences

Two or more sentences that run together are called **run-on sentences.** Use end marks and capital letters correctly to keep sentences from running together.

WRONG: Have you ridden on a train it is fun.
RIGHT: Have you ridden on a train? It is fun.

WRONG: Eva likes trains she takes train trips.
RIGHT: Eva likes trains. She takes train trips.

Guided Practice How can you correct these run-on sentences?

Example: The train is fast the wheels are loud.
The train is fast. The wheels are loud.

1. The train goes to cities it makes many stops.
2. Where else does it go it travels everywhere.
3. Does Eva see many farms once she saw cows.
4. She saw a big tractor a dog ran after it.
5. Eva waved to a farmer he waved back.

> ▶ Two or more sentences that run together are called **run-on sentences.**
> ▶ Do not run sentences together.

More Practice Write each run-on sentence as two sentences. Use capital letters and end marks correctly.

Example: I have a garden it is big.
I have a garden. It is big.

6. Would you like to see it do you have time?
7. I work in the garden myself my mother helps.
8. My garden is rocky I rake out the rocks.
9. I need to pull the weeds they grow so fast.
10. Some weeds are big I dig them out.
11. I planted flowers which ones do you like?
12. Some roses are red some roses are yellow.
13. Do you want to smell them they smell sweet.
14. The sunflowers are huge they are ten feet tall.
15. The bees love the garden they buzz loudly.
16. I also grow vegetables my tomatoes are the best.
17. Have you seen the tomatoes they are ripe.
18. Do you want some I cannot eat them all.
19. I see a ladybug it is on a tomato leaf.
20. We ate the beans they tasted crunchy.
21. Yesterday I planted carrot seeds I hope they grow.
22. A garden is fun you should try it.

Writing Application: Creative Writing
Pretend that you have an unusual plant. What things can it do? Write five sentences about your plant. Be sure you have not written any run-on sentences.

Building Vocabulary

The dachshund barked and wagged its tail.

Using Word Clues

Look at the picture above. What does the word *dachshund* mean? How do you know?

You do not always need a dictionary to find the meaning of a new word. Sometimes the other words in a sentence will give you a clue. What does the word *intelligent* mean in the sentence below?

Lynn is intelligent and learns very quickly.

The words *learns very quickly* give you a clue. The word *intelligent* means "smart."

Often another sentence will explain the meaning of a word.

Two colorful teals swam in the lake. They quacked softly as they swam along.

The sentences tell you that teals swim and quack. A teal, then, must be some kind of duck.

Practice

Write the word or words that have almost the same meaning as the underlined word.

Example: We saw a movie about a <u>baboon</u>. What big
     hands and a long tail it has!
     a. goat **b.** turtle **c.** monkey *monkey*

1. Al wore his <u>moccasins</u> and packed his sneakers.
 a. mittens **b.** shoes **c.** belts

2. The <u>starling</u> flew over us. It had dark, shiny feathers.
 a. dog **b.** plane **c.** bird

3. Cora saw a <u>beetle</u> eating the leaves on her plant.
 a. spot **b.** insect **c.** flower

4. We plan to <u>dwell</u> in this house for many years.
 a. live **b.** ski **c.** fly

5. Joseph did not get to school until after ten o'clock. The
teacher asked why he was <u>tardy</u>.
 a. quiet **b.** dirty **c.** late

6. Ricardo got <u>drenched</u> in the rain.
 a. very wet **b.** dry **c.** tired

7. Dee played the <u>flute</u> instead of the piano.
 a. game **b.** instrument **c.** radio

8. Grant was <u>concerned</u> about his sick bird.
 a. happy **b.** worried **c.** excited

Writing Application: Writing Sentences

Write five sentences. In each sentence, use a silly word in place of a real word. Give word clues for it. Have a friend use them to guess the real word.

The flower roared. The lion roared.

Grammar-Writing Connection

Combining Sentences: Compound Sentences

Good writers know how to make their writing interesting. You can do this, too, by using sentences with different lengths. Sometimes two short sentences have ideas that go together. You can join them to make one longer sentence. Use a comma (,) and the word *and* when you join two sentences.

Joy read about frogs.
Rob learned about toads.
> Joy read about frogs, and Rob learned about toads.

Because the two short sentences have similar ideas, they can be made into one longer sentence.

Revising Sentences

Make each pair of sentences into one sentence. Write the new sentences.

Example: Joy went on a hike. Rob sat by the pond.
Joy went on a hike, and Rob sat by the pond.

1. Joy found a toad by a tree. Rob saw a frog in the pond.
2. The tree had many branches. The pond was deep.
3. She studied the toad. He watched his frog.
4. The frog's skin was smooth. The toad's skin was bumpy.
5. The frog leaped into the air. The toad hopped slowly.
6. Joy lifted the toad onto a rock. Rob helped the frog into the water.

Creative Writing

A Sunday Afternoon on the Island of La Grande Jatte
by Georges Seurat, © Art Institute of Chicago

There are many ways to paint a sunny day at the park. Georges Seurat had a special way. He made shapes out of tiny dots of color. In fact, this painting is all dots!

• What feeling do the dots give the picture?

Activities

1. **Tell about your day.** Pretend that you are one of the people in the picture. Write about your day in the park.
2. **Plan your picnic.** What would you pack in a picnic? Where would you go? Describe your perfect picnic.

Check-up: Unit 1

What Is a Sentence? *(p. 2)* Read the two groups of words after each number. Write the group that is a sentence.

1. The sky turned dark.
   Many dark clouds.
2. The sun away.
   The sun disappeared.
3. Hurt my ears.
   I heard thunder.
4. It rained all day.
   Water for the flowers.
5. I wore my raincoat.
   Boots by the door.
6. Splashed in puddles.
   My feet got wet.

Statements and Questions *(p. 4)* Write each sentence correctly.

7. what is the weather like at the South Pole
8. it is very cold all year long
9. people cannot live there
10. has anyone ever been to the South Pole
11. an explorer named Amundsen reached it first
12. how did he get to the South Pole
13. he and his men rode on dog sleds

Commands and Exclamations *(p. 6)* Write *command* if the sentence is a command. Write *exclamation* if the sentence is an exclamation.

14. It is such a beautiful day!
15. Come to the beach with us.
16. Put the towel under the umbrella.
17. Here comes a huge wave!
18. Watch me swim, please.
19. Feel the water on your feet.
20. My feet are frozen!

The Subject of a Sentence *(p. 8)* Write each sentence. Underline the subject.

21. Lara plays the piano.
22. She practices every day.
23. Mrs. Emma Jones gives Lara lessons.
24. The neighbors listen to her music.
25. The dog howls loudly.
26. Her three brothers wait outside.
27. My Uncle John likes her music.

The Predicate of a Sentence *(p. 10)* Write each sentence. Underline the predicate.

28. A map is like a picture.
29. Most maps have symbols.
30. Symbols stand for real places or things.
31. Mr. Bono made a map.
32. The map showed everything in town.
33. Isabel saw her street on the map.
34. John found the library.

Run-on Sentences *(p. 12)* Write each run-on sentence as two sentences.

35. Mom tells stories some stories are about me.
36. One story is funny it is about my pet spider.
37. Does your family tell stories do you hear the same stories many times?
38. My uncle tells the best stories they are about his days as a sailor.
39. One time he saw a huge whale the whale was over fifty feet long!
40. The huge whale knocked against the boat then it quickly swam away.

Enrichment

Unit One: The Sentence

Invent a Cereal

Pretend that you work at a cereal company. Your job is to invent a new cereal. It must be healthy and also fun to eat. Draw an ad for your cereal. Use commands and exclamations to tell why people should buy it.

Animal Riddles

What are your favorite animal riddles? Fold and staple paper to make a book. Write a riddle on one side of each page. On the back, write a complete sentence to answer it. Draw pictures to go on each page of your book.

Supermarket Sentences

Most math problems use only numbers, like $2 + 3 = 5$. This problem can also be written in sentences.

> Josh bought two cans of carrots. He also bought three cans of corn. How many cans did Josh buy?

You try. Write three math problems with numbers. Then make supermarket word problems. Exchange papers. Can you solve your partner's problems?

Sentence Snakes

Think about life in the desert. Has a snake crawled into your imagination? Write a sentence about the desert. Put the subject first. Draw the outline of a snake around your sentence. Color the subject of the sentence red and the predicate blue. Cut out your sentence snake. Cut it apart between the subject and the predicate. Exchange the blue half of your snake with a partner. Join your partner's blue half with your own red half. Does this new sentence make sense? If not, think up and write a new subject half.

Sentence Scramble

Players—2. **You need**—25 index cards. Write on them *the, children, big, ran, in, after, when, a, parrots, little, saw, to, but, and, some, old, an, castle, were, with, and, the, we, monkey, they.*
How to play—Take turns making sentences with the cards, such as "We saw a castle." Say where capital letters and end marks should be. Ask your partner if your sentence is correct.
Scoring—2 points for each word in a correct sentence. Subtract 5 points for each run-on. The player with the highest score wins.

1 | What Is a Sentence? (p. 2)

● Make these words into sentences. Match the words below with words from the Word Box.

Example: The sun _____.
The sun shines brightly.

1. Many children _____.
2. _____ are in a bucket.
3. _____ is salty.
4. A balloon _____.
5. _____ plays in the sand.
6. A dog _____.
7. The egg sandwiches _____.

barks
A little girl
taste good
splash in the water
Pretty shells
shines brightly
sails into the air
The water

▲ Write *sentence* if the group of words is a sentence. Write *not a sentence* if it is not a sentence.

Example: I saw a puppet show.   *sentence*

8. Four puppets on strings.
9. One puppet had green hair.
10. The puppets sang a song.
11. On the stage.
12. Many people came to the show.
13. They liked the show.
14. Laughed out loud at the puppets.

■ Use each group of words to write a sentence.

Example: a paper bag puppet
Maria made a paper bag puppet.

15. small lunch bag
16. stuffed the bag
17. a funny face
18. string and yarn
19. buttons for eyes
20. large nose and teeth
21. colored the mouth
22. looked good

2 | Statements and Questions (p. 4)

● Write *statement* if the sentence tells something. Write *question* if the sentence asks something.

Example: When did dinosaurs live? *question*

1. Dinosaurs lived long ago.
2. Most dinosaurs were very large.
3. How big were they?
4. Some dinosaurs were seventy feet long.
5. Karen read a book about dinosaurs.
6. Where did she get the book?
7. She got the book from Chris.
8. I would like to borrow the book.

▲ Write each sentence. Use the correct end mark.

Example: What is a tiger *What is a tiger?*

9. A tiger is a wild cat
10. It has tan fur with black stripes
11. Is a tiger as big as a lion
12. Where does a tiger live
13. A tiger lives in the jungle
14. How fast does a tiger run
15. Would you like to see a tiger

■ Write each sentence correctly.

Example: have you ever seen a giant panda
        Have you ever seen a giant panda?

16. what does a giant panda look like
17. it looks like a large bear
18. the panda has black and white fur
19. where can you find giant pandas
20. they live in forests
21. some giant pandas are in zoos
22. what do the animals eat

● Write *command* if the sentence tells someone to do something. Write *exclamation* if the sentence shows strong feeling.

Example: Throw the football.
         command

1. Start the game.
2. We are ahead!
3. Listen to the coach.
4. Wear your helmet.
5. Jeff caught the pass!
6. This game is exciting!
7. Please score some points.

▲ Write each command or exclamation correctly.

Example: help me build the doghouse   (command)
         Help me build the doghouse.

8. this doghouse will be great   (exclamation)
9. get a hammer   (command)
10. bring the nails   (command)
11. fifi is running in circles   (exclamation)
12. count the boards   (command)
13. carry the wood   (command)
14. we finally finished   (exclamation)
15. fifi loves the doghouse   (exclamation)

■ Write *statement, question, command,* or *exclamation* for each sentence.

Example: Today is the big race!   *exclamation*

16. Will you enter the race?
17. Bring your red bicycle.
18. Take along some water.
19. My parents will watch the race.
20. The race will be close!
21. When does the race begin?
22. I hope I win!

4 | The Subject (p. 8)

● Write the subject of each sentence.

Example: The weather|is warm.   *The weather*

1. Apple trees|bloom in the spring.
2. Two robins|build a nest.
3. The children|picked pretty flowers.
4. Michael|washed the car.
5. A yellow kite|floated in the air.
6. Dogs|played behind a rock.
7. We|planned a picnic for Allen.

▲ Write the subject of each sentence.

Example: My family likes the winter.   *My family*

8. The wind feels cold.
9. We wear warm jackets and gloves.
10. Ed skates on the pond.
11. Tony carries his sled to the park.
12. My little sister slides down the hill.
13. She laughs.
14. Our funny snowman has a big head.
15. Dad chops wood in the backyard.

■ Change the silly subject in each sentence to a subject that makes sense. Write the new sentences. Underline the subjects.

Example: Radio won a prize.   *Linda won a prize.*

16. My parents sing in the trees.
17. The dog mows the lawn.
18. Baby helps him rake the leaves.
19. Our old car has a pool.
20. The tree gave a pool party yesterday.
21. The young pencils played tag.
22. My favorite fruit is the summer.

5 | The Predicate (p. 10)

● Write the predicate of each sentence.
Example: The sky|looks dark. *looks dark*
1. Lightning|flashes.
2. Rain|begins to fall.
3. Thunder|rumbles in the sky.
4. Some people|run for cover.
5. The storm|is over quickly.
6. The sun|shines again.

▲ Write each sentence. Draw a line between the subject and the predicate.
Example: Uncle Henry is a circus clown.
       Uncle Henry|is a circus clown.
7. His nose is big and red.
8. He juggles three balls in the air.
9. Funny cars chase him around the ring.
10. A black hat drops on the floor.
11. A helper counts to ten.
12. A large bird flies out of the hat.
13. All the people clap.

■ Write each sentence. Draw one line under the subject. Draw two lines under the predicate.
Example: The forest animals listened for danger.
       The forest animals listened for danger.
14. A deer leaped over the logs.
15. Two small rabbits were afraid.
16. The gray squirrels ran up a tree.
17. Raccoons ran behind a large rock.
18. A chipmunk family dug a hole.
19. Robins flew away.
20. Some owls hooted.

● Write each run-on sentence as two sentences. The line shows where the first sentence ends and the second sentence begins.

Example: Birds are fun | do you like them?
    Birds are fun. Do you like them?

1. What do birds eat | some birds eat seeds.
2. Robins often eat worms | owls eat mice.
3. Andy has a pet duck | it is big and fluffy.
4. The duck loves the water | it is a funny pet.
5. My parrot talks | what does it say?
6. It says my name | it asks for food.

▲ Write each run-on sentence as two sentences.

Example: The city is busy it is very noisy.
    The city is busy. It is very noisy.

7. People drive to work they honk their horns.
8. Buses pass by where are they going?
9. Workers build a bridge it is long.
10. A police officer blows her whistle a truck stops.
11. Stores are open do you want to shop?
12. Do you see that tall building Jimmy lives there.

■ Some sentences below are run-on sentences. Write each run-on sentence correctly. Write *correct* if the sentence is correct.

Example: Some stars are very bright. *correct*

13. Stars are many sizes they are many colors.
14. Our sun is a yellow star is it very hot?
15. Some people think that stars make pictures.
16. Do some groups of stars look like animals?
17. One group looks like a bear another is like a lion.
18. One star is the North Star it does not move.

Reading and Writing

My friend Charlie is a really good old friend. I couldn't like him any better than I do, even if he owned a pony.

"I had a good dream last night," I told Charlie. "I dreamed that I had a bike that could go anywhere."

James Flora
from *My Friend Charlie*

A Story About Yourself

Getting Ready Do you like to tell about something you have done? When you tell about an event, you try to help your listeners imagine what you saw and felt. In this unit, you will learn how to write about a true experience and make it interesting to others.

Activities

Listening Listen as the sentences on the opposite page are read. Who is telling the story—Charlie or his friend? How do you know? What is this person probably going to tell about?

Speaking Look at the picture. Imagine that you are going to tell this boy a story about yourself. With your class, make a list of different kinds of experiences that would be interesting to tell about. Have someone write the ideas on chart paper. Keep the list. Use it for story ideas later on.

LITERATURE

How is Jacob a good friend to Sammy?
How is Sammy a good friend to Jacob?

My Friend Jacob

By Lucille Clifton

My best friend lives next door. His name is Jacob. He is my very very best friend.

We do things together, Jacob and me. We love to play basketball together. Jacob always makes a basket on the first try.

He helps me to learn how to hold the ball so that I can make baskets too.

My mother used to say "Be careful with Jacob and that ball; he might hurt you." But now she doesn't. She knows that Jacob wouldn't hurt anybody, especially his very very best friend.

I love to sit on the steps and watch the cars go by with Jacob. He knows the name of every kind of car. Even if he only sees it just for a minute, Jacob can tell you the kind of car.

He is helping me be able to tell the cars too. When I make a mistake, Jacob never ever laughs. He just says, "No, no, Sam, try again."

And I do. He is my best best friend.

When I have to go to the store, Jacob goes with me to help me. His mother used to say "You don't have to have Jacob tagging along with you like that, Sammy." But now she doesn't. She knows we like to go to the store together. Jacob helps me to carry, and I help Jacob to remember.

"Red is for stop," I say if Jacob forgets. "Green is for go."

"Thank you, Sam," Jacob always says.

Jacob's birthday and my birthday are two days apart. Sometimes we celebrate together.

Last year he made me a surprise. He had been having a secret for weeks and weeks, and my mother knew, and his mother knew, but they wouldn't tell me.

Jacob would stay in the house in the afternoon for half an hour every day and not say anything to me when he came out. He would just smile and smile.

On my birthday, my mother made a cake for me with eight candles, and Jacob's mother made a cake for him with seventeen candles. We sat on the porch and sang and blew out our candles. Jacob blew out all of his in one breath because he's bigger.

Then my mother smiled and Jacob's mother smiled and said, "Give it to him, Jacob dear." My friend Jacob smiled and handed me a card.

HAPPY BIRTHDAY SAM
JACOB

He had printed it all himself! All by himself, my name and everything! It was neat!

My very best friend Jacob does so much helping me, I wanted to help him too. One day I decided to teach him how to knock.

Jacob will just walk into somebody's house if he knows them. If he doesn't know them, he will stand by the door until somebody notices him and lets him in.

"I wish Jacob would knock on the door," I heard my mother say.

So I decided to help him learn. Every day I would tell Jacob, but he would always forget. He would just open the door and walk right in.

My mother said probably it was too hard for him and I shouldn't worry about it. But I felt bad because

Jacob always helped me so much, and I wanted to be able to help him too.

I kept telling him and he kept forgetting, so one day I just said, "Never mind, Jacob, maybe it is too hard."

"What's the matter, Sam?" Jacob asked me.

"Never mind, Jacob," was all I said.

Next day, at dinnertime, we were sitting in our dining room when me and my mother and my father heard this real loud knocking at the door. Then the door popped open and Jacob stuck his head in.

"I'm knocking, Sam!" he yelled.

Boy, I jumped right up from the table and went grinning and hugged Jacob, and he grinned and hugged me too. He is my very very very best friend in the whole wide world!

Questions

1. Why are Sammy and Jacob best friends?
2. Why was Sammy so excited about the card?
3. Think about the ways Sammy and Jacob are friends. What kind of a person makes a good friend? Explain.
4. The author of "My Friend Jacob" used words such as I, me, my, and we when Sammy was talking. When a story is written as though one of the characters is telling it, we say it is written in the **first person**. Why do you think an author might choose to tell a story in the first person?

33

Vern

By Gwendolyn Brooks

When walking in a tiny rain
Across the vacant lot,
A pup's a good companion—
If a pup you've got.

And when you've had a scold,
And no one loves you very,
And you cannot be merry,
A pup will let you look at him,
And even let you hold
His little wiggly warmness—

And let you snuggle down beside.
Nor mock the tears you have to hide.

Questions

1. Why is a pup a good companion, or friend?
2. What do the words *tiny rain* mean?
3. "Vern" is a **poem**, or a description written in a special way. A poem uses words in special ways to paint pictures in your mind and express feelings. How do you think the writer of this poem felt?

RESPONDING TO LITERATURE

The Reading and Writing Connection

Personal Response What do you and a good friend like to do together? Keep a journal, or notebook, of things you do. Include words that tell what you think and how you feel.

Creative Writing Write the word *friend* down the left side of your paper, one letter to a line. Use each letter to begin a word or group of words that has to do with friends.

Creative Activities

Draw Make a birthday card for a special friend. Write a message. Draw a present on the inside of the card.

Read Aloud Work together as a class. Take turns reading aloud from "My Friend Jacob." First, find parts that tell how Jacob helped Sammy. Then find parts that tell how Sammy helped Jacob. Finally, talk about other ways friends help each other.

Vocabulary

The word **companion** means someone who helps, lives with, or travels with another person. What pet is a good companion? Why?

Looking Ahead

A Story About Yourself In this unit, you will write a story about yourself. You will write a good story title. Is the title "My Friend Jacob" a good one? Why?

Listening/Speaking/Thinking

Listening: For Order

Listen as your teacher or a classmate reads part of "My Friend Jacob" below. In what order did things happen?

> Next day, at dinnertime, we were sitting in our dining room when me and my mother and my father heard this real loud knocking at the door. Then the door popped open and Jacob stuck his head in.
>
> "I'm knocking, Sam!" he yelled.
>
> Boy, I jumped right up from the table and went grinning and hugged Jacob.

These events happened in an order that makes sense. First, there was knocking at the door. Then the door opened and Jacob stuck his head in. When Sam realized Jacob was knocking, he hugged him.

Follow these guides when listening for order.

Listening Guides

1. Listen for each event.
2. Picture the events in your mind.
3. Think how one event leads to another.

Practice

Listen as your teacher reads a story. Be ready to tell the order of events.

Speaking: Discussing Writing

Jacob and Sammy helped each other learn to do new things. You and your classmates can help each other learn, also. One way is by listening to each other's writing and discussing it. Talking about your work with someone else can give you new ideas to make your writing better.

When someone asks you for help with his or her writing, use these guides.

Discussion Guides

1. Listen carefully as the writer reads to you.
2. Tell something you liked about the writing or retell what you heard.
3. Ask questions about anything that is unclear. You might ask questions like this:
   Can you describe what happened in more detail? How did you feel when ___?
4. Make suggestions when the writer asks for help.
5. Be polite.

Joan wrote a story. Then she asked Manny to listen to it. Here is what Joan read.

> On Saturday Becky and I washed her dog Big Al. He really hates a bath. Big Al hid under the porch, but we got him to the pool. I held his leash, and Becky washed him. Then Becky and I both fell into the pool. What a mess! It was funny, and we laughed.

Joan and Manny discussed the story. Read their discussion on the next page.

➡

- How did Manny show that he listened to Joan's story?
- What helpful questions did he ask?
- What new details can Joan add to her story now?

Practice

A. Read this story. Write two questions you could ask to help the writer give a clearer picture.

We went to the park to fly our kites. My kite got stuck in a tree. I could not get the kite down. Then we got it down and went home.

B. Find a partner. Listen as your partner reads a story. Then do these things:

1. Tell something you liked about the story.
2. Ask two questions about the story.
3. Ask your partner if he or she got any new ideas.

Thinking: Drawing Conclusions

Suppose your friends were dressed in heavy coats and hats. Their warm clothing plus your own experience would help you draw a conclusion, or figure out, that it was cold outside.

You can draw conclusions when you read, also. Read this part of "My Friend Jacob." Which clues help you draw a conclusion about how old Sammy and Jacob are?

> On my birthday, my mother made a cake for me with eight candles, and Jacob's mother made a cake for him with seventeen candles. We sat on the porch and sang and blew out our candles.

The words *eight candles* and *seventeen candles* are clues. You know from your own experience that the number of candles on a cake is the same as a person's age. You could draw a conclusion that Sammy is eight years old and Jacob is seventeen.

Practice

Read each group of sentences. Answer the questions. What clues and experiences helped you?

1. Paul rolled up his pajama sleeves. He made toast. Then he ran to catch the school bus.

   Was Paul making breakfast, lunch, or dinner?

2. Anna looked out the window. What a busy place! Small trucks raced about. A jet took off.

   Was Anna at a train station or an airport?

Composition Skills

Writing a Good Beginning

Have you ever started to read a story and found you could not stop reading until the end? The story probably had a beginning that grabbed your attention right away. Which story beginning below grabs your attention?

> **1.** A new boy moved into the neighborhood. His name was Jeff. He was quiet. He told me that he liked to act in plays.
>
> **2.** The day Jeff moved into the neighborhood my life changed forever. Who would have thought that such a quiet, shy boy was actually a famous movie star!

The first beginning is dull and unexciting. The second one grabs your attention. You want to learn more about the movie star and how he changed the writer's life.

Prewriting Practice

A. Choose something exciting you have done that will make a good story. Write two different story beginnings.

B. Find a partner. Read your story beginnings to each other out loud. Which beginning does your partner like better? Why?

Using Details

In "My Friend Jacob," Sammy could have told you just this much.

> Jacob and I like to watch the cars go by.

Now read the sentences below. What other **details**, or information, does Sammy add?

> I love to sit on the steps and watch the cars go by with Jacob. He knows the name of every kind of car. Even if he only sees it just for a minute, Jacob can tell you the kind of car.

Sammy told you that he and Jacob sit on the steps when they watch cars. He also told you that Jacob remembers the name of every car.

Whenever you write, your words and sentences should paint a clear, lively picture for your reader. If you use enough details, your reader will have a better idea of what happens.

Prewriting Practice

Rewrite the story below. Add details that help your readers picture what happens. When you rewrite the story, be sure to answer these questions.

What is the game?   Where does everyone hide?
Who plays it?   Why is the game fun?

Every summer evening, we play the same game. We each find a place to hide. Sometimes I find a good place to hide. It is fun. When it gets dark, we go home.

Writing a Good Title

"My Friend Jacob" is a good title. It fits the whole story but does not tell too much. It is short, easy to remember, and makes you want to read the story. Would "My Birthday Party" be a good title for the story about Sammy and Jacob? It would not be a good title because it does not fit the whole story. Read the story and the three titles below.

> I woke up and looked at my clock. It was 8 o'clock. I had overslept! I was going to be late for school. I jumped out of bed. I put on my clothes and brushed my hair. I rushed into the kitchen to eat my breakfast. I grabbed my school books and started to run out the door. Then I stopped short. Today was Saturday.
>
> **Getting Ready for School**
> **The Day I Woke Up and Forgot It Was Saturday**
> **A Mixed-up Morning**

• Which title is best? Why?

Look at how capital letters are used in a title. The first word and each important word begin with a capital letter.

Prewriting Practice

Write two other titles for the poem "Vern." Compare your titles with those of your classmates. Which title do you like best?

The Grammar Connection

Avoiding Stringy Sentences

Stringy sentences have too many *and*'s or *and so*'s. Do not use stringy sentences when you write. Never use *and so* in your sentences.

STRINGY: My best friend's name is Jacob and he lives next door and so we do many things together.

BETTER: My best friend's name is Jacob. He lives next door. We do many things together.

BETTER: My best friend's name is Jacob, and he lives next door. We do many things together.

Practice Rewrite each stringy sentence two times. Write it as two sentences. Then write it as three sentences.

1. Jacob loves basketball and he teaches me how to play and so I can make baskets too.
2. Jacob and I go to the store and he helps carry packages and I teach him about traffic lights.
3. We celebrate our birthdays together and last year he made me a card and he kept it a secret.
4. My mother made me a cake and Jacob's mother made him a cake and so we blew out the candles.
5. I try to teach Jacob things and he keeps forgetting and I feel bad because he's always helping me.

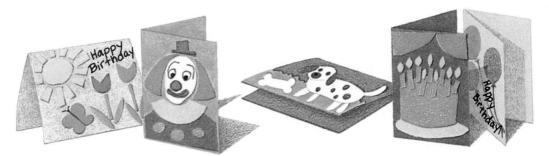

The Writing Process
How to Write a Story About Yourself

Step 1: Prewriting

Daniel made a list of some things he had done or that had happened to him. He thought about each topic.

my camping trip — There were too many things to tell about.

when I cut myself — He didn't remember this very well.

playing a game — This wasn't about one special time.

the hurricane — This had been exciting!

Daniel's grandmother would enjoy reading about the storm. He circled *the hurricane*.

On Your Own

1. **Think and discuss** Make a list of things you have done or that have happened to you. Use the Ideas page for help. Discuss your topics with a partner.
2. **Choose** Ask these questions about each topic.
   Do I remember exactly what happened?
   Would I enjoy writing about this?
   Circle the topic you want to write about.
3. **Explore** What will you write? What details will you include? Do one of the activities under "Exploring Your Topic" on the Ideas page.

Ideas for Prewriting

Choosing Your Topic

Topic Ideas

My friend's party
Getting a pet
An accident
A scary experience
My first bike ride
A plane trip
A new baby
An important day

Story Ideas

Read these questions for ideas.

What unusual things have happened to you?

What exciting things have you done?

Think about a special day in your life. Why was it special?

Exploring Your Topic

Brainstorm

Write everything you can think of about your topic for three minutes. Your ideas do not have to be in sentences. Here is part of Daniel's paper.

- branches from trees
- a loud crash
- flickering lights
- tape for windows

Draw It

Draw a picture of your story topic. Show details. Tell your story and show your picture to a partner. What questions does your partner have?

Step 2: Write a First Draft

Daniel was ready to write his first draft. He used the ideas he had brainstormed. He did not worry about making mistakes. He could correct them later.

Daniel's first draft

- What other ways could Daniel begin his story?
- Where could Daniel add more details?
- Why did he cross out some words?

> One day there was a hurricane.
> We had taped all the windows.
> We almost ran out of tape.
> Suddenly a branch crashed to the
> ground ~~and so~~ the lites flickered
> as if they weren't sure of
> something and went out. Then it
> was quiet the hurricane was over.

On Your Own

1. **Think about your story and your readers** Ask yourself these questions.
   Who will read my story?
   What do I want the reader to know and feel?
2. **Write** Write your first draft. Write a good beginning. Use details. Write on every other line. Do not worry about mistakes now.

Step 3: Revise

Daniel read the first draft of his story. He wrote a more interesting beginning. He added a title.

Then Daniel read his story to Amy. He asked Amy if he needed to add anything else.

Reading and responding

That was exciting! Why were the windows taped?

The tape kept the glass from shattering.

Weren't you frightened?

You bet! I'll add that.

Daniel thanked Amy. Then he made more revisions.

Part of Daniel's revised draft

The Scary Hurricane

"Daniel!" my sister shouted. "The hurricane is starting!" We were so scared that we hugged each other.

~~One day there was a hurricane.~~
to keep the glass from shattering
We had taped all the windows.

~~We almost ran out of tape.~~

Think and Discuss

- Is Daniel's title a good one? Why?
- Is his new beginning better? Why?
- What details did he add? Why?

On Your Own

1. **Think again** Read your story. Ask yourself these questions.

   Will my beginning catch my reader's interest?
   Where could I add more details?

2. **Revise** Make changes in your first draft. Write a new beginning. If you like your new one better, tape it over your first one. Add details. Write a good title. You may want to use words from the thesaurus below or the one beginning on page 414.

3. **Read/Listen/Respond** Read your story to a classmate or to your teacher.

Ask your listener:	As you listen:
"Is my beginning interesting?" "Did I tell enough?" "Where could I add details?"	I must listen carefully. Do I get a clear picture of what happened? What else would I like to know?

4. **Revise** Think about your partner's suggestions. Do you have any other ideas? Make those changes.

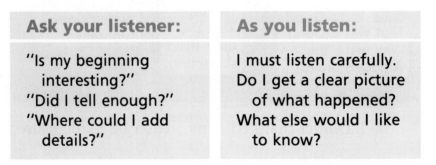

Thesaurus

big large, enormous, huge, tremendous
brave bold, daring
excited eager, enthusiastic
frighten scare, alarm, terrify

happen take place, occur
happy glad, cheerful, joyful, jolly
proud pleased, satisfied
sad unhappy, gloomy

Step 4: Proofread

Daniel proofread his story for mistakes in spelling, capitalization, and punctuation. He used a dictionary to check spellings. He used proofreading marks to make his changes. Here is the way Daniel's story looked after he proofread it.

Part of Daniel's proofread draft

Suddenly a branch crashed to the ground. ~~and so~~ the ~~lites~~ *lights* flickered as if they weren't sure of something and went out. Then it was quiet. the hurricane was over.

Think and Discuss

- Which spelling was corrected?
- Which end marks did he add? Why?
- Why did he change two small letters?

On Your Own

1. **Proofreading Practice** Proofread this paragraph. Correct the spelling mistake and run-on sentence. One word should have a capital letter. One sentence has the wrong end mark. Write the paragraph correctly.

    Grandpa took me to the zoo I loved it! I thought the seels were funny. have you seen the monkeys. They ate my peanuts. I laughed so hard.

Proofreading Marks

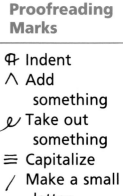

⌐	Indent
∧	Add something
℮	Take out something
≡	Capitalize
/	Make a small letter

2. Proofreading Application Now proofread your story. Use the Proofreading Checklist and the Grammar and Spelling Hints below. Use a dictionary to check spellings.

Proofreading Checklist

Did I

☑ **1.** begin and end each sentence correctly?

☑ **2.** make each sentence a complete thought?

☑ **3.** spell all words correctly?

The Grammar/Spelling Connection

Grammar Hints

Remember these rules from Unit 1.

- A sentence has a subject and a predicate.
- Use a capital letter to begin each sentence.
- End each sentence with the correct mark.
- Do not run your sentences together.

Spelling Hints

- The long *a* sound may be spelled *ai* or *ay*. (r<u>ai</u>n, pl<u>ay</u>)
- The long *e* sound may be spelled *ee* or *ea*. (s<u>ee</u>d, p<u>ea</u>ch)

Step 5: Publish

Daniel made a final neat copy of his story. He included all the changes and corrections he had made.

Daniel made a block picture story. He drew six boxes on a piece of paper. He drew pictures in the boxes and wrote part of the story under each picture. He drew the pictures in order. Daniel shared it with his grandmother.

On Your Own

1. **Copy** Copy your story in your neatest handwriting.
2. **Check** Read over your story again to make sure you have not left out anything or made any copying mistakes.
3. **Share** Think of a special way to share your story.

Ideas for Sharing

- Paste your story on a large sheet of paper. Add photographs.
- Make a mobile.
- Make a booklet for your story. Read and show your story to a friend.

Writing Across the Curriculum
A Story About Yourself

Literature and Creative Writing

The poem "Vern" told the ways a dog can be a friend. "My Friend Jacob" told of the friendship between two boys.

Have fun using what you have learned about writing a story about yourself. Do one or more of these activities.

Remember these things:
Write a good beginning.
Use clear, interesting details.
Write a good title.

1. **Tell Jacob's story.** Pretend that you are Jacob. Write a story that tells about your friendship with Sammy. Be sure to tell the ways that Sammy is your friend.

2. **Where did you get that pet?** You own a strange pet. What is it? Write a story. Tell how you came to own this pet.

3. **Travel with a friend.** Pretend that you and a friend took a trip. Write a story about one exciting thing that happened. Tell what happened and why you were glad to have your friend along.

Physical Education

Stories about games and sports are very exciting. Many people enjoy hearing and telling about them.

Choose one or more of the following activities. Follow the five steps learned in this unit to write your story.

1. **Choose a game.** The pictures below show children enjoying a field day. Do you see any games that you play? Write a story about a day that you spent playing games with a group of people.

Writing Steps
1. Choose a Topic
2. Write a First Draft
3. Revise
4. Proofread
5. Publish

2. **Share the thrill.** Can you ride a bike? turn a cartwheel? swim? Write a story about the day you learned how to do something all by yourself. You may want to use some of the words in the box. Share your story with a younger child who is just learning these things.

| bicycle |
| skate |
| dive |
| swim |
| catch |

Book Report

Writing a Book Report

Maria read "My Friend Jacob" and liked it very much. She wanted to read another book about making friends. Maria chose *Angel Child, Dragon Child* by Michele Maria Surat. This is the book report she shared with her class.

Title Angel Child, Dragon Child

Author Michele Maria Surat

About the Book This book is about a family who came to this country from Vietnam. The story is told by Ut. Ut has four older sisters and a baby brother. The children live with their father. Their mother had to stay in Vietnam. She will join them when they save enough money for her ticket. Ut misses her mother very much.

It is hard to start at a new school. Ut does not speak much English. The children tease her. One boy is the meanest. His name is Raymond. Ut tries to be good like an angel child and brave like a dragon child.

My Opinion Read the book and find out how Ut made a friend. I like the way it happened. I learned a lot about being a good friend.

Think and Discuss
- What is the title? Who is the author?
- Who is Ut? What kinds of problems does she have?
- Why does Maria like the book?

Share Your Book

Write a Book Report

1. **Title and Author** Write the complete title and the author's name.
2. **About the Book** Think about these things when you write this part of your report.
   - Who are the important people in the book? What are they like?
   - What part should I share? How can I tell what the story is about without telling too much?
3. **My Opinion** Write why you liked the book and why you think others would like to read this book.

Other Activities

- Draw pictures of important people in your book. Show your pictures when you share your book. Do not show pictures that tell the ending!
- Pretend you have just moved to the place where your story happens. Think of ways to make friends with the people in the book.
- Make a poster that shows things friends can do.

The Book Nook

Stevie	**The Hundred Dresses**
by John Steptoe	*by Eleanor Estes*
Robert is angry when little Stevie comes to live at his house. Stevie is a pest!	Wanda always wears the same dress. She says she has a hundred more dresses at home.

The geese on their
clay trumpets sound
false alarms.

Por nada los gansos
Tocan alarma
En sus trompetas de barro.

José Juan Tablada
"The Geese" (Los Gansos)

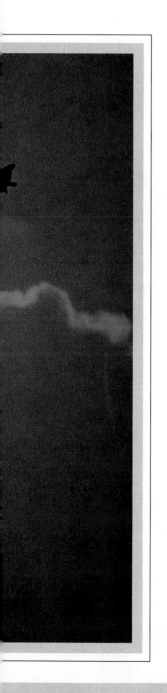

Nouns

Getting Ready Do you know the first word you spoke as a baby? It was probably a name. When you use a word to name a person, a place, or a thing, you are using a noun. Nouns are important words in our language. If we had no names for anything or anybody, we would have to make up some in a hurry! In this unit, you will learn more about nouns and how to use them.

Activities

Listening Listen as the poem on the opposite page is read. Listen for the words that name things. How many nouns do you hear? The poem is written in Spanish, also. Can you find the Spanish nouns? Every language has nouns.

Speaking Look at the picture. What do you see? Make a list of nouns that name things you see in the picture. What other nouns can you think of? Have someone list them on the board.

1 | What Are Nouns?

Some words name people, places, and things. A word that names a person, place, or thing is a **noun**.

PERSONS: My `brother` and his `friends` are excited.

PLACES: They're going to the `circus` . It's in `town` .

THINGS: The `bear` wore a funny `sign` .

person
grandmother

place
city

thing
apple

Guided Practice
One noun is underlined in each sentence. Find the other noun.

Example: The tent is filled with <u>children</u>.
The <u>tent</u> is filled with children.

1. The clowns have funny <u>noses</u>.
2. Their hats and <u>shoes</u> are floppy.
3. The elephants walk around the <u>ring</u>.
4. Their long trunks spray <u>water</u>.
5. The <u>lions</u> and tigers are scary.
6. A young <u>girl</u> rides on a pony.
7. The people always love the <u>show</u>.

Summing up

▶ A **noun** names a person, a place, or a thing.

More Practice Write the nouns in each sentence below. Each sentence has two nouns.

Example: This city has an airport.   *city   airport*

   8. A busy airport has many buildings.
   9. Some children watch the airplanes.
  10. A tall man carries a big bag.
  11. Several women buy tickets.
  12. Two girls walk to the gate.
  13. One child has a camera.
  14. Small shops sell gifts.
  15. Books and newspapers are also sold.
  16. A young boy waits for his friend.
  17. The plane flies high in the sky.
  18. The airplane goes through bumpy clouds.
  19. The people sit in their seats.
  20. A woman looks out the window.
  21. The houses and streets look small.
  22. Cars look like ants.
  23. One family plays a game.
  24. A girl and her brother read.
  25. A father holds a baby.
  26. The food is served on trays.
  27. The baby drinks some milk.
  28. A movie will be shown after lunch.
  29. Some people read magazines.
  30. Two men play checkers.

Writing Application: Creative Writing

Pretend that you are the pilot of an airplane. You have landed in a country where everyone is ten feet tall. Write five sentences about the country and its people. Circle the nouns.

2 | Common and Proper Nouns

You have learned that a noun names a person, a place, or a thing. A noun that names any person, place, or thing is called a **common noun**. A noun that names a particular person, place, or thing is called a **proper noun**.

Common nouns	Proper nouns
My friend swam today.	Suzy swam today.
Her dog went with her.	Buddy went with her.
The lake was cold.	Pine Lake was cold.

Proper nouns begin with capital letters. A proper noun, like *Pine Lake,* may have more than one word. Begin each important word in a proper noun with a capital letter.

Guided Practice Is each noun a common noun or a proper noun?

Example: Ash Road   *proper noun*

1. street   **3.** Mexico   **5.** teacher
2. country   **4.** John Wu   **6.** Thanksgiving

Summing up

▶ A **common noun** names any person, place, or thing.
▶ A **proper noun** names a particular person, place, or thing.
▶ Proper nouns begin with capital letters.

More Practice Write each noun. Then write *common* after each common noun and *proper* after each proper noun. Not all sentences have both common and proper nouns.

Example: My family visited Greenwood Zoo.
family   common   Greenwood Zoo   proper

7. The zoo is on River Road.
8. Aaron and Jessie came also.
9. A pony pulled a red wagon.
10. A camel ate some hay.
11. Arthur was a big gray elephant.
12. Jill fed the seals.
13. The fish swam in a huge pond.
14. A giraffe named Stretch was tall.
15. Next, my family visited a new museum.
16. The Stone Museum opened in May.
17. This building has a large center.
18. People can see the stars.
19. Jupiter, Mars, and other planets can be studied.
20. The North Star does not seem to move.
21. A movie shows pictures of the astronauts.
22. The first person on the moon was Neil Armstrong.
23. Another room has many telephones.
24. Mom liked the kites from Japan the best.
25. In July there will be a show about dinosaurs.
26. A scientist will talk about plants and animals.

Writing Application: Creative Writing
You have been chosen to ride along on a trip into space. What do you see? What kinds of experiments do you do? Give the space ship a name. Write five sentences about your trip.

3 | Nouns in the Subject

You know that the subject of a sentence tells whom or what the sentence is about. The main word in the subject is often a noun.

Spencer watched an animal show.

Some children fed the ducks.

A little girl petted a goat.

Seals did tricks.

Guided Practice The subject of each sentence is underlined. What is the noun in the subject?

Example: A helicopter landed. *helicopter*

1. Two children bought tickets.
2. Sandy wanted a ride.
3. The pilot waved.
4. A woman got on board.
5. My older sister sat down next to me.
6. Ramona buckled her seat belt.
7. The helicopter took off.
8. The blue sky seemed close to us.
9. Big houses looked tiny from the air.

Summing up

▶ A noun is often the main word in the subject.

More Practice Write the noun in the subject of each sentence.

Example: Green School held a field day.
Green School

10. The first race started at one o'clock.
11. Several classes entered the race.
12. The excited children rushed onto the field.
13. Adam Clarke wore his lucky sneakers.
14. The whistle blew loudly.
15. Teachers timed the race.
16. Peter ran fast.
17. Two girls passed Peter.
18. A tall boy moved ahead.
19. The race was close.
20. People cheered.
21. Adam was the winner.
22. His parents smiled.
23. Julia Wong came in second.
24. Several children tied for third place.
25. Mr. Perrone shook their hands.
26. First prize was museum tickets.
27. The runners went to Pike Park after the race.
28. The park has a lake.
29. The cold water felt good to the runners.
30. Mrs. MacDonald brought the food.

Writing Application: Writing About Yourself
Pretend that you have just won an Olympic medal in your favorite sport. A reporter wants to do a story about you. Write five sentences about what you will say when the reporter talks with you. Use a noun in the subject of each sentence.

4 | Singular and Plural Nouns

A noun that names only one person, place, or thing is a **singular noun**. A noun that names more than one person, place, or thing is a **plural noun**. Add *s* to most singular nouns to form the plural.

Singular	Plural
Julie climbed a tree. She played on a swing.	Julie climbed two trees. She played on some swings.

hat

hats

Guided Practice

A. Is each noun below singular or plural?

Example: elephants   *plural*

1. brother   **3.** baseballs   **5.** parade

2. crayons   **4.** trail   **6.** painters

B. What is the plural of each underlined noun?

Example: Two brothers rode to the <u>park</u>.   *parks*

7. The boys met a <u>friend</u>.

8. A <u>girl</u> walked her dogs.

9. One dog found a <u>bone</u>.

10. Ann bought a pretty <u>balloon</u>.

11. Three birds flew out of a <u>nest</u>.

Summing up

▶ A **singular noun** names one person, place, or thing.
▶ A **plural noun** names more than one.
▶ Add *s* to most singular nouns to form the plural.

More Practice

A. Write each underlined noun. Then write *singular* or *plural* beside each one.

Example: Grandmother came to visit the <u>girls</u>.   *plural*

12. She brought two <u>trunks</u> filled with old clothes.
13. Nancy showed the clothes to her <u>sister</u>.
14. They had a costume party with some <u>friends</u>.
15. Tina wore funny <u>shoes</u>.
16. Rita put on a straw <u>hat</u>.
17. One hat had yellow <u>ribbons</u>.
18. Another hat had five <u>flowers</u> on top.
19. Jon tried on an old <u>jacket</u>.
20. It had gold <u>buttons</u> down the front.

B. Write each sentence with the correct noun.

Example: Eva put on a long (coat, coats).
Eva put on a long coat.

21. The sleeves covered both (hand, hands).
22. The coat had two big (pocket, pockets).
23. She found a (key, keys) in one pocket.
24. How many (door, doors) would the key open?
25. Kerry wore a striped (skirt, skirts).
26. Dennis saw three blue (belt, belts).
27. Did you see this red (shirt, shirts)?
28. How did Donna look in those (glove, gloves)?

Writing Application: Sentences

Pretend that you and your friends are having a costume party. What kind of costumes do you wear? Write five sentences about the costumes. Use plural nouns in your sentences. Circle them.

5 | Plural Nouns with *es*

box

You know that you add *s* to most nouns to form the plural. Add *es* to form the plural of a singular noun that ends in *s, sh, ch,* or *x*.

SINGULAR: class   brush   lunch
PLURAL: class**es** brush**es** lunch**es**

boxes

Guided Practice What is the plural of each noun?

Example: bunch   *bunches*

1. fox   **2.** sash   **3.** beach   **4.** address

Summing up

▶ Add *es* to form the plural of a singular noun that ends in *s, sh, ch,* or *x*.

More Practice Make each underlined noun plural. Write the new word.

Example: Ted went to the <u>circus</u>.   *circuses*

5. Al met him after <u>class</u>.
6. The boys took a <u>bus</u>.
7. Ted ate a <u>sandwich</u>.

8. They sat on a <u>bench</u>.
9. A clown held a <u>dish</u>.
10. He stood on a <u>box</u>.

Writing Application: Creative Writing
Write five sentences about clowns. Use plurals of the words in the Word Box in your sentences.

box	circus	peach	lunch	class

6 | Plural Nouns with *ies*

You add *s* or *es* to most nouns to form the plural. If a noun ends with a consonant and *y*, change the *y* to *i* and add *es* to form the plural.

SINGULAR: penn**y**   cherr**y**

PLURAL: penn**ies**   cherr**ies**

cherr~~y~~ + es = cherries

Guided Practice What is the plural of each noun?

Example: story   *stories*

1. body   **2.** city   **3.** company   **4.** diary

Summing up

► If a noun ends with a consonant and *y*, change the *y* to *i* and add *es* to form the plural.

More Practice Make each underlined noun plural. Write the new sentences.

Example: Max picked the berry.   *Max picked the berries.*

5. He rode the pony.
6. The family watched.
7. The girl saw the bunny.

8. The baby stayed home.
9. The puppy slept.
10. The fly buzzed loudly.

Writing Application: Sentences

Write five sentences about spending the summer on a farm. Use plural forms of the words in the Word Box.

| pony | party | family | bunny | berry |

7 | Special Plural Nouns

Not every noun is made plural by adding *s* or *es*. Instead, their spelling changes in a special way. How does the spelling of *goose* change when it is plural?

SINGULAR: Molly fed one goose .

PLURAL: Sam fed two geese .

Look at the singular nouns below. How does the spelling of each noun change when it is plural?

mouse

mice

Singular	Plural
one man	three men
a woman	five women
one child	many children
a mouse	a few mice
the tooth	several teeth
one foot	two feet

Guided Practice Change each singular noun to a plural noun.

Example: man *men*

1. child
2. tooth
3. woman
4. mouse
5. foot
6. goose

Summing up

▶ Some nouns are made plural by changing the spelling in a special way.

More Practice

A. Use the plural of each noun in ( ) to complete the sentence. Write the sentences.

Example: The ____ waited for the bus.   (child)
The children waited for the bus.

7. One child hopped on both ____.   (foot)
8. A cat chased three ____.   (mouse)
9. A few ____ read newspapers.   (man)
10. The bus passed some ____.   (goose)
11. Many ____ were on the bus.   (woman)

B. Write the noun that completes each sentence correctly. Write *singular* or *plural* beside each one.

Example: Three (children, child) went to the pool.
children   plural

12. Two (woman, women) were diving.
13. A (men, man) was cleaning the pool.
14. Some (geese, goose) flew across the sky.
15. A baby was playing with two toy (mouse, mice).
16. A boy thought one toy (mouse, mice) was real.
17. He fell and hit his two front (tooth, teeth).
18. A (women, woman) helped him.
19. Two (man, men) looked in the boy's mouth.
20. The boy had not chipped one (tooth, teeth).

Writing Application: Creative Writing

Pretend that you are a grain of sand lying on the beach. Write five sentences that describe your day. Use words from the Word Box below. Make the words plural in your sentences.

child	man	woman	foot	goose

8 | Singular Possessive Nouns

A noun may show that a person or animal owns or has something. A noun that shows ownership is a **possessive noun**. Add an **apostrophe** (') and an *s* to a singular noun to make it a possessive noun.

Singular noun	Singular possessive noun
boy	boy's bike
Amy	Amy's game
cat	cat's paws

Look at the second column. *Boy's bike* means that the bike belongs to the boy. *Amy's game* means that Amy owns or has a game. What does *cat's paws* mean?

Guided Practice How would you form the possessive of each underlined singular noun?

Example: Nancy__ farm   *Nancy's*

1. horse__ stall
2. mother__ boots
3. Pablo__ airplane
4. neighbor__ barn
5. uncle__ tractor
6. puppy__ bones

Summing up

▶ A **possessive noun** shows ownership.
▶ Add an **apostrophe** (') and *s* to a singular noun to make it show ownership.

More Practice Change each singular noun in ( )
in the sentences below to the possessive form. Write
each sentence correctly.

Example: Mrs. Cohen read the ____ letter. (teacher)
Mrs. Cohen read the teacher's letter.

 7. Tonight ____ school had an open house. (Martha)
 8. ____ parents got a letter too. (Joe)
 9. ____ father went to school early. (Kathy)
10. He stopped at the ____ office. (principal)
11. Ms. Willis met ____ mother. (Robin)
12. Mr. DiSilva found ____ room. (Maria)
13. ____ class drew posters. (Kim)
14. The teacher showed each ____ art work. (child)
15. ____ drawing was in the middle. (Ben)
16. He drew a picture of his ____ farm. (cousin)
17. A pet show was held in ____ room. (Rosa)
18. On one table was ____ fish tank. (Paul)
19. All the parents saw the ____ cage. (hamster)
20. They laughed at the ____ funny hop. (rabbit)
21. ____ canary was sleeping. (Roberto)
22. ____ class had a science fair. (John)
23. ____ class showed their projects. (Mark)
24. ____ project won first prize. (Sally)

Writing Application: Sentences

Your school is having an open house. Your class will
put on a puppet show. Write five sentences about
what will happen at the puppet show. Use the
singular nouns in the Word Box in your sentences.
Make all of these nouns possessive.

| puppet | Lori | Manny | teacher | Steven |

9 | Plural Possessive Nouns

You know how to show that one person or animal owns or has something. How can you show that something belongs to more than one person or animal? Add just an apostrophe to a plural noun that ends in *s* to make it a possessive noun.

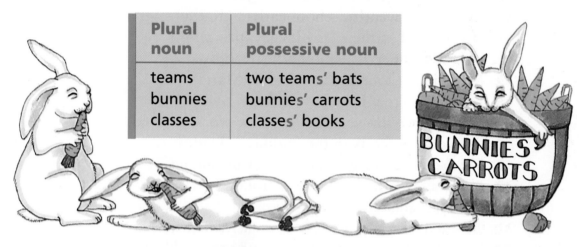

Plural noun	Plural possessive noun
teams	two teams' bats
bunnies	bunnies' carrots
classes	classes' books

Guided Practice How would you form the possessive of each underlined plural noun?

Example: two <u>girls</u>— closets *girls'*

1. three <u>babies'</u>— toys
2. <u>cats'</u>— fur
3. many <u>nurses'</u>— caps
4. three <u>boys'</u>— mother
5. <u>foxes'</u>— food
6. <u>teachers'</u>— maps
7. <u>friends'</u>— kites
8. <u>daughters'</u>— room

Summing up

▶ To show ownership, add just an apostrophe to a plural noun that ends in *s*.

More Practice Change each plural noun in ( ) to the possessive form. Write the sentences correctly.

Example: My ____ garage is messy.   (grandparents)
My grandparents' garage is messy.

9. My three ____ bikes have flat tires.   (cousins)
10. The ____ blocks are near the bikes.   (babies)
11. Where is the ____ basket?   (kittens)
12. The ____ collars feel greasy.   (puppies)
13. What happened to the ____ basketball?   (teams)
14. Help me find my ____ flowerpots.   (aunts)
15. I found the ____ ladders.   (painters)
16. The ____ old beds are against one wall.   (twins)
17. You are holding my ____ soccer shoes.   (brothers)
18. Did you see the two ____ costumes?   (girls)
19. Are the ____ jackets anywhere?   (boys)
20. My ____ hats are torn.   (uncles)
21. My ____ toys look dusty.   (sisters)
22. Can you find the ____ tools?   (workers)
23. My ____ camera is broken.   (parents)
24. The ____ rake is on a hook.   (gardeners)
25. Do you want to play the ____ records?   (neighbors)
26. Put their ____ books in boxes.   (friends)
27. The ____ tents can be folded.   (campers)
28. Grandma needs the ____ music.   (bands)
29. Her ____ radio is missing.   (brothers)
30. Are the ____ pictures ready?   (customers)

Writing Application: Writing About Yourself
Write a story about cleaning up your room. Use some plural possessive nouns in your paragraph. You may use some of the plural possessive nouns from the exercise above if you wish.

Building Vocabulary

Compound Words

The English language is changing and growing. New words are often added to the language. Sometimes two words are put together to make one new word. The new word is a **compound word**.

sun + flower = sunflower
dog + house = doghouse
basket + ball = basketball

You can tell the meaning of many compound words by looking at the words that make up the compound.

Bedtime is the time you go to bed .

A horseshoe is a shoe for a horse .

The picture at the top of the page shows compound words. What are they?

Practice

A. Write each underlined compound word. Then write the two words that form it.

> Example: Where did you get your <u>dollhouse</u>?
> *dollhouse doll house*

1. My sister's <u>birthday</u> is next week.
2. I might get her a <u>seashell</u>.
3. Is it cold <u>outside</u>?
4. <u>Everyone</u> is wearing jackets.
5. Is <u>Grandfather</u> here yet?
6. I thought I heard the <u>doorbell</u>.
7. We will go to the <u>playground</u>.

B. Answer each riddle with a compound word. Write each compound word.

> Example: I am a boat that sails. What am I? *sailboat*

8. I am a berry that is blue. What am I?
9. I am a house for a dog. What am I?
10. I am a paper full of news. What am I?
11. I am a light that can flash. What am I?
12. I am a coat to wear in the rain. What am I?
13. I am a brush for the hair. What am I?
14. I am a chair that you wheel. What am I?

Writing Application: Sentences

Each of the silly words in the Word Box is made up of two word parts. Put the correct word parts together to make real compound words. Use each of the correct compound words in a sentence.

airbox	butterplane	rainbook	mailbow	notefly

Grammar-Writing Connection

Combining Sentences: Compound Subjects

You have learned to make your writing more interesting by using sentences with different lengths. You can make your writing smoother and clearer too. Sometimes two short sentences have the same predicate. You can join, or combine, the subjects of both sentences to make one longer sentence. Use the word *and* when you combine the two subjects.

Carl went to the farm. ⟩ Carl and Abe went
Abe went to the farm. ⟩ to the farm.

The two short sentences have the same predicate, *went to the farm*. Because these sentences have the same predicate, the subjects *Carl* and *Abe* can be combined.

Revising Sentences

Write each pair of sentences as one sentence.

Example: The dog played. The cat played.
The dog and the cat played.

1. Ming fed the cows. Pat fed the cows.
2. Goats ate some hay. Horses ate some hay.
3. A truck stopped by the barn. A car stopped by the barn.
4. Peter heard something. Maria heard something.
5. A man shouted to them. A woman shouted to them.
6. Grandma picked corn. Grandpa picked corn.
7. The tomatoes were ripe. The cucumbers were ripe.

Creative Writing

A *Holiday* by Edward Henry Potthast
© Art Institute of Chicago

Edward Potthast used soft, fuzzy strokes to make this seashore look like a memory of a day at the beach.

• What are some of the people doing? How can you tell?

Activities

1. **What are they saying?** Imagine you can listen to the children in this scene. Write what they are saying.
2. **Send a postcard.** Pretend you visited this seashore. Write a postcard describing it to your best friend.
3. **Tell about your day.** Write a paragraph explaining how you usually spend a hot summer day.

Check-up: Unit 3

What Are Nouns? *(p. 58)* Write the nouns in each sentence.

1. My class went to the fair.
2. The bus waited for the students.
3. Children ate their lunches.
4. The girls went to see the chickens.
5. Cute chicks hatched from eggs.

Common and Proper Nouns *(p. 60)* Write *common* for each common noun and *proper* for each proper noun.

6. state	**8.** cat	**10.** winter	**12.** puppet
7. Ohio	**9.** Ann	**11.** Canada	**13.** Raul Garcia

Nouns in the Subject *(p. 62)* Write the noun in the subject of each sentence.

14. Vito entered his dog in a pet show.
15. Many people brought their dogs.
16. The dogs paraded around the room.
17. Judges looked closely at each dog.
18. The first prize was a blue ribbon.
19. Buddy won the blue ribbon!

Singular and Plural Nouns *(p. 64)* Write the noun that completes each sentence correctly.

20. My father drives a (truck, trucks).
21. His truck has sixteen (wheel, wheels).
22. Dad drives the truck to a (dock, docks).
23. Several (ship, ships) came into the dock today.
24. Dad loaded many (barrels, barrel) into his truck.
25. Then he drove to a (store, stores).

Plural Nouns with *es* and *ies* *(pp. 66, 67)* Write the plural form of each noun.

26. mystery   **28.** marsh   **30.** business   **32.** family
27. glass   **29.** speech   **31.** ax   **33.** inch

Special Plural Nouns *(p. 68)* Write the noun that completes each sentence correctly. Then write *singular* or *plural* beside each one.

34. A (man, men) bought some groceries.
35. The bag dropped on his two (foot, feet).
36. Several (woman, women) made the fruit salad.
37. One (child, children) ate all the blueberries.
38. The berries made all her (tooth, teeth) blue.

Singular Possessive Nouns *(p. 70)* Change the singular noun in ( ) to the possessive form. Write each sentence correctly.

39. ____ book report is finished.   (Sarah)
40. She put it on the ____ desk.   (teacher)
41. Amy wrote the ____ name under the title.   (author)
42. She drew a picture with her ____ crayons.   (brother)
43. The title of ____ book is <u>Beast</u>.   (Ramon)
44. He bought the book in his ____ store.   (aunt)

Plural Possessive Nouns *(p. 72)* Change each underlined plural noun to the plural possessive form. Write each sentence correctly.

45. My <u>sisters</u> dolls come from different countries.
46. The dolls are on a shelf in my <u>parents</u> room.
47. Many of the <u>dolls</u> dresses are colorful.
48. My <u>aunts</u> favorite doll comes from China.
49. Are your <u>friends</u> doll collections big?
50. They have thirty dolls at their <u>grandparents</u> houses.

Cumulative Review

Unit 1: The Sentence

What Is a Sentence? *(p. 2)* Read the two groups of words. Write the group that is a sentence.

1. I enjoy car rides.
  In a big red car.

4. Cars zoom by me.
  Trucks with loud horns.

2. The best seat.
  The front seat is best.

5. Always love the bumps.
  We go up the hills.

3. I look out the window.
  View of everything.

6. Interesting people.
  I wave at the people.

Kinds of Sentences *(pp. 4, 6)* Write each sentence correctly.

7. can you keep a secret

10. it is a great secret

8. do not tell anyone

11. what is the secret

9. Kim told me her secret

12. she got a new bike

Subjects and Predicates *(pp. 8, 10)* Write each sentence. Draw a line between subject and predicate.

13. Uncle Henry is a cook.

16. It tasted delicious.

14. He works at my school.

17. Some children had more.

15. He made soup today.

18. Mr. Lee ate three cups!

Run-on Sentences *(p. 12)* Rewrite each run-on sentence as two sentences.

19. What is your favorite hobby I collect rocks.

20. Some rocks are smooth other rocks feel rough.

21. I label all my rocks this rock is very old.

22. Do you see that orange rock it comes from Arizona.

23. Grandpa gave it to me he likes my collection.

Unit 3: Nouns

What Are Nouns? *(p. 58)* Write all the nouns.

24. My cousins own a huge pool.
25. My sister is having a party.
26. Noisy children are under the umbrella.
27. Two boys are swimming in the water.

Common and Proper Nouns *(p. 60)* Write *common* or *proper* for each noun.

28. Maine   30. pig   32. coat
29. book   31. Anita   33. Mill Road

Nouns in the Subject *(p. 62)* Write the noun in the subject of each sentence.

34. Many foods come from plants.
35. People eat different plant parts.
36. A fruit is part of a flowering plant.
37. A tomato is a fruit.
38. Carrots come from the root of a plant.

Singular and Plural Nouns *(pp. 64, 66, 68)* Write the plural form of each noun.

39. beach   41. class   43. child
40. story   42. fox   44. foot

Possessive Nouns *(pp. 70, 72)* Change each underlined noun to the possessive form. Write each new group of words.

45. Carrie pencil   48. a fox howl
46. two cousins football   49. puppies toys
47. some reporters desks   50. a boy shirt

Enrichment

Unit Three: Nouns

Alphabeasts

You run a large zoo with
many different animals.
Make an alphabeast book to
tell people about it. Think of
animals for as many letters
of the alphabet as you can. Create a page for each letter.
Write the letter at the top of the page. Write the name of
the animal under it. Then draw a picture of the animal
and write a sentence about it. Staple your pages in order.

Emergency!

Create a poster
for emergency phone
numbers. What will you
list? How about a doctor
or the fire department?
On cardboard, write seven
sentences with emergency
phone numbers. Use a
singular possessive noun in
each sentence.

Newspaper Fun

On a piece of paper,
write a common noun
like *car* or *city*. Draw the
shape of the thing named.
Using old newspapers,
cut out proper nouns that
are examples of your
common noun. Paste the
words onto the shape
you drew.

1 | What Are Nouns? (p. 58)

● Write the noun in each group of words.

Example: hat, run, happy *hat*

1. slowly, girl, tired
2. zoo, busy, early
3. bird, above, sleepy
4. muddy, played, aunt
5. under, lake, excited
6. funny, boat, up
7. farmer, near, sad
8. soft, truck, read

▲ Each sentence below has two nouns. Write each sentence. Underline the nouns.

Example: My teacher read to the class.
        My teacher read to the class.

9. The story came from my favorite book.
10. A king lived in a huge castle.
11. People from the town visited.
12. The queen showed each room.
13. Food was served on long tables.
14. The children played in the yard.
15. Some horses waited by the gate.

■ Write the nouns in each sentence. Then write *person, place,* or *thing* after each noun.

Example: Men and women do many jobs.
        Men—person   women—person   jobs—thing

16. Cooks prepare food.
17. Some people build houses.
18. Farmers grow fruits and vegetables.
19. Lifeguards watch swimmers at the beach.
20. Drivers take packages to cities.
21. Teachers show children how to read books.
22. Doctors and nurses help sick people.

2 | Common and Proper Nouns (p. 60)

● Write the proper noun in each pair of words.
Example: boy
Alex Wong *Alex Wong*

1. Baker School
   school
2. Chicago
   city
3. street
   Main Street
4. state
   Texas

5. Elk River
   river
6. Mrs. Arnez
   teacher
7. fish
   Puffy
8. day
   Monday

▲ Make two lists on your paper. Write all the common nouns in one list. Write all the proper nouns in the other list.
Example: ocean **Common Nouns   Proper Nouns**
                 ocean

9. Pluto
10. Iowa City
11. umbrella
12. Leslie Ross

13. painter
14. avenue
15. Jean
16. Oak Road

■ Finish each sentence with a proper noun for the word in ( ). Write the complete sentence.
Example: Jason goes to ____.   (school)
   Jason goes to Park School.

17. His school is on ____.   (street)
18. One day ____ joined the class.   (girl)
19. She came from ____.   (state)
20. She and ____ became friends.   (boy)
21. They played in ____.   (park)
22. The children went to ____.   (zoo)

● Choose a noun from the Word Box to finish each sentence. Write each sentence.

Example: A ___ visits a farm.
A boy visits a farm.

1. His ___ feeds the cows.
2. ___ moo loudly.
3. Three ___ pull tractors.
4. ___ lay eggs.
5. The ___ should be painted.
6. The ___ tastes good.

corn
Cows
boy
Hens
barn
horses
grandfather

▲ The subject of each sentence is underlined. Write the noun in the subject.

Example: <u>Two girls</u> planned a party. *girls*

7. <u>Jenny</u> cooked the food.
8. <u>Steven</u> wrapped the presents.
9. <u>His friend</u> brought the games.
10. <u>One boy</u> made party hats.
11. <u>Two games</u> were on the table.
12. <u>Three red balloons</u> popped.
13. <u>The young children</u> had a good time.

■ Write the subject of each sentence. Underline the noun in the subject.

Example: Many bats are small and furry.
Many <u>bats</u>

14. The animals fly like birds.
15. My older brother studied bats in school.
16. Insects are their favorite food.
17. The large wings are very strong.
18. All bats can hang upside down.
19. Dark caves are filled with bats.
20. Most bats sleep during the day.

4 | Singular and Plural Nouns (p. 64)

● Write *singular* if the underlined word in each sentence is singular. Write *plural* if the underlined word is plural.

Example: The <u>forest</u> was quiet. *singular*

1. We slept in our <u>tents</u>.
2. Our <u>friends</u> were camped next to us.
3. One <u>girl</u> heard a noise.
4. She hid under her <u>blanket</u>.
5. Five <u>raccoons</u> played nearby.
6. They walked on our picnic <u>table</u>.
7. We had forgotten to put away the <u>eggs</u>.
8. Tomorrow we will go to the <u>store</u>.

▲ Write the plural form of each noun.

Example: ship *ships*

9.	map	14.	ocean
10.	bird	15.	shore
11.	sailor	16.	storm
12.	cloud	17.	captain
13.	wave	18.	net

■ Change the singular noun in each sentence to a plural noun. Write the new plural noun.

Example: My sisters wrote a letter. *letters*

19. They took a trip with my cousins.
20. My uncle and my two aunts went along.
21. My aunts took a camera.
22. The train went through many towns.
23. My cousins looked out the window.
24. Many animals ran out of a big barn.
25. I took a picture of the animals.
26. A boy waved to my cousins.

5 | Plural Nouns with *es* (p. 66)

● Read each pair of nouns. Write the plural form.
Example: boss
          bosses *bosses*

1. ditches   **5.** beaches
      ditch   beach

2. dishes   **6.** lashes
      dish   lash

3. fox   **7.** dress
      foxes   dresses

4. gas   **8.** porch
      gases   porches

▲ Write the plural form of each noun.
Example: mess *messes*

9. ax   **13.** walrus
10. ranch   **14.** wax
11. bush   **15.** inch
12. church   **16.** waitress

■ Change each underlined singular noun to the plural form. Change each underlined plural noun to the singular form. Write the new sentences.
Example: Gail saw two <u>fox</u>. *Gail saw two foxes.*
17. The foxes hid behind the <u>bush</u>.
18. Gail tripped over some big <u>branch</u>.
19. Did you see the <u>patch</u> on her leg?
20. She will have to use the <u>crutches</u>.
21. Gail cannot go to the <u>beach</u> for six weeks.
22. Her mother bought her two <u>dress</u> and a book.
23. The children in her <u>class</u> brought her flowers.
24. Gail put the flowers in the pretty <u>glasses</u>.

6 | Plural Nouns with *ies* (p. 67)

● Write each noun. Then write *singular* or *plural* beside each one.

Example: cities *plural*

1. blueberry
2. countries
3. skies
4. strawberries
5. fly
6. penny
7. daisies
8. ladies

▲ Use the plural form of each noun in ( ) to complete each sentence. Write the sentences.

Example: Lara read some ____. (story) *stories*

9. Each story was about animal ____. (family)
10. Some animals like to eat ____. (berry)
11. She learned about animal ____. (baby)
12. Baby dogs are called ____. (puppy)
13. Baby rabbits are called ____. (bunny)
14. Allen read a story about ____. (pony)
15. Joseph found pictures of ____. (butterfly)
16. Lisa read two books about ____. (canary)

■ Write the noun that correctly completes each sentence. Then write *singular* or *plural* beside each one.

Example: Sam lives in the (country, countries).
         country   singular

17. He picks many (blueberry, blueberries).
18. A (bunny, bunnies) watches him.
19. He has two (hobby, hobbies).
20. Sam collects pictures of (butterfly, butterflies).
21. He is learning to ride a (pony, ponies).
22. His town has one (library, libraries).
23. Sam reads (story, stories) about insects and horses.
24. He found out that a (fly, flies) is an insect.

7 | Special Plural Nouns (p. 68)

● Write each noun. Then write *singular* or *plural* next to each one.

Example: children   *plural*

1. tooth
2. woman
3. men
4. feet
5. goose

6. mice
7. child
8. women
9. teeth
10. man

▲ Use the plural form of the noun in ( ) to complete each sentence. Write the sentences.

Example: The ___ went to the farm.   (child)
   The children went to the farm.

11. Some ___ worked in the field.   (man)
12. Two ___ painted the barn.   (woman)
13. I fed some ___.   (goose)
14. Field ___ ran across the road.   (mouse)
15. The farmer checked the horse's ___.   (tooth)
16. Two ___ sat on the fence.   (child)
17. We put our ___ in the pond.   (foot)

■ Find the noun in each sentence that should be plural. Write each sentence correctly.

Example: A few child walked to the pond.
   A few children walked to the pond.

18. Two man were singing.
19. Some goose started honking.
20. Two mouse heard the noise.
21. Several woman put some cheese on the ground.
22. Many child watched one mouse eat.
23. The mouse had two bad tooth.
24. It ran away on its four little foot.

● Write the possessive noun in each sentence.
Example: The family's dinner was ready. *family's*
   1. Greg's friend ate dinner with us.
   2. Mom poured soup into Jan's bowl.
   3. Some soup spilled on Ben's fork.
   4. Dad put vegetables on Dino's plate.
   5. Pam moved the baby's seat.
   6. Bob's napkin dropped to the floor.
   7. The dog sat near Jennifer's chair.
   8. The cat's food was too cold.
   9. She rubbed against Jill's leg.

▲ Change each underlined singular noun to the possessive form. Write each new group of words.
Example: <u>Ted</u> dog   *Ted's dog*
   10. <u>girl</u> balloon   14. <u>monkey</u> tail
   11. <u>father</u> hats   15. <u>Mr. Kirk</u> house
   12. <u>Ray</u> kite   16. <u>woman</u> letter
   13. <u>bird</u> feathers   17. <u>boy</u> trains

■ Rewrite each sentence. Use the possessive form of each underlined singular noun.
Example: The map that <u>Dad</u> has shows a path.
         Dad's map shows a path.
   18. The path begins at the house that <u>Steve</u> owns.
   19. The sister that <u>John</u> has leads the way.
   20. The children see tracks that belong to an <u>animal</u>.
   21. Sally takes the hand that belongs to <u>Melissa</u>.
   22. She points to a nest that belongs to a <u>bird</u>.
   23. Rico finds footprints that belong to a <u>bear</u>.
   24. Everybody looks for the den that the <u>fox</u> has.
   25. The path ends near the backyard that <u>Lin</u> owns.

● Read the two groups of words after each number. Write the group of words with the plural possessive noun in it.

Example: lions' den
       lion's den   *lions' den*

1. father's book
   fathers' book
2. farmers' corn
   farmer's corn
3. clown's shoes
   clowns' shoes
4. horses' saddles
   horse's saddles
5. sailors' boat
   sailor's boat
6. coach's hats
   coaches' hats

▲ Change the plural noun in ( ) to the possessive form. Write each sentence correctly.

Example: Many people shop at my (brothers) store
   Many people shop at my brothers' store.

7. Mr. Chen buys baskets for his (daughters) bikes.
8. Bruce looks at the racks of (boys) coats.
9. Mrs. Kane buys the (families) tents.
10. My two (friends) father buys a hammer.
11. Our (neighbors) son buys a hat.
12. The (dogs) leashes are next to the collars.
13. Jenny sees chairs for her (grandparents) house.

■ Write the possessive noun in each sentence. Then write *singular* or *plural* beside each one.

Example: I like my sisters' pets. *sisters'* *plural*

14. Anita's dog is big and spotted.
15. My other sister's cat has orange fur.
16. Both girls' pets have funny names.
17. The dog's name is Lefty.
18. Pumpkin is the cat's name.
19. Pumpkin eats Lefty's food.
20. Lefty eats the food in my parent's garden.

Reading and Writing

Mix a pancake,
Stir a pancake,
  Pop it in the pan;

Fry the pancake,
Toss the pancake,—
  Catch it if you can.

Christina Rossetti

Instructions

Getting Ready People explain to each other how to do many things. They give instructions. A friend might explain how to play a game. Your parents might explain how to set the table. Your teacher explains what to do during a fire drill. What can you explain? In this unit, you will learn how to give and write good instructions.

Activities

Speaking Look at the picture. The two pans of pancakes are at different points in cooking. Tell which steps in the poem have been followed for the pancakes in the pan on the left. Which steps have been followed for the pancakes on the right?

Listening Listen as the poem on the opposite page is read. What does it give instructions for making? What steps does it give? Could you make pancakes following these instructions? What other steps might be needed?

LITERATURE

A young boy dreams of finding "stars" under the desert sands. How does he make his dream come true?

Oasis of the Stars

By Olga Economakis

Abu's home was the desert, all of the desert, and that was the trouble. He didn't live in a house in one place like other children but in a tent with his father and mother. And their tent moved with them. And their animals moved with them—their sheep and goats and camels— while they looked for new pastures. Always looking. Never staying. From place to place in the desert they went—each new place like the one they had left and no place with even a name.

Summer was especially difficult. The hot sun would dry up the springs so that the grass wouldn't grow, and as Abu's father pitched the tent he would sigh, "Tomorrow we will move on again. Farther ahead there may be better pasture for the animals." So almost every day they would pack up their things, load the donkeys and camels and move on to a new place.

Most of the time Abu was happy. He liked to watch the sun rise like a big pink ball right out of the sand in the morning. And at night, when his mother and father sat outside the tent talking, he liked to hear the quiet sound of their voices in the night, murmuring like water running over rocks.

On nights when the sides of the tent were up to let in the cool night air, Abu would try to count all the shimmering little stars in the sky.

Other times, after a very hot day in search of a water hole, Abu would pretend that each star was a drop of water. "If we had all that water," he would murmur, "we would never have to move again. Then our tent would be a real home and Mother would not be so tired packing and unpacking. And Father could sit on a real chair instead of a camel saddle."

His father laughed at him and called him a dreamer. "When summer comes the water dries up and the grass dies. The stars are very beautiful but they are not water to drink. Would you want your animals to go thirsty?" Abu knew then that this was only another too-dry place, and they would have to pull up the tent poles again and strike out into the big desert that he had to call home.

One day Abu asked his father if they couldn't dig into the earth to see where the water went.

"I want to try to find my shimmering stars, my little drops of water," Abu said. "If I dig deep enough and long enough perhaps I shall find them."

"Dig for stars?" his father laughed. "Child, there is nothing under the sand but more sand. Soon we must move on again."

But Abu pleaded. "Please Father, may I just try?"

His father smiled. "Well, you may look. But remember that when our spring runs dry we must be on our way."

That very night Abu began his search. He found a spot where it seemed to him the grass was a little greener than any other place, and taking a shovel from his father's pack he began to work. First he cleared the area of grass and put it aside for the animals. Then he began to dig.

Night after night he dug. After a while his hole was deep enough so that he could stand in it up to his knees. Then it became waist deep. But there was no water there.

It was hard work. The sand often slipped back into the hole and he had to make a wall of rocks around it. Under the sand he found hard-packed earth and rocks. Sometimes he had to dig with his fingers around a large rock to pull it out. But still there was no water.

Deeper and deeper he went until only his head and shoulders showed above the hole. But the ground remained as dry as before.

Sometimes Abu became so tired that he wanted to put down his shovel and forget all about his hole. Then he would look up into the night and always the stars would be there, little shimmering stars spattered all over the sky, sparkling like tiny drops of water. And always, after seeing them, he would take up his shovel and dig some more. But Abu's water stayed in the sky. His little hole in the big desert was now over his head and there was no water at all.

Sometimes Abu's father would come and look down into his hole. "Abu, have you found them yet, your shimmering stars? Well, never mind. Summer is coming. We will find water elsewhere."

Then one hot day his father came to him to say that the spring had at last run dry. They would leave the next morning.

Abu cried that night as he dug deeper into his hole but he blinked his eyes and brushed his tears away furiously with the back of his hand. If only his tears could help, he thought, but tears were not enough. They could never fill up a hole so deep. He dropped his shovel and leaned back against the walls of his hole to rest. It was no use, he thought. The stars were in the sky. The earth was only desert. He stooped down for the shovel, ready to climb back to the top, but as he did, his hands touched the earth. And the earth was cool. Surely it was cool. Almost damp.

"It is only my silly tears," he said to himself. But he put down his shovel and taking a handful of dirt pressed it to his face. He tried again in another part of the hole. "It feels different," Abu thought, and he raised his voice.

"Father, Father, come!" he cried. "I think the ground is damp here. The water must be just below."

Abu's father was sitting in front of the tent as he always did in the evenings. He didn't get up but spoke gently. "It feels that way because the night air has cooled the earth," he explained. "Come, child. Stop your digging and sit here with me."

But Abu continued to dig. He couldn't see out of the hole any longer and in order to take the dirt out, he had to climb up some little steps he had made in the side of the hole. At last he was so tired that he fell asleep beside his hole and his father carried him into the tent. As he put Abu on his bed, he sighed. "The child is a dreamer and sometimes dreams hurt," he said. "But dreams, like water and food, make boys grow into men."

The next day, when the camels were packed and ready to go, Abu went to his hole for a final look. He looked at his rock wall with the sand piled around it. Then his eyes went down the little steps he had built one by one until finally he was looking at the bottom of his hole. At the bottom the sand was darker than it had been yesterday. He kicked off his sandals and started down his steps. Deeper and deeper he went until he had reached the last little step. Then he stepped into the bottom of the hole and felt his feet sink up to his ankles in wonderful, wet sand. He got to his knees and his robe soaked up the water from the sand. It was wet. Truly wet.

"Father, come quickly," he cried. "The water is here. It's here!"

Abu's father got down off his camel. He looked down at Abu kneeling in the bottom of the hole. Then he too climbed into the hole. He lifted a handful of sand out of the bottom and rubbed it in his fingers. Then he dug a little deeper and saw the sun glint off the smooth place he had made at the bottom. He lifted out some more sand, pressed it to his cheek and smelled it. It was indeed wet. Laughing out loud, he lifted Abu high up into the air. "My child, you were right," he said. "Your shimmering stars were there all the time, hiding under the sand. We shall stay here this summer."

100

So Abu and his father made the hole into a well. Now their tent has become a real home with a real chair for his father instead of a camel saddle, and a real hearth for his mother to cook on instead of a campfire.

And now, when the sun goes down and night falls on the desert, Abu looks into his well and counts the shimmering stars. He has named the place he lives. He calls it Wadi Nougoum, Oasis of the Stars.

Questions

1. How did Abu make his dream of finding water come true?
2. The **setting** is where a story takes place. What is the setting of "Oasis of the Stars"? Why did the desert cause so much trouble for Abu and his family?
3. What kind of person was Abu? Was he hard-working or lazy? Was he the kind of person who gives up easily? Explain.
4. Now Abu and his family can stay in one place by their well. How might this change their lives?

If you were to dig deep, deep into the earth, what would you find?

How to Dig a Hole to the Other Side of the World

By Faith McNulty

Find a soft place. Take a shovel and start to dig a hole. The dirt you dig up is called loam. Loam, or topsoil, is made up of tiny bits of rock mixed with many other things, such as plants and worms that died and rotted long ago.

When you have dug through the topsoil you will come to clay or gravel or sand. The digging will be harder. When the hole is five or six feet deep, you had better ask a friend to help. Your friend can pull up the clay or gravel in a bucket, while you stay at the bottom of the hole and keep digging.

Sooner or later you will come to rocks; all sorts of rocks; big rocks, little rocks; granite, limestone, sandstone. If you started your hole in Africa you might find diamonds. In Brazil you might find emeralds. In other places you might find coal—or gold or silver.

Wherever you dig watch for old bones and shells. The bones of many animals—dinosaurs, giant tigers, turtles, and other creatures of long ago—are buried everywhere. If you find some, dust them off carefully and save them.

When you have dug about fifty feet down—maybe more or maybe less—you will come to solid rock. This is the rocky skin of the earth, called the crust. It is mostly granite. To dig through it you will need a drilling machine. Start drilling.

You may hit water. Rain sinks through the topsoil and gathers in pools and underground rivers. If you come to water you should put on a diving suit.

You may come to a lake of black, gooey oil. If you hit oil it would be best to give up this hole and start another somewhere else.

Keep drilling. When you have drilled down a mile or so, the rock will be warm. This is because heat flows up into the rock from the center of the earth. You may hit boiling water or steam. This is because rainwater drips down through cracks onto very hot rock.

topsoil

clay

rocky matter

crust

In some places on earth, hot water bubbles up in springs or shoots up in geysers. Because of the boiling water and steam you will need an asbestos diving suit. Stay out of the way of geysers. If you got caught in a geyser it might carry you up to the surface and shoot you into the air. When you came down, you would have to start digging all over again.

Questions

1. What kinds of things might you find after you dig through the topsoil? What might you find in the earth's crust?

2. Suppose you got caught in a geyser. You were carried up to the surface. Why would you have to start digging again in another place?

3. The **author** is the person who wrote the story. Faith McNulty is the author of "How to Dig a Hole to the Other Side of the World." No one has really dug to the other side of the earth. How do you suppose Faith McNulty got these facts about what is found below the earth's surface?

RESPONDING TO LITERATURE

The Reading and Writing Connection

Personal Response Abu's dream came true. What do you dream about? Write a plan to make your dream come true. Your plan can be real or make-believe.

Creative Writing Pretend that you are digging. You find something wonderful. Write a story that tells what you have found and how it changes your life.

Creative Activities

Draw Pretend that you dug a hole in the earth. Draw the things you found. Show them from top to bottom. Next to each thing, write its name.

Read Aloud and Pantomime Work together as a class to act out parts of "Oasis of the Stars." One person should read aloud from the story. At the same time, another person should pantomime, or silently act out, what the words say to do.

Vocabulary

An **oasis** is an area in the desert where there are water, plants, and trees. It is very different from the dry desert around it. Why is an oasis like an island in the ocean?

Looking Ahead

Instructions In this unit, you will write instructions. Look at the first two paragraphs on page 102. What steps should you follow?

Listening/Speaking/Thinking

Listening: Following Directions

Sarah wondered why Anna's plant was losing its leaves. Anna said that she watered it once a week. Sarah said, "I told you to water it twice a week."

Use these guides when listening to directions.

Listening Guides

1. Listen carefully for each step.
2. Listen for the order of the steps.
3. Listen for words that tell you exactly what to do.
4. Ask questions if you are unsure of a step.

Listen as your teacher or a classmate reads the directions from "How to Dig a Hole to the Other Side of the World." What is the first thing you should do when you dig? Should you save the bones before you dust them off? Which words tell you what to do?

Wherever you dig <u>watch</u> for old bones and shells. The bones of many animals—dinosaurs, giant tigers, turtles, and other creatures of long ago—are buried everywhere. If you find some, <u>dust</u> them off carefully and <u>save</u> them.

Practice

Listen while your teacher reads directions. Follow the directions. Remember the Listening Guides.

Listening: For the Main Idea

Listen as your teacher or a classmate reads the sentences from "Oasis of the Stars" below. The one thing that all the sentences tell about is called the **topic**. The **main idea** sums up what all the sentences are telling about the topic. What are the topic and the main idea of these sentences?

> Summer was especially difficult. The hot sun would dry up the springs so that the grass wouldn't grow, and as Abu's father pitched the tent he would sigh, "Tomorrow we will move on again. Farther ahead there may be better pasture for the animals."

The topic of the group of sentences above is *summer*. The main idea is *summer was difficult*. When you listen for the main idea, follow these Listening Guides.

Listening Guides

1. First, listen to all the sentences.
2. Decide what one **topic** all of the sentences tell about.
3. Ask yourself what one idea the sentences are telling about the topic. That is the **main idea**.

Practice

Listen carefully as your teacher reads to you. Listen for the topic and the main idea of each group of sentences.

Speaking: Giving Instructions

You are digging to the other side of the world. Your hole is six feet deep. You must ask a friend for help. Your friend will want to know just what to do. How do you give your friend good directions? Follow these guides.

Speaking Guides

1. Think about what you need to explain. Break the work into steps.
2. Think about the order of the steps. Which one should you explain first? next? last?
3. Give step-by-step directions. Tell the steps in order from first to last.
4. Use **order words** to make the order clear. *First, next, then,* and *finally* are some order words. They tell when each step should be done.

Practice

Find a partner. Pretend that your partner has never learned to do these things.

1. Make a telephone call
2. Go from your classroom to the playground
3. Make a bed
4. Wrap a package

Choose one thing from the list above to explain to your partner. Follow the Speaking Guides on this page. Tell your directions to your partner. Can your partner follow your directions? Did you tell all the steps? Were they clear?

Thinking: Finding the Main Idea

You know that the topic is the one thing that a group of sentences is about. The main idea sums up what the sentences tell about the topic.

You have listened for the topic and the main idea. Can you find the topic and the main idea when you read a group of sentences?

A **paragraph** is a group of sentences that tells one main idea about a topic. The beginning of every paragraph is **indented**. To indent, leave a space before the first word.

What is the topic of the following paragraph? What is the main idea?

> Digging a hole can be hard work. You have to push on the shovel with your foot to loosen the dirt. Sometimes loose dirt trickles back into the hole. Then you have to dig it out again. Sometimes you hit big rocks. You have to dig around them with your fingers to get them out.

The topic of the paragraph above is *digging a hole*. Each sentence told you something about digging a hole. The main idea is *digging a hole can be hard work*.

Practice

Read each paragraph. Write the answers to the questions after each one.

Soil covers most of the earth's surface. There is soil under trees and under your feet. There is soil at the bottom of lakes and rivers. There is soil beneath lawns, roads, and sidewalks. Only bare rocks and the tops of some rocky mountains have no soil.

1. What is the topic?
   a. soil
   b. trees
   c. mountains
2. What is the main idea?
   a. Soil is under your feet.
   b. Soil covers most of the earth's surface.
   c. There is soil under roads.

What makes a geyser? Water drains into a crack in the earth's surface. If the water hits heated rock, it becomes hotter and hotter. It turns into steam. The steam pushes back up the crack. It carries water and mud with it. The steam, water, and mud shoot out of the ground right into the air.

1. What is the topic?
   a. steam
   b. geysers
   c. rocks
2. What is the main idea?
   a. making steam
   b. how a geyser is made
   c. cracks in the earth

Composition Skills

Topic Sentences and Supporting Details

You have already learned how to find the topic and the main idea when you read a paragraph. The topic is the one thing the paragraph tells about. The main idea sums up what the paragraph says about the topic.

A paragraph often has a sentence that states the main idea. This sentence is called the **topic sentence**.

What is the main idea of the paragraph below? Which sentence in the paragraph tells what the main idea is?

> You should do two things before you start to dig your hole. First, pick a good place to dig. Choose a place away from trees and plants. Find a spot where no one walks or plays. Second, gather all the shovels, buckets, and other tools you will need.

The main idea of the paragraph is *there are two things to do before you start to dig your hole*. The first sentence states that idea. The first sentence is the topic sentence.

The other sentences in the paragraph tell more about the main idea. They give **supporting details**. They tell what two things you should do before starting to dig a hole. What are the two things you should do?

Prewriting Practice

A. Read each paragraph. Then write the sentence that makes the best topic sentence for the paragraph.

1. You cannot see roots taking water from the dirt, but you can prove it. First, fill a jar with a cup of water. Next, stir in some blue food coloring. Then put a white flower in the water. In a short time you will notice that the white flower is turning blue.

    a. Food coloring is useful.
    b. Plant roots get water from dirt.
    c. A daisy is a white flower.

2. Collect samples of soil from different spots. Next, put each soil sample into a separate jar. Label each jar, telling where the soil came from. Then add water to the jars and stir. Rocky soil will settle first because it is heavy. Soil with clay in it will take longer to settle because it is lighter.

    a. Soil can be rocky.
    b. Label the jars.
    c. There are different kinds of soil.

B. The topic sentence is missing from the beginning of the paragraph below. Read the paragraph. Decide what the main idea is. Then write a good topic sentence for the paragraph.

[*Topic sentence goes here.*] First, get a jar, a cup of water, soil, several small green plants, and some white pebbles. Next, put about two inches of soil at the bottom of your jar. Put the plants in the soil. Then sprinkle the pebbles on the soil to make the planter look prettier. Finally, water the soil and put the lid on the jar.

Step-by-Step Order

Do you know how to make a sand castle? The paragraph below tells you how. Do the instructions make sense?

> It is easy to build a sand castle. Get very wet sand. Dig some holes through the walls to make doors. Pile one wet handful of sand on top of another to make walls. Decorate the castle with shells and pebbles.

These instructions are hard to understand. The steps are out of order. Which step is out of order?

Read the instructions below. Why are they clearer?

> It is easy to build a sand castle. First, get very wet sand. Next, pile one wet handful of sand on top of another to make walls. Then dig some holes through the walls to make doors. Finally, decorate the castle with shells and pebbles.

The steps are in the correct order. The order words *first, next, then,* and *finally* have been added.

Prewriting Practice

Write these steps for a fire drill in the correct order as a paragraph. Add order words.

Walk quickly and quietly outside.
Form a straight line.
Leave the room when your teacher tells you to.
Stand up and push in your chairs.
Follow these instructions for a fire drill.

Purpose and Audience

Why do you write something? You may want to tell a story or explain something. You always have a **purpose,** or a reason to write.

As you write, think about your **audience,** or your readers. Faith McNulty, the author of "How to Dig a Hole to the Other Side of the World," wrote for you. You were her audience. You too must think about your audience. Are you writing for a friend? a family member? your class? Some writing is done just for yourself.

Your writing will not always sound the same. It will change with your purpose and your audience.

Look at these instructions for a treasure hunt. Which one is written for someone new at school?

Clue

Go to the swings. Then look under the seat of the red swing. you will find your next clue.

Clue

Go to the playground. Look for the soccer field. To the right of the field are swings. Find the red swing. Look under the seat for the next clue.

Prewriting Practice

Write the answers to the questions below.

1. You want to tell your little brother how to wash his hair. Who is your audience? What is your purpose?
2. You want to give your classmates directions to your home. Who is your audience? What is your purpose?

The Grammar Connection

Using Exact Nouns

Which noun gives you a clearer picture?

> We would not have flowers without soil.
> We would not have daisies without soil.

The noun *daisies* is more exact than *flowers*. *Daisies* names a certain kind of flower. Use exact nouns to make your writing clearer and more interesting.

Practice Rewrite each sentence below. Change the underlined word to a more exact noun.

1. Without soil, we would not have <u>fruit</u> to eat.
2. <u>Animals</u> would not have grass to eat.
3. You could not buy warm <u>clothes</u> for the winter if there were no animals.
4. A young <u>child</u> would not have milk to drink.
5. Without trees, we could not build <u>things</u> from wood.
6. We would not have any wooden <u>furniture</u>.
7. There would be no paper for <u>people</u> to write on.
8. We would not have <u>places</u> for picnics.

The Writing Process
How to Write Instructions

Step 1: Prewriting

Kelly thought of all the things she could teach her classmates to do. She made a list of her topics.

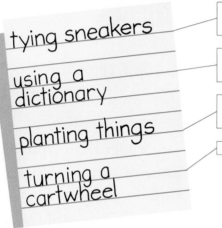

tying sneakers — Everyone knew how to do this.

using a dictionary — They learned this in school.

planting things — She had fun doing this. Others might like it too.

turning a cartwheel — This is easier to show.

Kelly remembered the oak tree she had grown. She circled *planting things*.

On Your Own

1. **Think and discuss** Make a list of the things you know how to do well. Use the Ideas page if you need help. Discuss your topics with a partner.
2. **Choose** Ask these questions about each topic.
   Do I know all the steps?
   Can I explain the steps clearly?
   Circle the topic you want to write about.
3. **Explore** What will be your topic sentence? What steps will you include? Do one of the activities under "Exploring Your Topic" on the Ideas page.

Ideas for Prewriting

Choosing Your Topic

Topic Ideas

Starting a rock
    collection
Making a sand box
Playing a game
Writing codes
Making breakfast
Making your bed
Taking a picture

Instruction Starters

What do you enjoy doing?
What do you know how to do
    well?
What do your friends ask you
    to teach them?
What have you learned to do
    recently?

Exploring Your Topic

Flow Chart

Make a flow chart for your
instructions. Write your topic
in a box. Write the steps in
order. Circle each step. Here
is Kelly's flow chart.

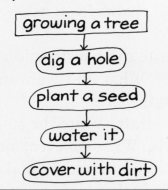

growing a tree
↓
dig a hole
↓
plant a seed
↓
water it
↓
cover with dirt

Pantomime

With a partner, act
out your
instructions for
your class.
Pantomime the
steps while your
partner tells what
you are doing.
Does the class have
any questions?

Step 2: Write a First Draft

Kelly was ready to write her first draft. She looked at her flow chart while writing. Kelly did not worry about making mistakes. Now she just wanted to get her ideas on paper.

Kelly's first draft

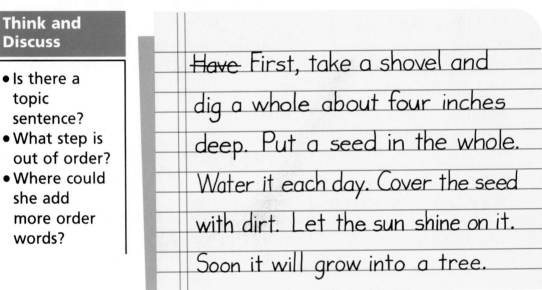

~~Have~~ First, take a shovel and dig a whole about four inches deep. Put a seed in the whole. Water it each day. Cover the seed with dirt. Let the sun shine on it. Soon it will grow into a tree.

Think and Discuss

- Is there a topic sentence?
- What step is out of order?
- Where could she add more order words?

On Your Own

1. **Think about purpose and audience** Ask yourself these questions.
   For whom shall I write these instructions?
   What is my purpose? What do I want my readers to know how to do?
2. **Write** Write your first draft. Write the steps in order. Use order words. Write on every other line so that you will have room to add or make changes. You can correct your mistakes later.

Step 3: Revise

Kelly read her first draft. She saw places where she could add order words to make the steps clearer.

Kelly wanted to know if someone else could follow her instructions. She read her first draft to Jenny.

Reading and responding

That sounds like fun, but at first I didn't know what the instructions were for.

I can add that at the beginning. Anything else?

What kind of seed should I use?

I'll make more changes.

Kelly thanked Jenny and made more revisions.

Kelly's revised draft

Growing your own oak tree is fun.
~~Have~~ First, take a shovel and
dig a whole about four inches
deep. Next, Put an acorn ~~a seed~~ in the whole.
Then Water it each day. Cover the acorn ~~seed~~
with dirt. Let the sun shine on it.
Soon it will grow into a tree.

Think and Discuss

- Which sentence did Kelly add? Why?
- Which sentence did she move? Why?
- What order words did she add?

On Your Own

1. **Think again** Read your instructions. Ask yourself these questions.

    Did I write a topic sentence?

    Are the steps in order?

    Where could I add order words and details?

2. **Revise** Make changes in your first draft. Underline your topic sentence. If you do not have a topic sentence, write one. Add order words and details. You may want to use words from the thesaurus below or the one beginning on page 414.

3. **Read/Listen/Respond** Read your instructions to a classmate or to your teacher.

Ask your listener:	As you listen:
"Are the steps in order?" "Are any steps missing?" "Can I add more details?"	I must listen carefully. Can I follow these instructions easily? What else should I know?

4. **Revise** Think about your listener's suggestions. Do you have any other ideas? Make those changes.

Thesaurus

cook bake, fry, broil
fasten tie, bind, close, seal
get gather, collect
last finally

make build, form, create
mix blend, stir
put place, lay, set
twist turn, twirl, spin

Step 4: Proofread

Kelly proofread her instructions. She used a dictionary. She used proofreading marks.

Here is the way Kelly's instructions looked.

Kelly's proofread draft

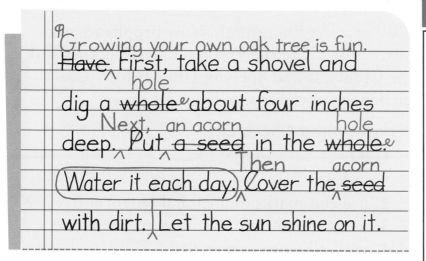

Think and Discuss

- Why did she add an indent mark?
- Which word did she correct for spelling?
- Why did she change two capital letters?

On Your Own

1. Proofreading Practice Proofread this paragraph. There is one spelling mistake. There is a wrong end mark, a missing apostrophe, and a mistake in paragraph format. Write the paragraph correctly.

```
It is fun to make fingerprint
paintinges.  First, put a dab
of paint on your fingertip.
Next, press down on your
paper?  Last, draw in details
with your sisters pen.
```

Proofreading Marks

⁊ Indent
∧ Add something
ℓ Take out something
≡ Capitalize
/ Make a small letter

2. Proofreading Application Now proofread your instructions. Use the Proofreading Checklist and the Grammar and Spelling Hints below. Use a dictionary to check spellings.

Proofreading Checklist

Did I

☑ **1.** indent?

☑ **2.** use end marks and capital letters correctly?

☑ **3.** use singular and plural nouns correctly?

☑ **4.** spell all words correctly?

The Grammar/Spelling Connection

Grammar Hints

Remember these rules from Unit 3.

- Add an apostrophe and *s* to a singular noun to make it show ownership. *(mother's, uncle's)*
- Add an apostrophe to a plural noun that ends in *s* to make it show ownership. *(boys', dogs')*

Spelling Hints

- If a singular noun ends with *s*, *sh*, *ch*, or *x*, add *es* to form the plural. *(fox<u>es</u>, dish<u>es</u>)*
- If a singular noun ends with a consonant and *y*, change the *y* to *i* and add *es*. *(berr<u>ies</u>, pon<u>ies</u>)*

Step 5: Publish

Kelly made a final neat copy of her instructions. She included all of her changes and corrections. She added the title "How to Grow an Oak Tree."

Then Kelly made a poster showing the steps for growing a tree. Her teacher asked her to read her instructions and show her poster during science class.

On Your Own

1. **Copy** Copy your instructions in your neatest handwriting.
2. **Add a title** Write a title for your instructions.
3. **Check** Read over your instructions again to make sure you have not left out anything or made any copying mistakes.
4. **Share** Think of a way to share your instructions.

Ideas for Sharing

- Draw a cartoon showing the steps.
- Read your instructions and show what to do to a group of classmates.
- Make an instruction booklet.

Writing Across the Curriculum
Instructions

Literature and Creative Writing

You never know what you might find when you dig. In "Oasis of the Stars," Abu found water. In "How to Dig a Hole to the Other Side of the World," you read about what you would find in the earth.

Use what you have learned about writing instructions. Do one or more of these activities.

> **Remember these things:**
> Write a topic sentence.
> Write the steps in order. Use order words.
> Think about your purpose and audience.

1. **Make it safe.** Write instructions for digging a hole. What will you do to make your hole safe? Tell what you plan to do and how a friend can help.

2. **Save the dinosaur bones.** You were digging, and you found some dinosaur bones. You must do something to save them. Write instructions on how to save dinosaur bones.

3. **Find the buried treasure.** You found a treasure chest, but you had to bury it. Write instructions for your family. Tell how to find your treasure.

Mathematics

In mathematics, you follow many kinds of instructions. When you solve problems and use numbers and measurements, you must put the steps in the right order.

Choose one or more of these activities. Follow the five steps you learned to write your instructions.

1. **Measure your height.** It is fun to know how tall people are. Write instructions for your friend. Tell how to measure your height and read the tape measure.

2. **Share a drawing.** Draw a simple shape on a sheet of paper. Write instructions telling how to make that shape. Give the instructions to a friend. Can your friend draw the shape by using your instructions?

3. **Be a paper artist.** Look at the things you can make by folding and cutting paper. Choose one of these items. Write instructions for a classmate telling how to make it. You may want to use some words from the Word Box.

Writing Steps
1. Choose a Topic
2. Write a First Draft
3. Revise
4. Proofread
5. Publish

half
quarter
paste
trim
design
fold

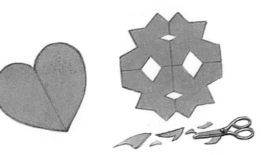

Book Report

Dressing Like a Book Character

Claudine enjoyed reading about Abu in "Oasis of the Stars." She liked to read about children who live in other countries. At the library she chose the book *Sumi and the Goat and the Tokyo Express* by Yoshiko Uchida. When she shared the book with her class, she wore a kimono like the one Sumi wears for holidays. Here is what she told them.

I read a book called *Sumi and the Goat and the Tokyo Express* by Yoshiko Uchida. I am dressed like Sumi, the main character in the book. Sumi lives in Sugi village in Japan.

Nothing much happens in Sugi village. Sumi makes friends with a new goat and gives it a red hat with holes for the goat's ears. She can't wait to tell her classmates about the goat.

But someone else has bigger news. A new railroad is being built for the Tokyo Express. The train will pass the village, but it will never stop there. Read the story to find out what happens.

Think and Discuss

• What did you learn about Sumi?
• What did you learn about Sugi village?

Share Your Book

Dress Like a Book Character

1. Choose an important character from your book.
2. Choose clothes that will make you look like the character. Find something to carry that is important in the story.
3. Wear this costume when you share your book with your class. Tell the title and author of your book. Tell a little about the character you are dressed as. Be careful not to tell too much of the story.

Other Activities

- Ask a classmate to dress like another character in the book. If the character is an animal, make the costume from a large paper bag. Use crayons to draw ears and whiskers. Tell about one thing the two characters do together in the book.
- Does your character have a special costume that he or she wears on special days? Draw a picture of your character wearing this costume. Tell about it.

 The Book Nook

Makota, the Smallest Boy *by Yoshiko Uchida* Makota is the smallest and slowest in his class. Old Mr. Imai helps him to be first.	**New Boy in Dublin** *by Clyde Robert Bulla* When Coady's family moves to Dublin, nothing in the city is the way he thought it would be.

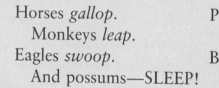

Horses *gallop*.
Monkeys *leap*.
Eagles *swoop*.
And possums—SLEEP!

Panthers *pounce*.
Rabbits *hop*.
Bullfrogs *dive*.
And donkeys—STOP!

Ilo Orleans
"Action"

Verbs

Getting Ready Our world is filled with action. People talk, run, eat, drive. Dogs bark. Planes fly. The wind blows. We cannot talk or write without using words that name actions. These words are called verbs. In this unit, you will learn how to use verbs correctly.

Activities

Listening Listen as the poem on the opposite page is read. Listen for the words that name actions. Can you hear all eight verbs? What are they?

Speaking What verbs could you use to tell what the frog is doing? Tell your verbs to the class. How many other verbs can you name? Make a class list on the board.

1 | What Are Verbs?

You have learned that a noun names a person, a place, or a thing. A word that tells what people or things do is a verb. **Verbs** are words that show action.

Ellen bought a ticket.

She rode on the bus.

Every sentence has a subject and a predicate. You know that the main word in the subject is often a noun. The verb is the main word in the predicate.

SUBJECT	PREDICATE
The driver	stopped at the library .

Guided Practice What is the verb in each sentence?

Example: Carmine flew to California. *flew*

1. He watched a movie on the airplane.
2. He stayed with his Uncle Jim.
3. Carmine visited many places.
4. He enjoyed the zoo in San Diego.
5. Carmine liked the lions the best.
6. One day he swam in the Pacific Ocean.
7. Children jumped over the big waves.

The lion s t r e t c h e d on the rock.

> ▶ A **verb** is a word that shows action.
> ▶ The verb is the main word in the predicate.

More Practice Write the verb in each sentence.

Example: Jan works for a newspaper. *works*

8. She writes news stories.
9. Jan likes her job.
10. Sometimes she stays at work very late.
11. Rico helps Jan with her work.
12. He takes pictures for the newspaper.
13. One day a lion escaped from the circus.
14. The lion trainer looked everywhere for it.
15. Police officers searched the streets.
16. People stayed in their houses.
17. Many stores closed early.
18. Rico grabbed his camera.
19. Jan raced out of the office.
20. They drove slowly through town.
21. Rico saw the lion in front of the pet store.
22. Jan heard a strange noise.
23. The lion snored very loudly.
24. They stopped the car.
25. Rico snapped a picture of the lion.
26. Jan's story made big news.

Writing Application: Creative Writing

Pretend that you are a newspaper reporter. Someone has discovered a footprint that is six feet long. Write five sentences about the footprint. Underline the verbs in your sentences.

2 | Verbs in the Present

Verbs show action in sentences. Verbs also tell when the action happens. The verb in each sentence below tells about an action that is happening now. Each verb is in the **present time**.

Mandy builds a snowman. Some friends help .

Verbs in the present have two forms. The correct form to use depends on what the subject of the sentence is.

1. Add *s* to the verb when the noun in the subject is singular.

The dog barks at the snowman. Jill laughs .

2. Do not add *s* to the verb when the noun in the subject is plural.

The boys shovel . Their parents start the car.

Guided Practice Is each subject singular or plural? What is the correct verb form for each sentence?

Example: Paul (love, loves) the snow.
singular   loves

1. Gregory (make, makes) big snowballs.
2. Toby (get, gets) the sled.
3. Their mother (take, takes) pictures.
4. The boys (race, races) to the hill.
5. Many children (slides, slide) down the hill.
6. Rebecca (skate, skates) on the ice.
7. Her sister (spin, spins) around in a circle.

Summing up

▶ Add *s* to a verb in the present when the noun in the subject is singular.

▶ Do not add *s* to a verb in the present when the noun in the subject is plural.

More Practice Choose the correct verb in ( ) to complete each sentence. Write the sentences.

Example: A koala (live, lives) in trees.
A koala lives in trees.

8. A snail (move, moves) slowly.
9. The horses (gallop, gallops) fast.
10. Rabbits (jump, jumps) into the bushes.
11. A bear (climb, climbs) trees.
12. Three worms (wiggle, wiggles) in the grass.
13. That monkey (swing, swings) on branches.
14. A turtle (hide, hides) in its shell.
15. Owls (hunt, hunts) at night.
16. Kangaroos (hop, hops) on their hind legs.
17. Squirrels (eat, eats) nuts.
18. A beaver (save, saves) food for the winter.
19. The duck (dive, dives) under the water.
20. Those hippos (stand, stands) in the lake.
21. Chipmunks (run, runs) over rocks.
22. Dolphins (travel, travels) in groups.

Writing Application: A Story

You have a chance to be an animal for a day. What animal would you like to be? Write a paragraph telling what you would see and do during that day. Use verbs in the present time. Underline the verbs.

3 | More Verbs in the Present

Plurals
crash + es = crashes
cry - y + ies = cries

Most verbs in the present end with *s* when the subject is a singular noun. Some verbs, though, end with *es* instead of *s*. Add *es* to verbs that end with *s*, *sh*, *ch*, or *x* when they are used with a singular noun in the subject. Do not add *es* when the noun in the subject is plural. Study the following chart to see how some verbs end with *es*.

Singular	Plural
Rob **tosses** a ball.	The boys **toss** the ball.
My grandfather **fishes**.	The girls **fish**.
Emily **mixes** the salad.	Friends **mix** the salad.
Mother **watches** us.	People **watch** us.

Some verbs end with a consonant and *y*. Change the *y* to *i* and add *es* when you use this kind of verb with a singular noun.

carr*y* + es = carr*ies*   hurr*y* + es = hurr*ies*

Guided Practice What is the correct present time of each verb in ( )?

Example: Uncle Joe ____ the food.   (pass)
          passes

1. A boy ____ his red kite.   (fly)
2. Tammy ____ in the lake.   (splash)
3. Father ____ me a game.   (teach)
4. Aunt Alice ____ the net.   (fix)
5. Krista ____ the ball.   (watch)

▶ Add *es* to a verb in the present that ends with *s*, *sh*, *ch*, *x*, or a consonant and *y* when it is used with a singular noun.

▶ If a verb ends with a consonant and *y*, change the *y* to *i* before adding *es*.

More Practice

A. Choose the correct verb in ( ) to complete each sentence. Write the sentences.

Example: Mr. Hogan (teach, teaches) at Taft School.
Mr. Hogan teaches at Taft School.

6. The students (study, studies) history.
7. Maria (reach, reaches) for more paper.
8. Pedro (try, tries) very hard.
9. Matt (guess, guesses) the correct answer.
10. The minutes (pass, passes).
11. Emil (finish, finishes) first.

B. Write the correct present time of each verb in ( ).

Example: The rain ____ on Julie. (splash) *splashes*

12. Julie ____ to her house. (hurry)
13. Sandy ____ after her. (rush)
14. Mom ____ them some hot soup. (fix)
15. Julie ____ out by the fireplace. (stretch)
16. The machine ____ the clothes. (dry)

Writing Application: Creative Writing
Pretend that you take a drink of water. Suddenly, you turn into a toy! Write five sentences about yourself. Use the words *try*, *push*, *catch*, *press*, and *fly*.

4 | Verbs in the Past

Verbs in the present tell about actions that happen now. Verbs can also tell that actions have already happened. A verb that tells about an action that has already happened is in the **past time**.

PRESENT

Kim steers the boat.

PAST

Kim steered the boat.

Add -*ed* to most verbs to show past time.

Present	kick	float	push	mix
Past	kicked	floated	pushed	mixed

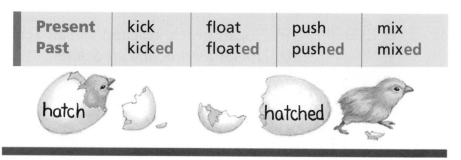

Guided Practice

A. Which verb shows past time in each sentence?

Example: Jerry (rows, rowed) his boat. *rowed*

1. The boat (passes, passed) two ducks.
2. Jerry (watched, watches) the ducks.
3. The ducks (quacked, quack) loudly.
4. Jerry (enjoys, enjoyed) the sound.
5. He (tosses, tossed) some bread to the ducks.
6. The ducks (rushes, rushed) to the bread.

B. What is the past time for each verb?

Example: play *played*

7. turn	**9.** talk	**11.** join	**13.** visit
8. pull	**10.** lift	**12.** patch	**14.** pick

▶ A verb in the **past time** shows that an action has already happened.
▶ Add -ed to most verbs to show past time.

More Practice

A. Write *present* if the underlined verb shows present time. Write *past* if the verb shows past time.

Example: The children <u>fix</u> the tree house.   *present*

15. Anita <u>patches</u> a hole in the floor.
16. Molly <u>sawed</u> the new boards.
17. Jeffrey <u>mixed</u> the paint.
18. Susan <u>paints</u> the boards.
19. Mark <u>washes</u> the paint brushes.
20. Carlos <u>hammers</u> the boards into place.
21. The children <u>worked</u> for hours.
22. Finally, the children <u>finished</u> their repairs.
23. The girls <u>climbed</u> into the tree house.
24. The boys <u>joined</u> them.
25. The tree house <u>looks</u> great.

B. Write the past time of these verbs.

Example: splash   *splashed*

26. help	**29.** cook	**32.** guess
27. laugh	**30.** walk	**33.** jump
28. wax	**31.** pitch	**34.** start

Writing Application: Instructions
Write instructions telling how to wash a puppy. Use the verbs *barked, leaped, washed,* and *finished.*

5 | More Verbs in the Past

You can make most verbs show past time just by adding *-ed*. However, the spelling of some verbs changes in other ways when you add *-ed*.

1. Some verbs end with *e*. Drop the *e* and add *-ed*.

   rac**e** + **ed** = rac**ed**   jok**e** + **ed** = jok**ed**

2. Some verbs end with a consonant and *y*. Change the *y* to *i* when you add *-ed*.

   cr**y** + **ed** = cr**ied**   worr**y** + **ed** = worr**ied**

3. Some verbs end with one vowel followed by one consonant. Double the consonant and add *-ed*.

   sto**p** + **p** + **ed** = sto**pped**   hu**g** + **g** + **ed** = hu**gged**

Guided Practice How is the past time of each verb spelled?

Example: like *liked*

1. pat   **3.** chase   **5.** drop   **7.** drag
2. marry   **4.** dry   **6.** save   **8.** copy

Summing up

▶ The spelling of some verbs changes when you add *-ed*.

More Practice Write the correct past time of each verb in ( ).

Example: Tina ___ at the post office. (stop) *stopped*

 9. A present ___ from her grandmother. (arrive)
10. A clerk ___ a box in front of her. (place)
11. Tina ___ home. (hurry)
12. She ___ the present into her house. (carry)
13. Quickly Tina ___ her present. (unwrap)
14. Tina ___ to open the present carefully. (try)
15. She ___ at the string. (tug)
16. A large clown puppet ___ at her. (stare)
17. The puppet ___ on strings. (move)
18. It ___ up and down. (dance)
19. It ___ back and forth. (hop)
20. Tina ___ the puppet Boomer. (name)
21. She ___ each part of the puppet. (study)
22. Then she ___ a puppet show. (plan)
23. Tina ___ to make a stage. (decide)
24. She ___ three friends to the show. (invite)
25. Boomer ___ at the children. (smile)
26. He ___ three balls. (juggle)
27. The children ___ the funny puppet. (love)
28. They ___ their hands loudly. (clap)

Writing Application: Sentences

Today is your birthday. You have just opened a present. It is just what you have always wanted. What kind of present is it? Does it talk? Do you have to put it together? Write five sentences about your present. Use the words in the Word Box.

| wrapped | amazed | invited | carried | planned |

6 | The Special Verb *be*

The verbs *am, is, are, was,* and *were* are all forms of the verb *be.* These verbs do not show action. They tell what someone or something is or was.

I am sleepy now.   I was tired last night.

Today we are in Maine.   Friday we were in Vermont.

It is a four-hour drive.   It was a long trip.

The verbs *am, is,* and *are* show present time. *Was* and *were* show past time.

Subject	Present	Past
I	am	was
you	are	were
he, she, it	is	was
singular noun *(John)*	is	was
we	are	were
they	are	were
plural noun *(dogs)*	are	were

Guided Practice Choose the correct verb for each sentence. Does the verb show present time or past time?

Example: The porch light (was, were) on. *was   past*

1. The key (is, are) in Mother's pocket.
2. The children (is, are) in the car.
3. My brothers (is, are) in the front seat.
4. I (is, am) in the back.
5. We (was, were) ready for our vacation.

> ▶ The verb *be* has special forms.
> ▶ *Am*, *is*, and *are* show present time.
> ▶ *Was* and *were* show past time.

More Practice

A. Choose the correct verb in ( ) to complete each sentence. Write the sentences.

Example: I (is, am) in class.   *I am in class.*

6. Mrs. Schultz (is, are) the teacher.
7. We (are, is) excited about the reports.
8. Kevin (is, are) the reporter today.
9. Lisa (were, was) the class reporter yesterday.
10. Her topic (was, were) George Washington.
11. Your report on Lincoln (was, were) terrific!

B. Each sentence is written in the present time. Change the underlined verb to show past time. Write the new verb.

Example: Frank <u>is</u> a roller skater.   *was*

12. We <u>are</u> members of a club.
13. The members <u>are</u> good skaters.
14. You <u>are</u> the best skater.
15. I <u>am</u> early for every lesson.
16. Ms. Ames <u>is</u> our teacher.

Writing Application: Creative Writing

Your bicycle club is building a bicycle. What will the bicycle look like? What can it do? Write five sentences about the bicycle. Use the verbs *am*, *is*, *are*, *was*, or *were* in at least two of your sentences.

7 | Helping Verbs

Sometimes the words *has* and *have* help other verbs to show past time. *Has* and *have* are called **helping verbs**.

1. Use the helping verb *has* with a singular noun in the subject and with *he, she,* or *it.*

   Ada has played the game.   She has enjoyed it.

2. Use the helping verb *have* with a plural noun in the subject and with *I, you, we,* or *they.*

   The boys have helped her.   I have watched .

Guided Practice Choose *has* or *have* to finish each sentence correctly.

Example: The game (has, have) started.   *has*

1. Amy (has, have) counted to ten.
2. She (has, have) peeked behind a tree.
3. Bob (has, have) run near the house.
4. I (has, have) crawled under a big bush.
5. Amy (has, have) found Bob.
6. We (has, have) played this game often.

Summing up

▶ *Has* and *have* are **helping verbs**.
▶ Use *has* with a singular noun in the subject and with *he, she,* or *it.*
▶ Use *have* with a plural noun in the subject and with *I, you, we,* or *they.*

More Practice Complete each sentence correctly with *has* or *have*. Write the sentences.

Example: My class ____ studied about sea animals.
My class has studied about sea animals.

7. David ____ read about sea turtles.
8. All turtles ____ hatched from eggs.
9. Some leatherback turtles ____ weighed about 1500 pounds.
10. They ____ measured eight feet long.
11. John ____ brought in his pet turtle.
12. We ____ learned that whales breathe through lungs.
13. Many whales ____ lived for more than forty years.
14. Suki ____ listened to a record about whales.
15. She ____ discovered that humpback whales sing.
16. Some songs ____ lasted for thirty minutes.
17. Julia ____ reported about seals.
18. Many fur seals ____ traveled great distances.
19. Harbor seals ____ spent most of their time on land.
20. They ____ performed funny tricks for people.
21. Julia's brother ____ fed some harbor seals.
22. Tyrone ____ collected books about sea life.
23. He ____ found many different books.
24. His teacher ____ added to Tyrone's collection.
25. Mrs. Dodge ____ bought a book about sea horses.
26. I ____ enjoyed the books.

Writing Application: A Story

Pretend that you and your family have gone fishing. A friendly whale has come along and has asked you to go for a ride. Where does the whale take you? What do you see? Write five sentences about your ride. Use the helping verbs *has* or *have* in each sentence.

8 | Irregular Verbs

Some verbs are special. They do not end with *-ed* to show past time. These verbs have one special spelling to show past time. They have another spelling when used with *has, have,* or *had.*

PRESENT: Many people run in Boston's big race.

PAST: William ran in the race last year.

WITH HAS: Anita has run in the race many times.

Study the chart below. Which two verbs have the same spelling in the present and when used with *has, have,* or *had*?

Present	Past	With *has, have,* or *had*
go	went	has, have, or had gone
see	saw	has, have, or had seen
do	did	has, have, or had done
run	ran	has, have, or had run
come	came	has, have, or had come

Guided Practice Choose the correct verb for each sentence.

Example: I had (saw, seen) the start of the race. *seen*

1. Wheelchair racers have (did, done) well.
2. Many racers (ran, run) all twenty-six miles last year.
3. One young man has (came, come) in first.
4. The crowd (saw, seen) him at the finish line.
5. He (went, gone) home with a medal.

▶ The verbs *go, see, do, run,* and *come* have special spellings to show past time.

More Practice Choose the correct verb in ( ) to complete each sentence. Write the sentences.

Example: My class (saw, seen) movies of space flights.
My class saw movies of space flights.

6. Mrs. Win had (ran, run) the film.
7. The films had (came, come) from Kennedy Space Center.
8. People have (went, gone) there to become astronauts.
9. The astronauts have (ran, run) many miles.
10. They have (did, done) exercises for many days.
11. Neil Armstrong (went, gone) to the moon in 1969.
12. He had (went, gone) for a moon walk.
13. Edwin E. Aldrin, Jr., had (went, gone) with him.
14. They had (came, come) home with moon rocks.
15. They (came, come) back to Earth with many pictures.
16. Many reporters (did, done) stories about their trip.
17. Mom (saw, seen) the moon landing on TV.
18. Maria has (saw, seen) moon rocks in a museum.
19. John Glenn (went, gone) into orbit in 1962.
20. He had (went, gone) around Earth three times.
21. We have (saw, seen) pictures of Sally Ride.
22. She has (went, gone) on a space shuttle.

Writing Application: Creative Writing
Pretend that you are living on the moon. Life on the moon is different from life on Earth. Write five sentences about your life on the moon. Use the past time of the verbs *go, see, do, run,* and *come.*

9 | More Irregular Verbs

You have learned that the verbs *go, see, do, run,* and *come* are special. They have special spellings to show past time.

The verbs *give, write, eat, take,* and *grow* are also special verbs. They have one special spelling to show past time. They have another spelling when used with *has, have,* or *had.*

PRESENT: I grow tomatoes in my garden.

PAST: Alexis grew carrots last summer.

WITH HAVE: We have grown many pretty flowers.

Study the chart below.

Present	Past	With *has, have,* or *had*
give	gave	has, have, or had given
write	wrote	has, have, or had written
eat	ate	has, have, or had eaten
take	took	has, have, or had taken
grow	grew	has, have, or had grown

Guided Practice Choose the correct verb for each sentence.

Example: Grandpa has (took, taken) pictures. *taken*

1. He (gave, given) me a camera for my birthday.
2. I (wrote, written) him a thank-you letter.
3. I have (grew, grown) sunflowers for a hobby.
4. We (took, taken) pictures of the sunflowers.
5. Some insects had (ate, eaten) a few of the flowers.

▶ The verbs *give, write, eat, take,* and *grow* have special spellings to show past time.

More Practice Choose the correct verb in ( ) to complete each sentence. Write the sentences.

Example: Last year a farmer (grew, grown) watermelons.
Last year a farmer grew watermelons.

6. He had (gave, given) Amanda a few.
7. Amanda (took, taken) the watermelons home.
8. The children (ate, eaten) them.
9. Chico (took, taken) the seeds out.
10. He (gave, given) some seeds to Grandma.
11. This year she has (grew, grown) her own watermelons.
12. One watermelon (grew, grown) very large.
13. Grandma (took, taken) it to the fair.
14. She had (wrote, written) Chico and Amanda a letter.
15. She (wrote, written) them about a contest.
16. Chico (took, taken) a trip to the fair.
17. The judges have (ate, eaten) Grandma's watermelon.
18. They (gave, given) Grandma first prize.
19. Chico (ate, eaten) a juicy slice.
20. Many people have (took, taken) pictures of Grandma.
21. Grandma (wrote, written) a story about her best plant.
22. She has (gave, given) courses on how to grow fruit.

Writing Application: Sentences
You have won a million dollars in a contest. What kind of contest was it? Write five sentences about the contest. Use the past time of the verbs *give, write, eat, take,* and *grow* in your sentences.

Sometimes two words are put together and shortened to make one word. The shortened form of the two words is a **contraction**. An apostrophe (') takes the place of any letter or letters that have been left out.

TWO WORDS	CONTRACTION
My radio does not work.	My radio doesn't work.
I cannot listen to it.	I can't listen to it.

Many contractions are made by putting together a verb and the word *not*.

Common Contractions with *not*

is not	isn't	do not	don't
are not	aren't	does not	doesn't
was not	wasn't	did not	didn't
were not	weren't	could not	couldn't
has not	hasn't	should not	shouldn't
have not	haven't	would not	wouldn't
had not	hadn't	cannot	can't

The contraction *won't* is special. It is formed from the words *will not*.

Guided Practice What are the contractions for the word or words below?

Example: do not   *don't*

1. were not	**3.** did not	**5.** is not	**7.** cannot
2. will not	**4.** are not	**6.** has not	**8.** was not

▶ A **contraction** is a shortened form of two words joined together. Use an apostrophe in place of the missing letter or letters.

More Practice

A. Write the contractions for the underlined words.

Example: We <u>are not</u> happy. *aren't*

9. The TV <u>is not</u> working.
10. We <u>do not</u> know what is wrong with it.
11. Mrs. Cabot <u>could not</u> fix the TV today.
12. It <u>cannot</u> be fixed until tomorrow.
13. I <u>have not</u> seen my favorite animal show.
14. My father <u>has not</u> watched the news.
15. Gina <u>will not</u> see the program about whales.

B. Write the words that make up each contraction.

Example: Mia <u>isn't</u> foolish like her friends. *is not*

16. She <u>doesn't</u> forget to follow safety rules.
17. Children <u>shouldn't</u> play in the street.
18. Carlos <u>didn't</u> cross at the crosswalk.
19. Brad <u>doesn't</u> fasten his seat belt.
20. Molly <u>wasn't</u> obeying the speed limit.
21. Chen <u>hadn't</u> signaled before a turn.
22. These children <u>weren't</u> using good sense.

Writing Application: Sentences
Pretend that you are a police officer. You are asked to teach third graders bicycle safety. Write five safety rules for bike riders. Begin each sentence with *Don't.*

Building Vocabulary

Prefixes

A **prefix** is a word part added to the beginning of a word. It changes the meaning of the word.

Prefix	Meaning	Example
un- re-	"not" or "the opposite of" "again"	unhappy repaint

The unhappy boy lost his toy boat.

Rebecca repainted the old fence.

Practice

Complete each sentence by adding *un-* or *re-* to the word in ( ). Write the sentences.

Example: Did you ____ the food for the party?   (pack)
Did you unpack the food for the party?

1. Mom has already ____ the chicken.   (heat)
2. It is ____ to touch the hot dish.   (safe)
3. John is very ____.   (happy)
4. He is ____ to be here until later.   (able)
5. I had to ____ Rita's invitation.   (write)

Suffixes

You know that a prefix is added to the beginning of a word. A **suffix** is a word part too. When it is added to the end of a word, it changes the meaning.

Suffix	Meaning	Example
-er	"someone who does something"	farmer
-less	"without"	fearless

A farmer is a person who farms.

A person without fear is fearless .

Practice

Complete each sentence by adding *-er* or *-less* to the word in ( ). Write the sentences.

Example: Julian is a ___ for the newspaper.   (report)
Julian is a reporter for the newspaper.

1. Is that stray kitten ___?   (home)
2. My favorite ___ is giving a concert.   (sing)
3. That broken baseball bat is ___.   (use)
4. The blue sky is ___.   (cloud)
5. Did your ___ give you a test today?   (teach)

Writing Application: Creative Writing

Pretend that you are a flower. Someone picks you. What happens to you after you are picked? Write five sentences. Use the words in the Word Box.

gardener	unwrap	harmless	refill	fearless

Grammar-Writing Connection

Combining Sentences: Compound Predicates

You know that combining sentences often makes your writing stronger. Sometimes you can combine two short sentences that have the same subject. Combine the predicates of both sentences to make a longer sentence. When you combine two predicates, use the word *and*.

Tony ran fastest .

Tony won the race .

> Tony ran fastest and won the race .

Notice that *Tony* is the subject of both sentences. You can combine the predicates *ran fastest* and *won the race* to make one longer sentence.

Revising Sentences

Write each pair of sentences as one sentence.

Example: The coach smiles. The coach nods his head.
The coach smiles and nods his head.

1. Amy sits in her wheelchair. Amy practices basketball.
2. She goes to the gym. She exercises for three hours.
3. Everyone is ready to play. Everyone wants to win.
4. The teams line up. The teams wait for the whistle.
5. Theresa gets the ball. Theresa passes it to Amy.
6. Amy shoots a basket. Amy scores a point.
7. The crowd cheers. The crowd claps.
8. Mrs. Parks smiles at Amy's team. Mrs. Parks gives them a trophy.

Creative Writing

Balloon by Grandma Moses
© Grandma Moses Properties Co.

Do you think someone your age painted this picture? No—a grandmother did! Grandma Moses began painting at the age of seventy-six. Her simple paintings show farm scenes.

• Why does this picture seem busy and happy?

Activities

1. **Write a poem.** What if you could go riding in this balloon? Write a poem about your ride.
2. **Write a story.** Who are the children waving and jumping in this painting? Write a story about them.
3. **Describe what you saw.** Have you ever spotted something wonderful in the sky? Describe it.

Check-up: Unit 5

What Are Verbs? *(p. 130)* Write the verb in each sentence.

1. Claudia took a trip to Egypt.
2. Her sister Libby went with her.
3. They rode camels.
4. Then they visited the pyramids.
5. Libby sent me a postcard.

Verbs in the Present *(pp. 132, 134)* Choose the correct verb in ( ) to complete each sentence. Write the sentences.

6. A bee (fly, flies) to a flower.
7. Pollen (stick, sticks) to the bee's legs.
8. The bee (rush, rushes) the pollen to the hive.
9. The worker bees (make, makes) honey.
10. The children (watch, watches) them.
11. Uncle Phil (take, takes) the honey from the hive.

Verbs in the Past *(p. 136)* Write the past time of the following verbs.

12. climb   14. fix   16. wish   18. look
13. touch   15. miss   17. lift   19. march

More Verbs in the Past *(p. 138)* Write the correct past time of each verb in ( ).

20. The wind ____ through the trees.   (whistle)
21. The rain ____ against the windows.   (slam)
22. A cat ____ in the rain.   (cry)
23. Maria ____ to the front door.   (hurry)
24. Her cat ____ into the warm kitchen.   (race)
25. Maria ____ the cat.   (dry)

The Special Verb *be (p. 140)* Choose the correct verb for each sentence. Write the sentences.

26. A kitten (was, were) for sale.
27. Kittens (is, are) playful animals.
28. Ollie (is, are) black and white.
29. His paws (is, are) tiny.
30. Once Ollie (was, were) up on the roof.
31. He (was, were) scared.

Helping Verbs *(p. 142)* Complete each sentence correctly with *has* or *have*. Write the sentences.

32. Rosita ____ been to a Mexican festival.
33. She ____ enjoyed the fireworks and bells.
34. Her grandparents ____ marched in the parade.
35. Some festivals ____ started before daylight.
36. Many Mexicans ____ worn colorful costumes.

Irregular Verbs *(pp. 144, 146)* Choose the correct verb in ( ) to complete each of the sentences below. Write the sentences.

37. Aunt Joan has (went, gone) to Africa.
38. She has (saw, seen) many giraffes.
39. The giraffes had (ate, eaten) leaves from tall trees.
40. Aunt Joan (came, come) to my class.
41. She (gave, given) a talk about Africa.
42. My class (took, taken) notes.
43. I have (wrote, written) a story about giraffes.

Contractions with *not (p. 148)* Write the contraction for each word or words.

44. do not
45. cannot
46. have not
47. should not
48. was not
49. will not
50. has not
51. did not
52. would not

Enrichment

Time Out!

How do you and your friends spend time? Make a large paper clock. Draw hands on it to show a time of day. What do you usually do at this time? Write a sentence about it on the clock.

Example: At 4:00 P.M., I play basketball.

Now ask three classmates what they do at this time. Write their sentences on the clock too. Use verbs that show present time.

Listen! Listen!

Each place has its own set of sounds. Find this out for yourself. Listen to the sounds in your classroom. Make a list of everything you hear. Write complete sentences with verbs in the past time. Underline each verb in your sentences.

The chalk squeaked across the board.

Plant Care

Pretend that your family is taking a vacation. A friend promises to take care of the house plants. Write a list of instructions. Begin each sentence with a command—for example, "Talk nicely to the plants for ten minutes every day."

VERB ACCORDIONS

You can use one subject with many action verbs. Prove this to yourself by making a verb accordion. First, cut a strip from the top of a piece of paper. Think up and write the subject of a sentence on this strip. Next, fold the rest of the paper back and forth to make an accordion. Write an action verb on each section of the accordion. Use the past time. Read each sentence to be sure it makes sense. Tape the accordion to the end of the strip.

⊞ Contraction Cards

Players—2. **You need**—14 index cards. Label them *is, did, are, should, was, would, were, could, have, does, had, do, has, can.* **How to play**—Mix the cards and place them face down in a pile. Draw one card at a time, taking turns. Add *not* to the word on the card to form a contraction. Use each contraction correctly in a sentence.

Example: My dog can't find its tail!

Ask your partner whether the sentence is correct. **Scoring**—2 points if you spell the contraction correctly; 1 point for a correct sentence. Play until someone scores 15 points.

1 | What Are Verbs? (p. 130)

● Write the verb in each sentence.

Example: The band|marches down the street.   *marches*

1. We|watch it go by.
2. Many children|follow the band leader.
3. A tall boy|carries the flag.
4. The flag|waves in the wind.
5. Two clowns|dance.
6. Hana|beats the drum.

▲ Write the verb in each sentence.

Example: My family works in the yard.   *works*

7. Mom cuts the grass.
8. Randy trims the bushes.
9. I rake the leaves into a pile.
10. Lee plants some vegetables.
11. My sisters paint the old fence.
12. Dad waters the roses and the tulips.
13. Then we drink some cold fruit juice.

■ Think of a verb that makes sense in each sentence. Then write the sentences.

Example: Nick ____ to the mailbox.
        Nick walks to the mailbox.

14. He ____ a letter to his pen pal Eric.
15. Eric ____ in Toronto, Canada.
16. Once Nick ____ Eric.
17. He ____ to Canada in an airplane.
18. Nick ____ with them for a week.
19. The boys ____ a hockey game.
20. They ____ in Lake St. Louis two times.

● Choose the correct present time of the verb in each pair of sentences below. Write the correct sentences.

Example: Your body <u>works</u> hard.
Your body <u>work</u> hard.   *Your body works hard.*

1. Your nose <u>smells</u>.
Your nose <u>smell</u>.

4. Your eyes <u>see</u>.
Your eyes <u>sees</u>.

2. Your ears <u>hears</u>.
Your ears <u>hear</u>.

5. Your teeth <u>chews</u> food.
Your teeth <u>chew</u> food.

3. Your brain <u>think</u>.
Your brain <u>thinks</u>.

6. Your heart <u>pump</u> blood.
Your heart <u>pumps</u> blood.

▲ Choose the correct verb in ( ) to complete each sentence. Write the sentences.

Example: Children (need, needs) good food.
Children need good food.

7. Your body (use, uses) food in many ways.
8. Bananas (give, gives) us energy.
9. Beans (make, makes) the body stronger.
10. Tomas (pack, packs) a cheese sandwich for lunch.
11. Melissa (drink, drinks) milk every day.
12. The Kennetts (eat, eats) three healthy meals a day.

■ Write the correct present time of each verb in ( ). Then write whether the subject is singular or plural.

Example: Mrs. Gibson ____ us about the heart.   (tell)
tells   singular

13. Hearts ____ blood.   (pump)
14. Each beat ____ blood to the rest of the body.   (send)
15. Tubes ____ to and from the heart.   (lead)
16. The lungs ____ blood.   (get)
17. The brain ____ blood too.   (need)
18. Sarah's heart ____ ninety times a minute.   (beat)

3 | More Verbs in the Present (p. 134)

● Write the verb in each pair that is spelled correctly.

Example: carryes
carries *carries*

1. mixs
mixes

3. pushs
pushes

5. fixs
fixes

7. hurryes
hurries

2. teaches
teachs

4. marries
marrys

6. cries
cryes

8. catchs
catches

▲ Choose the correct verb in ( ) to complete each sentence. Write the sentences.

Example: Spiders (catch, catches) bugs in their webs.
Spiders catch bugs in their webs.

9. A spider (push, pushes) a silk thread into the air.
10. The thread (fly, flies) through the air.
11. Strong winds (carry, carries) the silk to a tree.
12. The spider (stretches, stretch) silk to make a web.
13. The animal (finish, finishes) its work.
14. Bugs (flies, fly) into the web.
15. Then the spider (rush, rushes) to its meal.

■ Write the correct present time of each verb in ( ). Then write *singular* if the subject is singular. Write *plural* if the subject is plural.

Example: Scientists ___ dolphins. (study)
study plural

16. A mother dolphin ___ her baby. (touch)
17. The mother ___ it to the top of the water. (push)
18. The baby ___ for a breath of air. (rush)
19. Other dolphins ___ through the water. (hurry)
20. One scientist ___ two dolphins tricks. (teach)
21. Another trainer ___ the dolphins some food. (toss)
22. Many people ___ the dolphins. (watch)

● Write the word in each pair that shows past time.

Example: jump

jumped *jumped*

1. splashed
   splash
2. watched
   watches
3. plays
   played

4. packed
   packs
5. laughed
   laugh
6. twists
   twisted

7. pitched
   pitches
8. barks
   barked
9. yelled
   yell

10. rush
    rushed
11. crosses
    crossed
12. add
    added

▲ Change the verb in ( ) to show past time. Write each sentence.

Example: Long ago people ___ in groups.   (travel)
Long ago people traveled in groups.

13. Early people ___ wild animals for food.   (hunt)
14. Hunters ___ berries and nuts.   (gather)
15. Then people ___ new ways of doing things.   (learn)
16. They ___ with simple tools.   (work)
17. Men and women ___ seeds.   (plant)
18. They ___ some of their food over a fire.   (cook)

■ Change the verb in each sentence to show past time. Write the sentences.

Example: I learn about Christopher Columbus.
I learned about Christopher Columbus.

19. Columbus talks to the Queen of Spain.
20. He asks for three ships.
21. His ships sail across the ocean.
22. The sailors reach a new land in 1492.
23. They land in America!
24. The ships stay in America for a few months.
25. Then Columbus returns to Spain.

EXTRA PRACTICE: UNIT 5

● Write the past time for each verb below. Drop or add letters as needed.

Example: copy + ed = *copied*

1. dry + ed =   **7.** marry + ed =

2. hike + ed =   **8.** trot + ed =

3. hop + ed =   **9.** pin + ed =

4. tag + ed =   **10.** hurry + ed =

5. sneeze + ed =   **11.** decide + ed =

6. hope + ed =   **12.** grab + ed =

▲ Write each verb below to show past time.

Example: drip   *dripped*

13. taste	**17.** nod	**21.** shop
14. worry	**18.** skate	**22.** bake
15. drag	**19.** try	**23.** step
16. bounce	**20.** carry	**24.** cry

■ Change the verb in each sentence to show past time. Write the sentences.

Example: George Washington Carver lives on a farm.
          George Washington Carver lived on a farm.

25. He loves plants.

26. Some people name him the "plant doctor."

27. George chops wood for money.

28. He saves money for school.

29. The young boy stops at nothing.

30. George studies all about plant life.

31. He raises many kinds of plants.

32. He moves to Iowa in 1891.

33. George tries many experiments with peanuts.

34. His good work pleases many people.

35. George Washington Carver cares about his work.

● Choose the verb in ( ) to complete each sentence correctly. Write the sentences.

Example: It (is, are) time for school.
It is time for school.

1. I (am, is) on the bus.
2. Kathy (is, are) on the bus.
3. The bus (is, are) late.
4. We (is, are) late for school.
5. My teacher (was, were) worried.
6. The class (is, are) already busy.

▲ Each sentence shows present time. Change the underlined verb to show past time. Write the new verbs.

Example: Two letters <u>are</u> in the mail.
Two letters were in the mail.

7. One letter <u>is</u> from Lisa.
8. It <u>is</u> very interesting.
9. Her family <u>is</u> in Texas for two weeks.
10. She <u>is</u> president of her class.
11. Her brothers <u>are</u> in a contest.
12. Sam <u>is</u> the winner.

■ Use _am, is, are, was,_ or _were_ to complete each sentence correctly. Write the sentences.

Example: We ____ at the library today.
We are at the library today.

13. The library ____ a busy place now.
14. The librarians ____ always very helpful.
15. Yesterday we ____ in the reading room.
16. The reading room ____ quiet.
17. Three children ____ at our table.
18. We ____ tired at the end of the day.

● Choose the verb in ( ) to complete each sentence correctly. Write the sentences.

Example: The frog (has, have) hopped onto a rock.
The frog has hopped onto a rock.

1. Lions (has, have) roared in the jungle.
2. The squirrels (has, have) cracked some nuts.
3. A bird (has, have) flapped its wings.
4. A horse (has, have) trotted down the street.
5. Bees (has, have) buzzed near the flowers.
6. The dog (has, have) barked all day.

▲ Complete each sentence correctly with *has* or *have*. Write the sentences.

Example: I ____ read all about animal life.
I have read all about animal life.

7. Animals ____ protected themselves well.
8. A skunk ____ sprayed its enemies.
9. Worms ____ crawled under rocks.
10. Prairie dogs ____ dug holes in the ground.
11. An insect ____ turned brown like a twig.
12. A tiger ____ hidden in the tall grass.

■ Rewrite each sentence by adding the helping verb *has* or *have* to the main verb.

Example: Army ants lived in large groups.
Army ants have lived in large groups.

13. The groups moved from place to place.
14. They traveled only by night.
15. The queen settled down in one spot.
16. Many ants hatched from her eggs.
17. Each worker gathered food.
18. Soldiers guarded the queen.

● Choose the verb in ( ) to complete each sentence correctly. Write the sentences.

Example: Carolyn has (came, come) to Missouri.
Carolyn has come to Missouri.

1. She (saw, seen) her grandfather one day.
2. They (went, gone) to a World Series game.
3. The pitcher (ran, run) after a ball.
4. The batter had (ran, run) to third base.
5. Both teams have (did, done) their best.
6. Carolyn has (saw, seen) a terrific baseball game.

▲ Write the correct past time of each verb in ( ).

Example: A flower show has ____ here. (come) *come*

7. Today we ____ to the show. (go)
8. Nick had ____ with us. (come)
9. We have ____ Japanese trees at the show. (see)
10. Sam ____ to the roses first. (run)
11. He ____ beautiful yellow roses. (see)
12. Nick has ____ a report about the show. (do)

■ Use the correct past time of the verbs in the Word Box to complete each sentence. Write the sentences.

go	run	see	come	do

Example: Officer Hill has ____ to my school.
Officer Hill has come to my school.

13. He ____ with a film and safety posters.
14. Officer Hill ____ a film on bicycle safety.
15. Lori's class had ____ the film and taken notes.
16. They ____ bicycle accidents in the film.
17. One child ____ to the hospital in a police car.
18. Some classes have ____ a safety show.

EXTRA PRACTICE: UNIT 5

● Choose the verb in ( ) to complete each sentence correctly. Write the sentences.

Example: I (wrote, written) about Maria Tallchief.
I wrote about Maria Tallchief.

1. Maria Tallchief (took, taken) dance lessons.
2. She had (took, taken) many music lessons too.
3. She (grew, grown) up to be a famous dancer.
4. Maria (gave, given) many shows.
5. She has (took, taken) trips to several cities.
6. Reporters have (wrote, written) about her life.

▲ Write the correct past time of each verb in ( ).

Example: Derek _____ a trip to the West. (take) *took*

7. His family _____ picnic lunches along the way. (eat)
8. Mr. Jones had _____ a photo of the Rockies. (take)
9. Derek _____ me a letter from California. (write)
10. He _____ me a cactus from Arizona. (give)
11. It had _____ in a cactus garden. (grow)
12. I have _____ it some water. (give)

■ Use the correct past time of the verbs in the Word Box to complete each sentence. Write the sentences.

take	write	give	eat	grow

Example: Pat has _____ about Amelia Earhart.
Pat has written about Amelia Earhart.

13. Amelia _____ excited about her flight alone.
14. Her flight across the Atlantic _____ over fifteen hours.
15. She _____ very little food during her flight.
16. President Hoover had _____ her a medal.
17. Many people have _____ about her trip.
18. They have _____ talks about Amelia Earhart.

10 | Contractions with *not* (p. 148)

● Write the contraction in each sentence.

Example: Dad doesn't have his car keys.   *doesn't*

1. They aren't in his pocket.
2. Dad isn't happy at all.
3. He can't drive the car.
4. Mom hasn't seen the keys.
5. I don't see them anywhere.
6. Couldn't they be in the car?
7. We haven't looked there.
8. Shouldn't we have an extra set?
9. Then Dad won't be late for work.

▲ Write the contractions for the words below.

Example: did not   *didn't*

10. were not
11. could not
12. have not
13. are not
14. had not
15. cannot
16. should not
17. does not
18. will not
19. is not

■ Write each sentence. Replace a word or words in each sentence with a contraction.

Example: Tabby was not home.   *Tabby wasn't home.*

20. I did not hear her bell.
21. She cannot have gone too far.
22. We have not fed her yet.
23. The kittens are not with her.
24. Tabby would not hide in a tree!
25. She could not be in the garage.
26. We were not worried about Tabby.
27. The cat will not be gone for long.
28. She does not like rainy weather.

Reading and Writing

Long years ago, at the edge of a small mountain village in the snow country of Japan, there lived an old man and his wife. They had little in this world that they could call their own, but they were happy in their life together.

Miyoko Matsutani
from "The Crane Maiden"

Story

Getting Ready Some stories take place in a long-ago time. Some stories are set in the present. Some stories are about real people, and some are make-believe. What kind of a story would you like to tell? Who would your characters be? In this unit, you will read a story and write one of your own.

Activities

Listening Listen as the story beginning that is on the opposite page is read. Where does it take place? When does it take place? Who are the characters in the story?

Speaking Look at the picture. Could this be the setting for the story? What could the story be about? Have someone write your class's ideas on chart paper. Use it later to help you think of story ideas.

LITERATURE

What was the biggest problem Arthur faced as director of the Thanksgiving play?

Arthur's Thanksgiving

By Marc Brown

Arthur's class was so quiet, you could hear a pin drop. Mr. Ratburn was about to announce the director for the Thanksgiving play, *The Big Turkey Hunt.*

Arthur chewed his pencil. "I hope he picks me," whispered Francine. They all held their breath.

"I've chosen Arthur to direct the play," said Mr. Ratburn. He handed Arthur the script.

"Me? The director?" said Arthur.

"Oh, no," grumbled Francine. "This is going to be a disaster."

Arthur's first job as director was to assign parts. The narrator would have the most to say, but the turkey, the symbol of Thanksgiving, had the most important role of all.

Secretly, Arthur was glad he wouldn't have to be the turkey. But who would play that part?

Francine shared her lunch with Arthur. She wanted to be the narrator. Buster let Arthur borrow his Captain Zoom spaceman. He wanted to be Governor William Bradford. Being the director seemed like fun.

Arthur thought Francine would make a good turkey. "Never!" said Francine. "I want to be the narrator. Besides, I have the loudest voice." No doubt about that. Francine would be the narrator.

Arthur showed Muffy a drawing of the turkey costume. "Lots of feathers," said Arthur. "It's a very glamorous role."

"Yuk!" squealed Muffy. "I should be the Indian princess. I have real braids."

"Brain, I've saved the most intelligent part for you," explained Arthur.

"No way will I be the turkey," answered the Brain. "I'll be the Indian chief."

"Buster, you're my best friend," began Arthur. "The part is real easy. Only one line, and it's the best in the play."

"I want to be Governor Bradford," said Buster.

Arthur even asked Binky Barnes. "The turkey's a strong and powerful animal," argued Arthur.

"Yeah, without saying a word, it can make you look like a fool in front of the entire school," said Binky.

The play was only six days away. Where would Arthur find a turkey?

"I wouldn't be caught dead in that outfit," said his sister, D.W.

"The best part in the Thanksgiving play is still open," said Arthur over the PA system at school. "If you're interested, please come to the office at once." No one came to the office. Arthur put posters in the cafeteria and placed ads in the school paper, but nothing worked.

Arthur had other problems, too. Muffy complained about everything. Francine would not take off her movie-star glasses, and she was having a hard time seeing what she was doing. Buster couldn't remember his lines. "In 1620," he recited, "we sailed to America on the cauliflower."

The rehearsals went from bad to worse.

"When the Pilgrims and Indians decided to celebrate their friendship," narrated Francine, "they began to hunt for a turkey. They finally found one, and there was great rejoicing. Today when we think of Thanksgiving, we think of *turkey*." She glared at Arthur.

"Don't worry," Arthur promised. "I'll find a turkey in time."

As a last resort Arthur decided to rent a turkey— but that wasn't such a good idea.

"If you don't get a turkey by tomorrow's performance," said Francine, "I quit."

Everyone agreed. No turkey—no play.

Arthur went home to think. He thought about turkeys while he did arithmetic. He thought about turkeys while he played the piano. And he thought about turkeys while he and D.W. did the dishes.

"If you want something done right, you have to do it yourself," said D.W.

The next morning, Francine, Muffy, and Buster stood before Arthur. They weren't taking any chances. "Do we have a turkey?" they asked.

Arthur just smiled.

The whole school filed into the auditorium.

"Oooo!" said the kids when the lights went out.

"Shhhh!" said the teachers as the curtain went up.

"In 1620, we sailed to America on the *Mayflower*," recited Buster, proudly.

"Phew!" said Arthur.

The play continued smoothly. Muffy didn't drop the cranberries. The Brain had his costume on correctly. Sue Ellen said her lines in a loud, clear voice. And Francine had even taken off her movie-star glasses.

Then it came time for Francine's big speech. She crossed her fingers and began. "When the Indians and Pilgrims finally found a turkey, there was great rejoicing. Today, when we think of Thanksgiving, we think of turkey."

There was a lot of fumbling behind the curtain.

Arthur took a deep breath and walked onstage.

As soon as he did, the audience began to laugh. Arthur turned bright red. This was going to be even worse than he had thought it would be.

"The turkey," Arthur began, "is a symbol, a symbol of . . . of . . ."

173

"Of togetherness and Thanksgiving!" said a chorus of voices behind him.

Arthur turned around and smiled. "O.K., turkeys, all together now. Let's hear the last line, loud and clear."

"Happy Thanksgiving!"

Questions

1. What problem did Arthur have?
2. The people or animals in a story are the **characters**. We learn what the characters are like by what they say and do and by how the author describes them. Arthur and Francine are two characters in this story. Who are other main characters in the story? What are they like? Explain.
3. What reasons did Arthur use to try to persuade Muffy, Buster, the Brain, and Binky to be the turkey? How did each reason fit each character?
4. Why do you think Arthur's friends dressed up as turkeys at the end of the play?

RESPONDING TO LITERATURE

The Reading and Writing Connection

Personal Response What would you have done if you had been Arthur? Use this sentence starter: *If I had been Arthur, I would have . . .* Read your answer to your classmates.

Creative Writing Someone has to play the worm in an apple in the class play. How would you talk a classmate into taking the part? Write what you and that person would say.

Creative Activities

Make Puppets Turn a paper bag into a puppet. Choose a character from the story. Make the paper bag into that character. Draw a face and hair. Use the puppets to act out "Arthur's Thanksgiving."

Readers Theater Take turns reading "Arthur's Thanksgiving" in small groups. Choose students to read the words the characters say and someone to read the story.

Vocabulary

People write **ads** to sell something or find someone to do something. Arthur put an ad in the school newspaper. Write an ad for someone to play the part of the turkey.

Looking Ahead

Story In this unit, you will write a story. A story ending tells how the story happenings work out. Does "Arthur's Thanksgiving" have a good ending? Why?

Listening/Speaking/Thinking

Listening: For a Purpose

People have different reasons for speaking. Arthur tried to talk his friends into playing the turkey. He tried to **persuade** them. A speaker might also want to **entertain** you, or let you enjoy something. Some speakers want to **inform** you. They want to tell you facts. You will understand better what a speaker is trying to say if you understand the speaker's purpose.

Maria is the director of her class play. What is the purpose of each group of sentences below?

1. "Tryouts will be held on Thursday afternoon."

2. "The tree is the best part. The costume is great, and the tree stays on stage all the time."

3. "This play is really exciting! Let me tell you the story. Once upon a time there was a boy . . ."

Use these guides when listening for a purpose.

Listening Guides

1. Pay attention to what the speaker is saying.
2. Decide if the speaker is trying to **entertain, inform,** or **persuade.**
3. Keep in mind the speaker's purpose as you listen.

Practice

Listen as your teacher reads to you. Be ready to tell each speaker's purpose.

Speaking: Reading a Story

How do you suppose the characters in "Arthur's Thanksgiving" said these sentences?

> "Me? The director?" said Arthur.
> "Oh, no," grumbled Francine. "This is going to be a disaster."

Arthur did not believe he was chosen, so he spoke in a surprised voice. He asked questions. How should you read the words Francine said?

Reading a story out loud can be fun for your audience, but you must read with expression. Your voice should show what the characters think and feel. Follow these guides.

Speaking Guides

1. Practice reading the story out loud to yourself or to a friend. Practice until you read it smoothly.
2. Read loudly and clearly.
3. Think about how the characters in the story think and feel. Then read the words as if the characters were really saying them.
4. Read parts that are not spoken as if you were the author.

Practice

Practice reading aloud from "Arthur's Thanksgiving." Follow the Speaking Guides above. Then pick a partner. Take turns reading a page aloud. Discuss why you read it the same or differently.

Speaking: Giving Reasons

When you want someone to do something, give a good reason. If you give good reasons, the person may agree with your ideas.

Arthur tried to talk his classmates into playing the turkey. Muffy thought that she was pretty, so Arthur showed her a picture of a beautiful turkey costume. He used a reason that would interest Muffy.

Suppose you wanted a friend to go swimming with you on a hot day. Which reason would you use?

1. Swimming makes you feel cool in hot weather.
2. I like going to the pool with my friends.
3. The pool gets crowded early.

Reason 1 is good because it tells why swimming is a good sport in the summer. Reason 2 tells why *you* like to go swimming. It is not a good reason. Reason 3 does not make sense.

Remember these guides when giving reasons.

Speaking Guides

1. Use reasons that make sense.
2. Give reasons that will interest your listener.

Practice

A. Lee thinks everyone should learn to ride a bike. Which reason might persuade someone to learn?

1. Some bikes have baskets.
2. You can go places faster on your bike.

B. Give two more reasons to learn to ride a bike.

Thinking: Clustering

Do you have trouble finding ideas to write about? One way to get ideas is to make a **cluster**. A cluster is a special drawing. It shows how ideas connect to one main idea. Circles show the ideas. Lines show how the ideas are connected. As you draw, new ideas will pop into your head. You will see how your ideas go together.

Clustering can help you get ideas for stories or story characters. Begin with a main word, name, or topic. What other words do you think of? Write them around your main word. Circle them. Draw lines to connect them to the main word.

This cluster is about Francine. What does this cluster tell you about her?

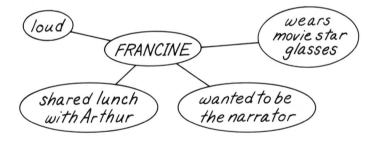

Practice

Draw a cluster to help you think of a story about Thanksgiving. Write the word *Thanksgiving*. Think of two or three words about Thanksgiving. Add them to the cluster. Circle the words. Draw lines to connect them to *Thanksgiving*. Add as many words to your cluster as you can think of. What story idea does it suggest? Tell your story idea to a partner.

Characters and Setting

You have learned that every story has a beginning, a middle, and an end. Every story also has characters and a setting.

The **characters** are the people and animals in a story. The characters in "Arthur's Thanksgiving" are funny, make-believe animals who talk like people.

When you write your own story, your characters can be anyone or anything you want them to be. Will they be animals or strange, scary creatures? Will they be just like you and people you know? How will your characters look, talk, and act?

The **setting** tells *where* and *when* a story takes place. Most of "Arthur's Thanksgiving" took place at Arthur's school. It took place in the present, in the fall of the year.

What setting will you choose for your story? Will it take place in your neighborhood, in a far-off land, or on another planet?

When will your story take place? Will it take place long, long ago? Will it happen now or far in the future? As the writer, you make the choice.

Prewriting Practice

A. Draw a picture of a setting for the story you planned in the last two lessons. Then draw a picture of one or more characters for your story. Draw as many details as you can.

B. Show your pictures and tell about your story.

The Grammar Connection

Using Exact Verbs

Which verb below gives a clearer, more lively picture?

Muffy complained about everything.
Muffy grumbled about everything.

The verb *grumbled* gives a more exact picture than *complained*. Use exact verbs to make your writing clear and exciting.

Practice Rewrite each sentence below. Change the underlined word to a more exact verb. Use the words in the box.

shuffled	shouted	handed
appeared	recited	hung

1. Mr. Ratburn gave Arthur the script.
2. Francine said, "I want to be the narrator."
3. Arthur put posters everywhere.
4. Arthur walked onstage in the costume.
5. He looked embarrassed.
6. Arthur spoke his part.

The Writing Process
How to Write a Story

Step 1: Prewriting

Luis wanted to write a make-believe story. He thought he would share the story with his sister's first-grade class. He made a list of topics.

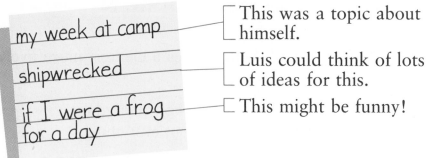

my week at camp — This was a topic about himself.

shipwrecked — Luis could think of lots of ideas for this.

if I were a frog for a day — This might be funny!

After thinking more about his last two topics, Luis decided that he had better ideas for *shipwrecked*.

On Your Own

1. **Think and discuss** Make a list of story ideas. Use the Ideas page to help you. Discuss your ideas with a partner.
2. **Choose** Ask these questions about each topic.
   Would this idea make an interesting story?
   What ideas do I have for the beginning, middle, and end?
   Circle the topic you want to write about.
3. **Explore** What kind of story will you write? What will happen? Do one of the activities under "Exploring Your Topic" on the Ideas page.

Ideas for Prewriting

Choosing Your Topic

Topic Ideas

The Valentine's
   Day play
The lost bicycle
   mystery
Meeting a giant in
   the woods
Finding a bag of
   money
A ride on an
   octopus

Story Starters

Read these starters for ideas.

Once upon a time there was
a man who lived in the sea . . .

Katie felt a wet nose on
her face. She opened one eye
and . . .

Rob and his mother were
walking in the woods.
Suddenly they saw . . .

Pat ate some popcorn. In a
few seconds, he turned into . . .

Exploring Your Topic

Cluster

Make a cluster about your story.
Here is Luis's cluster.

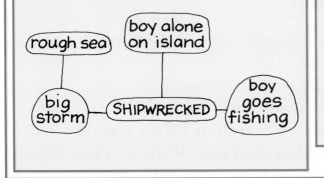

Order It

Think of the order
of events in your
story. Make a
cartoon strip.
Show your cartoon
strip and tell your
story to a
classmate.

Step 2: Write a First Draft

Luis began his first draft. He did not worry about mistakes. He wrote down the story events first.

Luis's first draft

Think and Discuss

- Does Luis's story have a beginning, middle, and end?
- Does it have a good ending? Why or why not?
- Why did he cross out a word?

Boom! Thunder ~~sounded~~ crasht.
The motor on Toms fishing boat
wouldnt start. he would never get
back to the campsite before the
storm hit. The sea got very rough
It began to rain. The storm ended.
Tom was all alone on an island.
He went to sleep.

On Your Own

1. **Think about purpose and audience** Ask yourself these questions.
   Who will be reading my story?
   What kind of story will I write?
2. **Write** Write your first draft. Write a good beginning, middle, and end. Write on every other line. You can correct your mistakes later.

Step 3: Revise

Luis read his first draft. He added a word and changed one verb. Luis read his story to Tricia. He asked Tricia if he needed to make more changes.

Reading and responding

> The beginning is exciting, but your ending is too short.

> Should I tell what Tom did on the island?

> That's a good idea. Also, does Tom get saved?

> I'll think about that.

Tricia's questions made Luis think more about his story. He added details and wrote a new ending.

Part of Luis's revised draft

Tom was all alone on ^an island.
                    a deserted

~~He went to sleep.~~ He went exploring. He saw a cabin. It looked familiar. "I smell hamburgers!" said Tom. He walked a little farther. There was his family eating lunch! He wasn't on a deserted island. He had landed on the other side of his family's vacation island!

Think and Discuss

- Why is Luis's new ending better?
- What details did he add?

On Your Own

1. **Think again** Read your story. Ask yourself these questions about your story.

   Does it have a beginning, a middle, and an end?
   Is my story about one main idea?
   Does my ending make sense?

2. **Revise** Make changes in your first draft. Use exact verbs. If you do not like your ending, write a new one. You may want to use words from the thesaurus below or the one beginning on page 414.

3. **Read/Listen/Respond** Read your story to a classmate or to your teacher.

Ask your listener:	As you listen:
"Is my story clear?" "Can you picture what happens?" "Does it have a good beginning, middle, and end?"	I must listen carefully. Is the story about one main idea? Where are more details needed? Is the ending good?

4. **Revise** Think about your listener's suggestions. Do you have any other ideas? Make those changes.

Thesaurus

end finish, stop, complete, quit
funny amusing, silly
look see, glance, gaze, stare
nice pleasant, fine

run race, hurry, jog
say speak, tell, state, exclaim
save rescue, recover
strange odd, weird, peculiar

Step 4: Proofread

Luis proofread his story. He used a dictionary to check spellings. He used proofreading marks.

Here is part of Luis's story after proofreading.

Part of Luis's proofread draft

Boom! Thunder ~~sounded~~ ~~crasht~~ crashed. The motor on Tom's fishing boat wouldn't start. he would never get back to the campsite before the storm hit. The sea became ~~got~~ very rough.

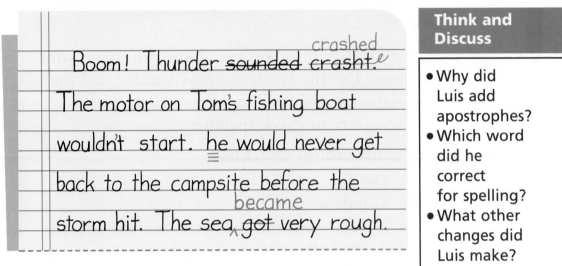

Think and Discuss

- Why did Luis add apostrophes?
- Which word did he correct for spelling?
- What other changes did Luis make?

On Your Own

1. **Proofreading Practice** Proofread this paragraph. Correct three spelling mistakes and add an end mark. One word should have a capital letter. Write the paragraph correctly.

    One morning food was missing from our camper. We heard scraching outside. My family lookd. We had fownd the thief a raccoon was enjoying our food.

Proofreading Marks

- ¶ Indent
- ∧ Add something
- ℓ Take out something
- ≡ Capitalize
- / Make a small letter

2. **Proofreading Application** Now proofread your story. Use the Proofreading Checklist and the Grammar and Spelling Hints below. Use a dictionary to check spellings.

Proofreading Checklist

   Did I

☑ **1.** indent?

☑ **2.** begin and end each sentence correctly?

☑ **3.** spell all words correctly?

The Grammar/Spelling Connection

Grammar Hints

Remember these rules from Unit 5.

- When a noun in the subject is singular, verbs in the present end with *s*. *(Pat laughs.)*
- When a noun in the subject is plural, verbs in the present do not end with *s*. *(Birds sing.)*

Spelling Hints

- The vowel sound in *town* and *found* may be spelled *ow* or *ou*. *(brown, round)*
- The letters *wr*, *kn*, and *tch* sometimes spell one consonant sound. *(write, knock, catch)*

Step 5: Publish

Luis made a final copy of his story. He included all the changes he had made. He wrote it as neatly as he could. He added the title "Shipwrecked." He shared his story with his sister's class by making a TV show.

On Your Own

1. **Copy** Copy your story in your neatest handwriting.
2. **Check** Read over your story again. Make sure you have not left out anything or made any copying mistakes.
3. **Add a title** Write a title for your story.
4. **Share** Think of a special way to share your story.

Ideas for Sharing

- Draw a poster showing a scene from your story.
- Make your story into a play. Have your classmates act it out.
- Make a story booklet with a cover.

Writing Across the Curriculum
Story

Literature and Creative Writing

In "Arthur's Thanksgiving," Arthur directed the class play. He could not find anyone who wanted to be the turkey. At the end of the play, though, Arthur's classmates all dressed as turkeys. The play was a huge success.

Have fun using what you have learned about writing a story. Try one or more of these activities.

Remember these things:

Be sure your story has a beginning, a middle, and an end.

Write a good ending.

Include details about the characters and setting.

1. **Francine's the turkey!** Pretend that Francine took the part of the turkey. Would she have settled for saying so few lines? Would she have worn the turkey costume? What would have happened if the audience had laughed? Write a story about Francine playing the part of the turkey.

2. **Buster directs the play.** Arthur's friend Buster was forgetful. What would have happened if Buster had directed the Thanksgiving play? Write a funny story about it.

Art

Stories sometimes help artists create pieces of art. Sometimes, though, art helps writers think of stories.

Choose one or more of the following activities. Follow the five steps for writing a story.

1. **What is your favorite color?** Think of three of your favorite colors. What does each color make you think of? How does each one make you feel? What would each color be like if it were a person? Write a story. Let the colors be the characters. Draw a picture for your story.

Writing Steps
1. Choose a Topic
2. Write a First Draft
3. Revise
4. Proofread
5. Publish

2. **Make a collage.** Cut out several pictures from magazines or newspapers. Paste the pictures on a large sheet of construction paper in an interesting way. Write a story about the pictures.

3. **Is the statue alive?** Choose one of the statues below. Write a story for your classmates about the day it came to life. What did it do and say? You may want to use some of the words in the box.

freedom
torch
cowhand
bronco

Book Report

Putting on a Play with Masks

Rachel thought "Arthur's Thanksgiving" was a funny story. She asked her teacher if she could put on a short play about the book she had read. The book was *A Toad for Tuesday* by Russell E. Erickson.

Rachel made masks out of poster board for the two main characters. She wrote what each character would say on a large piece of paper. As she spoke each character's part, she held up a different mask in front of her face. Here is Rachel's play.

RACHEL: You are about to meet two characters from *A Toad for Tuesday* by Russell E. Erickson. One is an owl named Owl. The other is a toad named Warton.

OWL: What's your name?

WARTON: Warton. Will I be your dinner?

OWL: Yes, you will! Next Tuesday is my birthday and a little toad will be a special treat. So until Tuesday, Warty, you may do as you please. Besides, you can't get down from this tree!

RACHEL: Does Warton get eaten? What can he do? Why can't he get down from the tree? Read the book to find out.

Think and Discuss

• What did you learn about each character?
• Where does the story take place?
• Why did Rachel choose this part of the story?

Share Your Book

Put on a Play with Masks

1. Choose an interesting part of your book. Choose a part that has at least two characters.
2. Write a play. Tell the title and author in the beginning. You may use words the characters said in the book or your own words.
3. Make a mask for each character in your play. Draw the shape of each mask on poster board. Next, draw places for your eyes, nose, and mouth. Then carefully cut out your masks. Color them and glue on pieces of cloth, paper, or yarn. Your masks do not have to look like the book characters.
4. Present your play. Hold the different characters' masks in front of your face as you read their parts. Try to speak as each character would speak.

Other Activities

- Make a poster to tell about your play.
- Draw costumes each character might wear. Draw pictures of the setting for the story.
- Ask classmates to take different characters' parts.

The Book Nook

Warton and Morton *by Russell E. Erickson* Two toad brothers go on a trip and find trouble and adventure.	**Arthur's Eyes** *by Marc Brown* Arthur is worried about the new glasses he has to wear.

UNIT 7 | Grammar

Red horse, roan horse, black horse, and white,
Feeding all together in the green summer light.
White horse, black horse, spotted horse, and gray,
I wish that I were off with you, far, far away!

Elizabeth Coatsworth
from "The Horses"

Adjectives and Adverbs

Getting Ready When you look at a painting, the colors help you know what the picture looks like. When you read, words called adjectives tell you how people and places look and sound, how foods taste, how the air smells, or how something feels to touch. Words called adverbs tell you how people and things move and act. In this unit, you will learn how to use adjectives and adverbs.

Activities

Listening Listen as the poem on the opposite page is read. Which words describe how the horses look?

Speaking Look at the picture. What words can you use to describe how the trees look? how the water sounds and feels? how the stream flows?

1 | What Are Adjectives?

Words that describe, or tell about, nouns are called **adjectives**. Adjectives make sentences more interesting. They give details that make your meaning clearer.

Loud sirens woke me up.   (What kind of sirens?)

The old barn was on fire.   (What kind of barn?)

The adjectives in the sentences above tell *what kind*. Notice that an adjective usually comes before the noun it describes.

rat **CAT**

Guided Practice What is the adjective that describes each underlined noun?

Example: Trucks rushed to the enormous fire.   *enormous*

1. A black dog barked at the trucks.
2. A tall man watched the fire.
3. Firefighters sprayed water on the angry flames.
4. The empty building burned quickly.
5. Thick smoke came out the windows.
6. Soon the tired firefighters were done.
7. They rested on the cool grass.

Summing up

▶ An **adjective** is a word that describes a noun.
▶ Some adjectives tell what kind.

More Practice

A. Write the adjective that describes each underlined noun.

Example: Leaves fell from the bushy <u>trees</u>.   *bushy*

8. Manuel raked the leaves into a huge <u>pile</u>.
9. A yellow <u>butterfly</u> flew onto the leaves.
10. A frisky <u>kitten</u> ran after the butterfly.
11. The dry <u>leaves</u> went everywhere.
12. He packed the leaves into brown <u>bags</u>.
13. He put the bags into the old <u>truck</u>.
14. Then Manuel heard a funny <u>noise</u>.
15. The nosy <u>kitten</u> had jumped into the truck.

B. Write each sentence. Underline the adjective that tells *what kind*.

Example: The tulips blossomed in the large yard.
The tulips blossomed in the <u>large</u> yard.

16. The dog wiggled under the long fence.
17. Grandma wore a green hat.
18. She dug a deep hole near the garden.
19. We planted a tiny tree.
20. My brother trimmed the tall bushes.
21. The ripe apples fell to the ground.
22. We ate the shiny apples.

Writing Application: A Story

Read this story beginning.

> Grandma found a piece of paper. It said, "Hidden under the big oak tree is a treasure."

Write a middle and an ending for the story. Use adjectives that tell *what kind*.

You have learned that adjectives can tell *what kind*. Adjectives such as *one, ten, many,* and *several* tell *how many*.

Two families traveled to New York.

They passed many towns along the way.

An adjective that tells *how many* comes before the noun it describes.

Guided Practice What is the adjective that describes each underlined noun?

Example: The trip took five hours.   *five*

1. They spent seven days in New York.
2. New York City has several museums.
3. One museum has stuffed animals that look real.
4. The three brothers took a ferry ride.
5. They took ten pictures of the Statue of Liberty.
6. Some people climbed the stairs inside the statue.
7. A few children ran to the top.
8. The children saw two bridges.
9. Many cars crossed the bridges.
10. One truck broke down.
11. Several boats sailed by.
12. Four helicopters flew overhead.

many cars

Summing up

▶ Some adjectives tell *how many*.

More Practice

A. Write the adjective that describes each underlined noun.

Example: One <u>day</u> the families went to the Bronx Zoo.
One

13. The zoo has many <u>animals</u>.
14. It took several <u>hours</u> to see everything.
15. Six <u>seals</u> put on a show.
16. A trainer fed some <u>lions</u>.
17. Four <u>elephants</u> drank water.
18. Two <u>goats</u> walked up to the fence.
19. Some <u>tigers</u> were sleeping on a rock.
20. Several <u>monkeys</u> made faces at us.

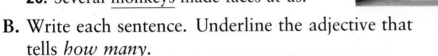

B. Write each sentence. Underline the adjective that tells *how many.*

Example: Next, they drove to the beach in two cars.
Next, they drove to the beach in <u>two</u> cars.

21. A few children walked on the sand.
22. One girl stepped on a shell.
23. They brought four baskets of food.
24. Chad ate some sandwiches and fruit.
25. Several people sat on blankets.
26. Some boys played a game in the water.
27. Jody made a castle with nine towers.
28. Three women dried their towels in the sun.

Writing Application: A Description

Pretend that you have entered a sand-castle contest.
How long did it take to build the castle? How big is
it? Write five sentences describing your castle. Use
adjectives that tell *how many.*

3 | Using *a*, *an*, and *the*

The words *a*, *an*, and *the* are special adjectives. They are called **articles.** Follow the rules below when you use articles.

1. Use *a* and *an* with singular nouns. Use *a* before words that begin with a consonant sound. Use *an* before words that begin with a vowel sound.

   Jess stands in a long line.

   Our plane leaves in an hour.

2. Use *the* before both singular and plural nouns.

   I wait at the gate.   Jess buys the tickets.

Guided Practice Which article in ( ) may be used before each word below?

Example: (a, an) airplane *an*

1. (the, an) pen
2. (a, an) fat cat
3. (a, an) egg
4. (a, an) old farm
5. (a, an) heavy jacket
6. (a, an) kite

7. (the, an) frisky animal
8. (an, a) huge garden
9. (the, an) yellow flower
10. (a, an) apple
11. (a, an) wool hat
12. (the, an) funny joke

Summing up

▶ *A*, *an*, and *the* are special adjectives called **articles.**
▶ Use *a* before a word that begins with a consonant sound. Use *an* before a word that begins with a vowel sound.

More Practice Choose the correct article in ( ) to complete each sentence. Write the sentences.

Example: Buddy is (a, an) hearing ear dog.
Buddy is a hearing ear dog.

13. (The, An) dog helps deaf children.
14. Buddy trains with Tim in (a, an) special program.
15. Tim gives (the, an) dog hand signals.
16. Buddy makes Tim aware of (the, an) important sounds.
17. They walk to (an, a) toy store.
18. Buddy wears (an, a) special leash.
19. Tim starts to cross (a, an) street.
20. Buddy hears (a, an) car.
21. (The, An) dog steps in front of Tim.
22. Tim stops at (the, an) curb.
23. They arrive at (the, an) toy store safely.
24. Tim buys (a, an) airplane for himself.
25. He picks out (a, an) ball for Buddy.
26. They walk for (a, an) hour.
27. Tim sets (a, an) alarm clock every night.
28. Buddy wakes Tim when (a, the) alarm rings.
29. He licks Tim when (the, an) doorbell rings.
30. Tim is on (a, an) softball team.
31. Buddy stays on (the, an) field near Tim.
32. Buddy always keeps (a, an) eye on him.
33. Sometimes Tim takes Buddy to (a, an) open field.
34. Buddy brings (a, an) favorite stick with him.
35. Tim throws (the, an) stick for Buddy.

Writing Application: Sentences

Imagine that you are fishing and lose your jacket. Your dog helps you find it. Write five sentences about this adventure. Use the words *a, an,* and *the*.

4 | Comparing with Adjectives

Jupiter

Mars

smaller

You know that adjectives describe nouns. They can also show how people, places, or things are alike or different. Study the two rules below for comparing with adjectives.

1. Add *-er* to most adjectives to compare *two* people, places, or things.

> Mars is a smaller planet than Jupiter.

2. Add *-est* to most adjectives to compare *more than two* people, places, or things.

> Pluto is the smallest planet of all.

Jupiter

Mars

Pluto

smallest

Guided Practice Which adjective form in ( ) will complete each sentence correctly?

Example: Uranus is a (smaller, smallest) planet than Saturn. *smaller*

1. Pluto has a (longer, longest) year than Neptune.
2. Mercury is (nearer, nearest) of all to the sun.
3. Uranus is (warmer, warmest) than Neptune.
4. Saturn is the (warmer, warmest) of the three.
5. Earth is (nearer, nearest) the sun than Mars is.

Summing up

▶ Add *-er* to most adjectives to compare two people, places, or things.
▶ Add *-est* to most adjectives to compare more than two people, places, or things.

More Practice

A. Write the correct form of the adjective in ( ) to complete each sentence. Write the sentences.

Example: The planet (nearer, nearest) to Earth is Venus.
The planet nearest to Earth is Venus.

6. Mars is (nearer, nearest) to Earth than Saturn is.
7. The planet with the (longer, longest) year is Pluto.
8. Uranus is (cooler, coolest) than Saturn.
9. Neptune is the (cooler, coolest) of the three.
10. Jupiter has a (longer, longest) year than Mars.
11. Earth is (warmer, warmest) than Mars.
12. The (warmer, warmest) planet of all is Venus.

B. Use the correct form of the adjective in ( ) to complete each sentence. Write the sentences.

Example: Mars is a ____ planet than Venus.   (small)
Mars is a smaller planet than Venus.

13. Mercury is the ____ of the three.   (small)
14. The ____ planet of all is Venus.   (bright)
15. Earth has a ____ day than Mars.   (short)
16. Mercury has the ____ year of all.   (short)
17. The ____ planet of all is Pluto.   (cold)
18. Jupiter is ____ than Venus.   (cold)
19. Uranus has ____ moons than Saturn.   (few)
20. Neptune has the ____ moons of the three.   (few)

Writing Application: Creative Writing

Pretend that your plane has accidentally landed near the North Pole. What do you see? What is the climate like? Compare life at the North Pole with life in your town. Write five sentences. Use adjectives that end with *-er* and *-est*.

5 | What Are Adverbs?

You have learned that adjectives describe nouns. Words that describe verbs are called **adverbs**.

Kim walked up to the horse <u>bravely</u>.   (walked how?)

She <u>carefully</u> sat on the horse.   (sat how?)

The horse stood <u>quietly</u>.   (stood how?)

<u>Suddenly</u> it galloped.   (galloped how?)

The adverbs above tell you *how* an action happened. Most adverbs that tell *how* end in *-ly*.

The wind blew gently.

The wind blew fiercely.

Guided Practice Which word in each sentence is an adverb?

Example: Kim's horse ran swiftly.   *swiftly*

1. Suddenly they came to a fence.
2. The horse jumped the fence nicely.
3. It landed safely on its feet.
4. Kim patted the horse's head softly.
5. Kim easily won the blue ribbon in the horse show.

Summing up

▶ A word that describes a verb is an **adverb**.
▶ Adverbs that tell *how* usually end in *-ly*.

More Practice Write each sentence. Underline the adverb that tells *how*.

Example: The sun shone brightly in the sky.
         The sun shone <u>brightly</u> in the sky.

6. Suki's alarm clock buzzed loudly.
7. She excitedly hopped out of bed.
8. She walked cheerfully into the kitchen.
9. Suki and her Dad planned their day carefully.
10. Mr. Ono gladly promised her riding lessons.
11. They talked eagerly about horses.
12. Clearly, Mr. Ono had a surprise for Suki.
13. They drove quickly to the stable.
14. One pony ate lunch hungrily.
15. Suddenly a man brought a brown pony to Suki.
16. Mr. Ono had secretly bought the pony for Suki for her birthday!
17. Happily she named the pony Daisy.
18. Suki calmly put the saddle on Daisy.
19. Gently Daisy poked Suki with her nose.
20. Suki spoke quietly to Daisy.
21. They rode around the stable slowly.
22. Suki held the reins tightly.
23. Daisy easily carried Suki on her back.
24. Daisy held her head proudly.
25. Suki certainly had a wonderful time.
26. Sadly Suki had to go home.

Writing Application: A Story

Think of a wonderful gift to give someone. What kind of gift would you give? Whom would you give it to? Write about something special you might give. Use adverbs that tell *how*.

6 | Other Kinds of Adverbs

You know that adverbs describe verbs. They can tell *how* an action happens. Adverbs can also tell *when* and *where* an action happens.

WHEN: Yesterday my family drove to Florida.

WHERE: We arrived there at night.

The chart below shows adverbs that tell *when* and *where*.

Adverbs telling *when*		Adverbs telling *where*	
always	soon	ahead	here
first	then	around	nearby
later	today	away	out
next	tomorrow	everywhere	there
often	yesterday	far	upstairs

Guided Practice
What is the adverb in each sentence? Does each adverb tell *where* or *when*?

Example: Dad always takes his map. *always* *when*

1. He searched everywhere for it.
2. Soon we left without the map.
3. Dad turned the car around.
4. Then the children giggled.
5. We drove away.

Summing up

▶ Adverbs can tell *when* and *where* an action happens.

More Practice

A. Write each underlined adverb. Then write *when* or *where* after each one.

Example: We <u>soon</u> found the hotel. *soon   when*

   6. We went <u>upstairs</u> and unpacked.

   7. I looked <u>out</u> at the ocean.

   8. <u>Then</u> we took a bus tour.

   9. We visited the Monkey Jungle <u>next</u>.

  10. Many baby monkeys played <u>there</u>.

  11. Their mothers stayed <u>nearby</u> and slept.

  12. I walked <u>around</u> and took pictures.

  13. <u>Soon</u> we ate lunch.

B. Write each sentence. Underline the adverb. Then write *when* or *where* after each one.

Example: We reached the beach later.
          We reached the beach <u>later</u>.   when

  14. The children raced ahead.

  15. We looked for shells everywhere.

  16. Today Mom took diving lessons.

  17. Her boat goes far.

  18. First, she learned about safety rules.

  19. Tomorrow she will take another lesson.

  20. Then she can take pictures of the fish.

Writing Application: Sentences

Pretend that you have sailed to a beautiful island. No one has ever been there before. Write five sentences about your discoveries. Use words in the Word Box.

far	everywhere	here	first	soon

7 | Using *to*, *two*, and *too*

The words *to*, *two*, and *too* sound exactly alike, but they are spelled differently and have different meanings. The clues in a sentence can help you decide which word to use. Study the following chart to learn what each word means.

Word	Meaning	Example
to	in the direction of	I went to school.
two	a number (2)	I ate two plums.
too	also more than enough	I ate pears too. I ate too much.

Guided Practice Would you use *to*, *two*, or *too* to complete each sentence?

Example: Mom took me ____ her office.   *to*

1. Her office is ____ blocks from our house.
2. She took my best friend ____.
3. We walked ____ the elevators.
4. There were ____ many buttons to push.
5. We rode up ____ floors.

Summing up

▶ *To*, *two*, and *too* sound alike but have different meanings.
▶ *To* means "in the direction of."
▶ *Two* is a number.
▶ *Too* means "also" or "more than enough."

More Practice Complete each sentence with *to*, *two*, or *too*. Write the sentences.

Example: Shana and I went ____ the state park.
Shana and I went to the state park.

6. Her parents came ____.
7. The trip took ____ long.
8. We sang ____ songs in the car.
9. We played games ____.
10. ____ rangers greeted us.
11. They pointed ____ a long trail.
12. The trail led ____ a beautiful lake.
13. Mr. Kass carried ____ fishing poles.
14. He carried the food ____.
15. I wondered if that was ____ heavy for him.
16. Shana caught ____ fish.
17. Mrs. Kass caught a fish ____.
18. I saw ____ owls in a tree.
19. I walked up ____ them.
20. We hiked for ____ hours.
21. The long hike was ____ much for us.
22. Finally, we hiked ____ the end of the trail.
23. Mr. Kass gave the food ____ us.
24. I ate ____ big sandwiches.
25. Mrs. Kass was hungry ____.
26. Will you hike ____ the lake with us next week?

park trail ⇧

Writing Application: Sentences

You are camping with your family. Suddenly you hear a strange noise. Where is the noise coming from? What is making the noise? What do you do about it? Write five sentences. Use *to*, *two*, and *too* in your sentences.

Building Vocabulary

Synonyms

Words with almost the same meaning are called **synonyms**.

The boys looked for their lost puppy.

They searched everywhere.

In the sentences above, *looked* and *searched* have almost the same meaning. They are synonyms.

Practice

Replace each underlined word with a synonym from the Word Box. Write the new sentences.

Example: Lisa and I were walking quickly.
Lisa and I were walking fast.

1. We looked up at a noisy airplane.
2. Lisa did not see the big rock.
3. She tripped over it.
4. Lisa landed in a muddy puddle.
5. Her cap was crushed.
6. She got her boots wet.
7. I began to laugh.
8. Lisa looked awfully funny!

loud
silly
hat
soaked
huge
fast
started
fell
dirty

Antonyms

Words that have opposite meanings are called **antonyms**. Study the antonyms in each sentence.

The big dog has a small tail.

The happy clown has a sad face.

In these sentences, *big* is the opposite of *small,* and *happy* is the opposite of *sad*.

Practice

Replace each underlined word with an antonym from the Word Box. Write the new sentences so that the silly story makes sense.

Example: The snow stopped falling.
The snow started falling.

sad
up
easy
heavy
better
play
started
wet
cold

1. The strong winds made Pepe feel hot.
2. He put on a light sweater.
3. Pepe was very happy.
4. He could not work outside.
5. He could not climb down a tree.
6. His clothes might get dry.
7. It would not be hard to keep busy.
8. Pepe hoped the weather would get worse.

Writing Application: A Story

Write a silly story using the words in the Word Box. Then write the story again. Replace the words in the Word Box with antonyms so the story makes sense.

big	happy	lost	old	laugh

Grammar-Writing Connection

Writing Clearly with Adjectives

Good writers choose words that give their readers a clear and interesting picture. You can do this, too, if you choose the right adjective.

Adjectives add important details to sentences. If you change an adjective, you can change the meaning of a sentence. You can give your reader a different picture. How do you picture the animals in these sentences?

The brown dog chased the black cat.

The friendly dog chased the mean cat.

Revising Sentences

Write each sentence twice. Use different adjectives in each sentence to change the meaning of the sentence.

Example: The ____ men carried the ____ boxes.
The tired men carried the heavy boxes.
The tall men carried the big boxes.

1. Mr. Simms read the class a ____ story.
2. The ____ team wanted to win the game.
3. Some ____ clouds floated in the sky.
4. I saw a ____ movie on Saturday.
5. A ____ lion came toward us.
6. The ____ house has ____ stairs.
7. The ____ girl walked into the ____ room.
8. The ____ wind blew the ____ leaves everywhere.
9. The ____ elevator went to the tenth floor.

Creative Writing

This boy's thoughts seem faraway. That is how the painting got its name. *Faraway* shows the artist Andrew Wyeth's son. He is daydreaming in a field of grass.

• Does this painting seem lonely or peaceful? Why?

Activities

1. **Describe the boy's thoughts.** What is the boy thinking and daydreaming about? Write down his thoughts.
2. **Write your conversation.** Suppose you and this boy meet by accident. Write your conversation with him.
3. **Tell about your private place.** Do you have a place where you like to sit and think alone? Describe it.

Cumulative Review, continued

Verbs in the Past *(pp. 136, 138)* Write the past time of each verb.

52. hum   **55.** rake   **58.** scare
53. bury   **56.** miss   **59.** chop
54. match   **57.** spy   **60.** lift

Helping Verbs *(p. 142)* Complete each sentence with *has* or *have*. Write each sentence.

61. Anna ____ started a coin collection.
62. She ____ collected coins from different countries.
63. My grandparents ____ discovered a great coin shop.
64. They ____ surprised Anna with a Japanese coin.
65. Grandpa ____ bought a Greek coin for himself.

The Verb *be* and Irregular Verbs *(pp. 140, 144, 146)* Write each sentence. Use the correct verb in ( ).

66. Ted has (ate, eaten) something bad.
67. We (was, were) upset.
68. Mom (took, taken) him to the doctor.
69. The doctor has (gave, given) him some medicine.
70. I have (saw, seen) the mail.
71. Ted's friends (wrote, written) him cards.
72. He (is, are) much better today.
73. He (went, gone) back to school.

Contractions with *not* *(p. 148)* Write the contraction for each word or words.

74. will not   **77.** is not   **80.** had not
75. do not   **78.** cannot   **81.** were not
76. has not   **79.** should not   **82.** did not

Unit 7: Adjectives and Adverbs

Adjectives *(pp. 198, 200)* Write the adjective in each sentence. Do not write *a, an,* or *the*.

83. Some people are fixing a road.
84. They wear warm jackets and hats.
85. A woman runs a huge machine.
86. The machine carries heavy piles of dirt.
87. Sometimes I can hear the loud drill.

Using *a, an, the* and ***to, too, two*** *(pp. 202, 210)* Write each sentence. Use the correct word.

88. Marta has taken (too, two) riding lessons.
89. Each lesson lasted (a, an) hour.
90. Today she rode (to, too) (the, a) old brook.
91. Her riding teacher went (to, too).
92. Marta brought (a, an) sweater with her.

Comparing with Adjectives *(p. 204)* Write each sentence. Use the correct form of the adjective in ( ).

93. Yesterday was ＿＿ than today.   (damp)
94. Today is the ＿＿ day of the week.   (bright)
95. The nights are ＿＿ than the days.   (cool)
96. Tuesday was ＿＿ than Wednesday.   (bright)
97. Winter nights are ＿＿ of all.   (cold)

Adverbs *(pp. 206, 208)* Write each adverb.

98. Yesterday Sam was painting his room.
99. The telephone rang loudly.
100. Sam ran upstairs and answered it.
101. Sam's curious puppy carelessly kicked the can.
102. The paint spilled everywhere!

Enrichment

Shape Poems

Write a poem using the following form:

> Clouds—
> Dark, gray, rainy—
> Move
> Quickly away today.

noun—
adjective, adjective, adjective *(describes the noun)*—
verb
adverb, adverb, adverb *(tells how, when, or where).*

Cut out the shape of the noun in your poem. Copy the poem onto the shape.

Floor Plans

Pretend you are planning a new store. It can be any kind you like. First, make a list of things to sell in the store. Use an adjective to describe each one, such as "large bicycle." Draw a line under the adjective. Next, draw a floor plan of your store. Show where things on your list will be.

Thank-You Mobile

Make a mobile for someone who helped you. Draw a large, smiling face on cardboard. Below the mouth, write a note like "Thank you! You are super!" Cut out the face. On more cardboard, write four adjectives that praise the person. Draw shapes around them and cut them out. String together the parts of the mobile.

Extra Practice: Unit 7

1 **What Are Adjectives? (p. 198)**

● Write the adjective that describes the underlined noun.

Example: Josh got a new <u>bike</u> yesterday. *new*

1. He rode it down a bumpy <u>street</u>.
2. Daniel heard the loud <u>horn</u>.
3. They rode to the sandy <u>beach</u> together.
4. The boys jumped into the cool <u>water</u>.
5. Josh brought a huge <u>sandwich</u>.
6. He forgot to bring his purple <u>towel</u>.

▲ Write each sentence. Underline the adjective that tells *what kind*.

Example: Gina and I carried the heavy suitcases.
Gina and I carried the <u>heavy</u> suitcases.

7. We put them into the brown car.
8. Mom packed juicy apples for the ride.
9. Soon we saw the busy airport.
10. Noisy airplanes were landing everywhere.
11. We handed a young man the tickets.
12. The plane took off with a loud roar.

■ Write each sentence. Use a different adjective to describe each underlined noun.

Example: The <u>bus</u> went by. *The noisy bus went by.*

13. It stopped at the <u>park</u>.
14. My <u>sister</u> and I got off the bus.
15. We wore <u>hats</u> and light jackets.
16. A <u>baby</u> was sleeping in a carriage.
17. A man walked a <u>dog</u> along the sidewalk.
18. Some women fed the <u>squirrels</u>.

● Complete each sentence with an adjective that tells *how many*. Write the sentences. Use the Word Box.

Example: Tony and Alex explored ___ caves.
    Tony and Alex explored two caves.

| some |
| two |
| several |
| three |
| five |
| many |
| eight |

1. Alex took ___ flashlights with him.
2. Tony packed ___ sandwiches.
3. The boys climbed over ___ rocks.
4. Tony saw ___ footprints.
5. Alex discovered ___ eggs.
6. Then ___ birds flew into the cave.

▲ Write each sentence. Underline the adjective that tells *how many*.

Example: The movie about the desert took two hours.
    The movie about the desert took <u>two</u> hours.

7. One desert is called the Sahara Desert.
8. Did you notice the five camels?
9. They can go for many months without water.
10. Deserts may not get rain for several years.
11. A few deserts do have water holes.
12. Some plants and animals live in the desert.

■ Write each sentence with an adjective that tells *how many*. Underline the noun each adjective describes.

Example: ___ people took a trip to Africa.
    Several <u>people</u> took a trip to Africa.

13. Ann and Jamie set up ___ tents.
14. The group watched ___ animals in the jungle.
15. Bob saw ___ elephants.
16. Casey discovered ___ monkeys.
17. ___ hippos swam in the water with their babies.
18. The trip lasted ___ days.

● Choose the correct group of words in each pair. Write the correct group.

Example: a ox

      an ox   *an ox*

1. an peach
   a peach

2. a tall tree
   an tall tree

3. an long story
   a long story

4. an bird
   a bird

5. an orange
   a orange

6. a quiet deer
   an quiet deer

7. an old eagle
   a old eagle

8. an uncle
   a uncle

9. a aunt
   an aunt

▲ Write each sentence. Use the correct article.

Example: Walt Disney was (a, an) artist.
      Walt Disney was an artist.

10. He wanted (a, an) animal for his cartoons.
11. Disney thought about his early life on (a, an) farm.
12. He remembered (a, an) pet mouse named Mortimer.
13. Mortimer was (a, an) interesting mouse.
14. Disney drew (a, an) cartoon mouse named Mickey.
15. (An, The) first Mickey Mouse film opened in 1928.
16. Mickey Mouse is (an, the) star of many cartoons.

■ Complete each sentence with *a, an,* or *the*. Write the sentences. Be sure that your answers make sense.

Example: Why is Sally Ride ____ famous person?
      Why is Sally Ride a famous person?

17. Sally Ride is ____ astronaut.
18. She was ____ first American woman in space.
19. She was ____ youngest astronaut to go into orbit.
20. In 1983 Sally took ____ exciting trip.
21. She flew on one of ____ space shuttles.
22. Sally quickly became ____ celebrity.

4 | Comparing with Adjectives (p. 204)

● Make three columns on your paper. In the first column, copy the adjectives. In the middle column, write the adjectives with *-er*. In the third column, write the adjectives with *-est*.

Example: loud

Adjective	**With -er**	**With -est**
loud	*louder*	*loudest*

1. new	**3.** tall	**5.** fast	**7.** young
2. soft	**4.** old	**6.** short	**8.** smooth

▲ Use the correct form of the adjective in ( ) to complete each sentence. Write the sentences.

Example: A zebra is (taller, tallest) than a tiger.
A zebra is taller than a tiger.

9. A giraffe is the (taller, tallest) of the three.
10. The hummingbird is the (smaller, smallest) of all birds.
11. A bluejay lives (longer, longest) than a robin.
12. A lion can run (faster, fastest) than a goat.
13. A leopard is the (faster, fastest) animal of all.
14. A robin is (smaller, smallest) than a parrot.

■ Use the correct form of the adjective to complete each sentence. Write the sentences. Then underline the adjectives that compare more than two nouns.

Example: The sailboat is the ___ boat of all.   (long)
The sailboat is the longest boat of all.

15. The canoe is ___ than the rowboat.   (long)
16. My fishing pole is ___ than yours.   (new)
17. John's fishing pole is the ___ of all.   (new)
18. The lake is ___ than the pond.   (deep)
19. This fish is the ___ of the three.   (short)
20. Is your fish ___ than mine?   (short)

● Write each sentence. Complete each sentence with an adverb that tells *how*. Use a different adverb in each sentence. You may use the Word Box.

Example: Birds fly ____. *Birds fly easily.*

	quietly
	swiftly
	loudly
	noisily
	easily
	slowly
	carefully

  1. Baby chicks hatch ____.

  2. ____ a robin builds its nest.

  3. Hummingbirds flap their wings ____.

  4. Woodpeckers drill ____ into trees.

  5. Most birds awaken ____ at dawn.

  6. ____ seagulls move through the air.

▲ Write each sentence. Underline the adverb.

Example: Cranes fly smoothly. *Cranes fly smoothly.*

  7. Whooping cranes live together noisily.

  8. They usually lay two eggs a year.

  9. Normally one chick lives.

10. Scientists eagerly help the birds.

11. They quickly remove one of the eggs.

12. Gently they place the egg in another nest.

13. Another bird hatches the egg successfully.

■ Use a different adverb that tells *how* to complete each sentence. Write the sentences.

Example: ____ Eva hurried to the field day.
      Eagerly Eva hurried to the field day.

14. She ____ waited for the sack race to begin.

15. The whistle blew ____.

16. Three children ____ took the lead.

17. The crowd yelled ____.

18. ____ Eva was winning the race!

19. She crossed the finish line ____.

20. ____ she showed her award to the crowd.

● Write the adverb. The word in ( ) tells you what kind.

Example: Dad drives a bus everywhere.   (where)
   Dad drives a bus everywhere.

1. He leaves for his job early.   (when)
2. Today people climbed onto the empty bus.   (when)
3. They could always get seats.   (when)
4. The bus travels far.   (where)
5. Dad turns the bus around at the last stop.   (where)
6. Tomorrow Dad will take me with him.   (when)
7. I will look out at the people.   (where)

▲ Write each sentence. Underline the adverb.

Example: The Wright Brothers often talked about planes.
   The Wright Brothers often talked about planes.

8. They soon built one.
9. Then the brothers tested the airplane.
10. The airplane flew around for a short time.
11. Later they took another short trip.
12. Today airplanes travel far.
13. They can fly everywhere.

■ Write the sentences with adverbs from the Word Box. Underline the verbs.

Example: ＿＿ I rode in a helicopter.
   Today I rode in a helicopter.

14. We ＿＿ stayed seated.
15. We flew ＿＿.
16. I saw tiny houses ＿＿.
17. ＿＿ the pilot changed direction.
18. He turned the helicopter ＿＿.
19. ＿＿ we passed a huge cloud.
20. I would love to go for a ride ＿＿!

| below |
| then |
| around |
| once |
| again |
| everywhere |
| always |
| today |

● Write each sentence. Use the correct word in ( ).
  Example: Nina and Paul went (to, two) the pet shop.
           Nina and Paul went to the pet shop.
  1. Paul bought (too, two) fish.
  2. He bought some food for them (too, to).
  3. Nina walked over (to, two) the puppies.
  4. She watched (two, too) brown ones.
  5. The children stayed at the store (to, too) long.
  6. They ran (to, two) Allison's house.

▲ Write each sentence with *to, two,* or *too.*
  Example: Grandpa went ____ school.
           Grandpa went to school.
  7. He took ____ courses.
  8. Each course lasted ____ months.
  9. One course was ____ crowded.
  10. Grandpa used ____ kinds of computers in class.
  11. He watched films ____.
  12. Grandpa took me ____ a class.
  13. I used a computer ____.

■ Write *correct* if the underlined word is correct. If it is not, write the sentence correctly.
  Example: A ship sailed <u>too</u> an island.
           A ship sailed to an island.
  14. The trip takes <u>two</u> hours.
  15. A sailor moved <u>too</u> the controls.
  16. The captain was at the controls <u>to</u>.
  17. She turned the wheel <u>to</u> the right.
  18. In <u>too</u> seconds the boat gained speed.
  19. Did she turn the wheel <u>too</u> much?
  20. The boat got <u>two</u> the island exactly on time.

EXTRA PRACTICE: UNIT 7

When the day is cloudy,
The thunder makes a low rumble
And the rain patters against the lodge,
Then it's fine and nice to sleep,
    isn't it?

(Crow)

Description

Getting Ready How would you describe an orange to someone who has never seen one? What does it look like? How does the skin feel? What does an orange smell like? How does it taste? Choose words that will make each detail come to life in your reader's mind. In this unit, you will read a good description and write one of your own.

Activities

Listening Listen as the poem on the opposite page is read. What kind of day is described? What sound does the thunder make? What word describes the sound of the rain?

Speaking Look at the picture. Imagine yourself in this place. How do the plants look? What sounds do you hear? What can you smell? How do the stones feel?

LITERATURE

Always Wondering

By Aileen Fisher

Roads run by
and paths run by
and tracks
Where trains go thundering
And green and brown
of field and town
and over-ing and under-ing.

Brooks run by
and creeks run by
and rivers
big and blundering,

And where they end,
around what bend,
I'm always, always wondering.

Questions
1. What things does the poet wonder about?
2. What do the words *over-ing* and *under-ing* mean?
3. Like all poems, this poem has **rhythm**, or a pattern of repeated beats. Tap out the beats in the first four lines. What does the rhythm sound like? Explain.

What makes a town the best town in the world?

The Best Town in the World

By Byrd Baylor

All my life I've heard
    about
a little, dirt-road,
one-store,
country town
not far from a rocky
    canyon
way back
in the Texas hills.

This town had lots of
    space
around it
with caves to find
and honey trees
and giant rocks to climb.

It had a creek
and there were panther
    tracks
to follow
and you could swing
on the wild grapevines.
My father said it was
the best town in the
    world
and he just happened
to be born there.
How's that for being
lucky?

We always liked
to hear about
that town
where everything was
perfect.

Of course it had a name
but people called the
    town
and all the ranches
and the farms around it
just *The Canyon*,
and they called each
    other
Canyon People.
The way my father
    said it,
you could tell
it was a special thing
to be
one of those people.

All the best cooks
in the world lived there.
My father said
if you were walking
    down the road,
just hunting arrowheads
or maybe coming home
    from school,
they'd call you in

and give you
sweet potato pie
or gingerbread
and stand there
by the big wood stove
and smile at you
while you were eating.

It was that kind
of town.

The best blackberries
in the world
grew wild.

My father says
the ones in stores
don't taste a thing
like those
he used to pick.
Those tasted just like
a blackberry should.

He'd crawl into
a tangle
of blackberry thicket
and eat all he wanted
and finally
walk home
swinging his bucket
(with enough for
    four pies)
and his hands

234

and his face
and his hard bare feet
would be stained
that beautiful color.

The dogs were smarter
    there.
They helped you herd the
    goats
and growled at
    rattlesnakes
before you even saw them.
And if you stopped
to climb a tree
your dogs stopped, too.
They curled up and
    waited
for you to come down.
They didn't run off
by themselves.

Summer days
were longer there
than they are
in other places,
and wildflowers grew
    taller
and thicker on the hills—
not just the yellow ones.
There were all shades of
lavender and purple

and orange and red
and blue
and the palest kind of
    pink.
They all had butterflies
to match.

Fireflies lit up
the whole place
at night,
and in the distance
you could hear
somebody's fiddle
or banjo
or harp.

My father says
no city water
ever tasted half as good
as water that he carried
in a bucket from the well
by their back door.

And there isn't
any water
anywhere
as clear
as the water
in that ice cold creek
where all the children
    swam.
You could look down
and see the white sand
and watch the minnows
flashing by.

But
when my father came to
    the part
about that ice cold water
we would always say,

"It doesn't sound
so perfect
if the water was
ice cold."

He'd look surprised
and say,
"But that's the way
creek water
is supposed to be—
ice cold."

So we learned that
however
things were
in that town
is just exactly how
things *ought* to be.

Questions

1. What are some reasons why the author's father thinks the town where he grew up is the best town in the world?
2. The author carefully chose certain words to describe her father's home town. She wanted those words to form **images**, or pictures, in your mind. Do you think this town was friendly or unfriendly? What images make you think so?
3. Do you think the town can be as perfect as the father remembers it to be? Why or why not?

RESPONDING TO LITERATURE

The Reading and Writing Connection

Personal Response Think about your city or town. Why is it a good place to live? Are there lots of things to do? Make a list of the things you like about it. Compare lists.

Creative Writing What do you wonder about? Write each thing on a separate slip of paper. Put together your slips of paper to form a poem called "I Wonder." Read the poem to someone.

Creative Activities

Create a Scene Make a shoe box scene of "The Best Town in the World." Use stones and other natural things to make your scene look real.

Choral Reading Practice reading aloud "Always Wondering" with a small group. One person reads the first part. Another person reads the second part. Everyone reads the last part together.

Vocabulary

Look up *blunder* in a dictionary. Why was *blunder* a good word to use to describe rivers in "Always Wondering"?

Looking Ahead

Description You will write a description in this unit. Which words did the author use to describe the sights, tastes, and sounds in "The Best Town in the World"?

Listening/Speaking/Thinking

Listening: To Poetry

Poetry has a language of its own. In "Always Wondering," you listened for the rhythm, or pattern of repeated beats. Poems may have other patterns too. Sometimes you may hear the same beginning sounds repeated. Listen as a classmate reads this poem. Which beginning sounds are repeated?

The Meal

Timothy Tompkins had turnips and tea.
The turnips were tiny.
He ate at least three.
And then, for dessert,
He had onions and ice.
He liked that so much
That he ordered it twice.
He had two cups of ketchup,
A prune, and a pickle.
"Delicious," said Timothy.
"Well worth a nickel."
He folded his napkin
And hastened to add,
"It's one of the loveliest breakfasts I've had."

Karla Kuskin

Timothy and *Tompkins* both begin with the sound the letter *t* stands for. What other words in the first two lines begin with that sound? What other words in one line have the same beginning sounds?

Sometimes poets use words that sound just like the sounds they name. Listen as two groups of classmates read this poem. What sound words do you hear?

> **The Fourth**
>
> GROUP 1:   Oh
> GROUP 2:   CRASH!
> GROUP 1:   my
> GROUP 2:   BASH!
> GROUP 1:   it's
> GROUP 2:   BANG!
> GROUP 1:   the
> GROUP 2:   ZANG!
> GROUP 1:   Fourth
> GROUP 2:   WHOOSH!
> GROUP 1:   of
> GROUP 2:   BAROOOM!
> GROUP 1:   July
> GROUP 2:   WHEW!
>
> Shel Silverstein
>
> From *Where the Sidewalk Ends: The Poems & Drawings of Shel Silverstein.* Copyright © 1974 by Snake Eye Music, Inc. Reprinted by permission of Harper & Row, Publishers, Inc. and Jonathan Cape Ltd.

Remember these guides as you listen to poems.

Listening Guides

1. Listen for words that begin with the same sound.
2. Listen for sound words.

Practice

Listen to some poems. Which words repeat the same beginning sounds? What sound words do you hear?

Listening: For Details

In "The Best Town in the World," the author used details to paint pictures in your mind. Listen as a classmate reads these lines. What images, or pictures, do you see?

He'd crawl into
a tangle
of blackberry thicket
and eat all he wanted
and finally
walk home
swinging his bucket

(with enough for four pies)
and his hands
and his face
and his hard bare feet
would be stained
that beautiful color.

Details such as *a tangle of blackberry thicket* helped you form a clear picture in your mind. What other images could you "see"? What details helped? Remember these Listening Guides.

Listening Guides

1. Listen for details that tell how something looks, sounds, feels, smells, and tastes.
2. Try to form clear pictures in your mind.

Practice

Listen as your teacher reads part of a story. Use the Listening Guides. Then draw a picture of the story. Be sure to use details.

Speaking: Giving a Description

Suppose you received a kitten for your birthday. You want to describe the kitten to your friend. It is important to choose details that will help your friend clearly picture the kitten.

What room in school is Lila describing? Which details help you to know?

I'm thinking of a warm, noisy place. The air smells of fish. Trays, plates, and silverware rattle loudly.

When you describe something, choose your details carefully. Use details that will help your listeners picture what you are describing.

Speaking Guides

1. Think about what you want to describe. How does it look? sound? taste? feel? smell?
2. Use details that will help your listeners paint pictures in their minds.

Practice

Use the Speaking Guides as you do these activities.

A. Picture in your mind the best meal you have ever eaten. Then describe it to a classmate.

B. Describe an animal to a classmate. Have your classmate guess which animal it is. Use words that tell how the animal looks, sounds, feels, and smells.

Thinking: Classifying

Byrd Baylor wrote about blackberries, rocks, and wildflowers. These things are all alike in one way. They are all things that are found in nature.

Things that are alike in some way can be grouped together, or **classified**. The name of the group tells how the things are alike. How are the following things alike?

Apples, milk, carrots, and eggs are all kinds of food. A hammer does not belong in this group because it is a tool. Does a bike belong in this group? Why or why not? What else can be added to this group?

Things can belong to more than one group. Study the group below. What things belong to it and also to the group *Food*?

Growing Things	
trees	fish
blackberries	wildflowers

Blackberries and fish are kinds of food. They also grow. They can be classified in both groups.

Food	
apples	carrots
milk	eggs

Practice

A. Read the name of each group below. Then write the words that belong in each group.

1. Jumping Animals	frog	snake	rabbit
2. Flying Things	bird	kite	hill
3. Flowers	leaf	daisy	tulip
4. Toys	dolls	desk	puzzles
5. Colors	blue	orange	paper
6. Sports	grape	soccer	tennis

B. Read the names of the groups in the box. Then read the list of words beside each number. Write the name of the group that goes with each list.

Round Things	**Things to Write With**
Bodies of Water	**Clothes**
Things to Ride In	**Girls' Names**

7. pencils, pens, chalk, markers
8. ponds, lakes, rivers, creeks
9. full moon, ball, apple, plates
10. shoes, belts, gloves, pants
11. bus, car, train, airplane
12. Maria, Kim, Ann, Kristen

C. Write the headings *Things That Are Round, Words That Begin with B,* and *Fruit* on your paper. Write each of the words below under the correct heading. Some of the words will go under more than one heading. Then add the names of two new things to each group.

blanket	peach	blueberry
orange	boat	ball
strawberry	Earth	plate

Composition Skills

Using Your Senses

The author of "The Best Town in the World" wanted you to taste the blackberries, see the wildflowers, and feel the creek. She used sense words, such as *grew wild, shades of lavender and purple,* and *ice cold.* **Sense words** tell how something looks, sounds, feels, smells, and tastes.

Here are some sense words arranged in groups.

Sense Words			
Sight	yellow spotted	pale round	tiny pointed
Sound	hum	buzz	squeaky
Taste	bitter	sweet	spicy
Touch	smooth prickly	soft sandy	bumpy damp
Smell	fresh	fishy	smoky

When you write, use sense words to make your description come alive.

Prewriting Practice

Write at least two sense words to describe each item.

1. a dog

2. a lemon

3. sandpaper

4. a kitchen

5. a campfire

6. peanuts

7. an ice cube

8. spaghetti

9. a clock

Writing Topic Sentences and Choosing Details

When you write a description, begin with a topic sentence that states the main idea. Then choose details that support the main idea to create the picture you want.

The paragraph below describes a sled.

> It was a beautiful sled. Father had made it of hickory. It was long and slim and swift-looking; the hickory runners had been soaked and bent into long, clean curves that seemed ready to fly. Almanzo stroked the shiny-smooth wood.
> from *Farmer Boy* by Laura Ingalls Wilder

- What is the main idea?
- What is the topic sentence?
- What details did the author choose to support the main idea?

Suppose the author wanted to describe the sled in a different way. Read the paragraph below. Why did the author use different details in this paragraph?

> The old sled needed repair. The red paint was chipped, and spots of rust covered the nails. The edges were rough, and the rope that was attached to the sled was ragged.

The main idea of this paragraph is that the old sled needed repair. The author chose details that supported that main idea. What details did the author use?

Prewriting Practice

A. Choose a topic below or a topic of your own. Write two topic sentences to describe each one.

a hiding place   a bike
a show you saw   an animal

B. Think of three supporting details for each topic sentence you wrote. List them on your paper.

Using Exact Words

Read these descriptions of a creek. Which one gives a clearer picture?

1. You could see the bottom and the fish swimming.
2. You could look down and see the white sand and watch the minnows flashing by.

The second description, from "The Best Town in the World," is better. The words *white sand, minnows,* and *flashing by* helped you to picture the sand and the fish. These words are more exact.

When you describe something, your choice of words creates a certain picture. Read the description below. How well can you picture the lake?

The lake looked pretty.

Now read these two exact descriptions of the lake.

1. Sunset colors shone in the clear, calm lake.
2. White-tipped waves rippled across the dark, icy lake water.

• What picture formed in your mind each time?
• Which exact words helped you picture the lake?

Prewriting Practice

Rewrite each sentence. Use a more exact word in place of each underlined one.

1. The <u>bad</u> weather lasted for a week.
2. The <u>happy</u> children waited in line.
3. The kitten's fur felt <u>nice</u>.
4. Lee <u>went</u> after the ball.
5. Fresh fruit from the garden tastes <u>good</u>.

The Grammar Connection

Using Adverbs to Change Meaning
Adverbs can change the meaning of a sentence.

Two beavers swam lazily to the dam.
Two beavers swam playfully to the dam.

Choose adverbs carefully to make your meaning clear.

Practice Write each sentence twice. Use two different adverbs to create different pictures.

1. The children ____ boarded the school bus.
2. ____ we heard the sound of the parade.
3. Leave your hats, mittens, and coats ____.
4. They climbed ____ up the mountain.
5. The radio played ____.
6. ____ I will mail the letter.

The Writing Process
How to Write a Description

Step 1: Prewriting

Amanda listed people and things she could describe. Then she thought about each one.

my grandmother ⎤ She had not seen her grandmother for a while.

a day at school ⎤ There was too much to tell.

a season ⎤ She could use a lot of sense words for this!

Amanda's favorite season was autumn. She thought that her pen pal in Hawaii might like to read about autumn too. Amanda circled *a season*.

On Your Own

1. **Think and discuss** Make a list of things you can describe. Use the Ideas page to help you. Discuss your list with a partner.
2. **Choose** Ask these questions about each topic.
   Is this about one main idea?
   Can I look at this before I write?
   Can I use at least three of my senses?
   Circle the topic you want to write about.
3. **Explore** What sense words will you use? What details will you include? Do one of the activities under "Exploring Your Topic" on the Ideas page.

Ideas for Prewriting

Choosing Your Topic

Topic Ideas

A place in my
   town
My pet
My favorite toy
A flower
A car
An apple
An airplane ride
A walk in the
   woods
The beach

Picture This!

Look at the pictures for ideas.

Exploring Your Topic

Classify

Write the headings
*Sight, Sound, Taste,
Touch,* and *Smell*
at the top of your
paper. Under each
heading, write as
many sense words
about your topic as
you can.

Description Riddles

Write a riddle about your
topic. Use sense words and
exact words. Have a classmate
try to guess what it is.

Example: What is small, juicy,
   and green and grows
   in bunches?   (a grape)

Step 2: Write a First Draft

Amanda was ready to write her first draft. She did not worry about making mistakes. She would have a chance to correct them later.

Amanda's first draft

> ~~Fall is fun.~~ Autumn is the best season. it is pretty leaves falling on the ground? Fall things are up. The grass starts to frost. The wind is cold. Then you go home and eat pumpkin bred

On Your Own

1. **Think about purpose and audience** Ask yourself these questions.

   Who will be reading my description?

   What is my purpose?

   What do I want my reader to see, smell, hear, taste, and feel?

2. **Write** Write your first draft. Write a topic sentence. Use as many senses as you can. Use exact words. Write on every other line so that you can make changes. Do not worry about mistakes.

Step 3: Revise

Amanda read her first draft. She realized that she needed a sentence that told how autumn smelled. She also changed one word to be more exact.

Amanda wanted to know if her description of autumn was clear. She read her first draft to Eve.

Reading and responding

Amanda made more revisions on her paper.

Amanda's revised draft

~~Fall is fun.~~ Autumn is the best
                    red and yellow
season. it is ʌ pretty leaves
crackling
falling ʌ on the ground? Fall ʌ things   decorations
        You can smell chimney smoke.
are up. The grass starts to frost.
        slashes against you like a whip.
The wind ʌ is cold. Then you go

home and eat pumpkin bred

Think and Discuss

• What sentence did Amanda add? Why?
• What details did she add?
• What words did she change? Why?

On Your Own

1. **Think again** Ask yourself these questions.
   Did I write a good topic sentence?
   Did I choose details that support the topic
      sentence?
   What details could I add?
   Have I used several senses?
2. **Revise** Make changes in your first draft. If you do
   not have a topic sentence, write one. Add exact
   words and details to make your description clearer.
   You may want to use the thesaurus below or the
   one beginning on page 414.
3. **Read/Listen/Respond** Read your description to a
   classmate or to your teacher.

Ask your listener:	As you listen:
"Does my description paint a picture?" "Did I use my senses?" "Where could I add details?"	I must listen carefully. Is this about one main idea? Where are details needed?

4. **Revise** Think about your listener's suggestions. Do
   you have any other ideas? Make those changes.

Thesaurus

cold chilly, frosty	**smell** scent, odor,
hot spicy, sharp, tangy	aroma
loud noisy, roaring	**soft** delicate, tender,
quiet calm, silent,	fluffy
peaceful, still	**sour** tart, bitter

Step 4: Proofread

Amanda proofread her description. She used a dictionary to check spellings. She used proofreading marks. Here is her description after proofreading.

Amanda's proofread draft

~~Fall is fun.~~ Autumn is the best
season. it is ^red and yellow^ ~~pretty~~ leaves
crackling~~ing~~ decorations
falling on the ground~~?~~. Fall ^things^
^You can smell chimney smoke.^
are up. The grass starts to frost.
^slashes against you like a whip.^
The wind ^is cold.~~ Then you go
bread
home and eat pumpkin ~~brede~~.

Think and Discuss

- Which spelling did she correct?
- Which end mark did she change? Which one did she add?
- Why did she add a capital letter?

On Your Own

1. **Proofreading Practice** Proofread the paragraph below. Correct the two spelling mistakes. There is one adjective mistake and one wrong end mark. Write the paragraph correctly.

```
    Tim and I had a excellent
day at the circus. The air
smelld of peanuts. The lion
was biger than the tiger. Did
you like the clowns.
```

Proofreading Marks

¶	Indent
∧	Add something
ℓ	Take out something
≡	Capitalize
/	Make a small letter

➡

2. Proofreading Application Proofread your description. Use the Proofreading Checklist and the Grammar and Spelling Hints. Use a dictionary.

Proofreading Checklist

Did I

☑ **1.** begin and end each sentence correctly?

☑ **2.** spell all words correctly?

☑ **3.** use adjectives and adverbs correctly?

The Grammar/Spelling Connection

Grammar Hints

Remember these rules from Unit 7.

• Add *-er* to most adjectives to compare two people, places, or things. *(small, smaller)*

• Add *-est* to most adjectives to compare more than two people, places, or things. *(small, smaller, smallest)*

Spelling Hint

• When a one-syllable word ends with a single vowel and a consonant, double the consonant before adding *-er* or *-est*. *(big, bigger, biggest)*

Step 5: Publish

Amanda made a final copy of her description. She included all the changes she had made. She added the title "Autumn Is." She wrote it as neatly as she could. Then she made a scrapbook of photographs and autumn leaves. She glued her description on the first page. She mailed her scrapbook to her pen pal.

On Your Own

1. **Add a title** Write a title for your description.
2. **Copy** Copy your description in your neatest handwriting.
3. **Check** Read your description again. Make sure you have not left out anything or made any copying mistakes.
4. **Share** Think of a special way to share your description.

Ideas for Sharing

- Make a fingerpainting. Attach it to your description. Read your description to a friend.
- Make a greeting card. Put your description inside.

Writing Across the Curriculum
Description

Literature and Creative Writing

In "The Best Town in the World," a writer describes the town where her father grew up as the best place to live.

Have fun using what you have learned about writing a description. Try one or more of these activities.

Remember these things:
Use sense words.
Use details that support the topic sentence.
Use exact words.

1. **Describe a best town.** Pretend that you live in a perfect town. What would your town be like? Describe it.
2. **Write a travel folder.** Make a travel folder about the area where you live. Describe the area, and tell why it is the best place in the world to visit.
3. **Make a sign.** Pretend that you have moved to a town where no one has ever heard of popcorn. You want to sell popcorn in your new store. Write a sign for your store window describing popcorn.

Science

Scientists describe the world around us. They are always careful to include exact details.

Choose one or more of the following activities. Follow the five steps for writing a description.

1. **Write a weather report.** Describe the weather for a day. Was it sunny? rainy? hot? What noises did you hear?
   Extra! Make a weather chart. Record the weather for a week. Write the high and low temperature for each day. Measure the rainfall. Write a description for each day.

Writing Steps
1. Choose a Topic
2. Write a First Draft
3. Revise
4. Proofread
5. Publish

2. **Describe a picture.** The scientist John James Audubon painted many pictures of birds. (Because he was most interested in the birds, he sometimes did not finish other parts of the paintings.) He wrote a description for each picture. Write your own description of the spoonbill shown below. You may want to use words from the Word Box.

feathers
slender
rosy
beak
claws

Book Report

Making a Poster

John read "The Best Town in the World" and wished he could go there. He lived in Boston and thought it might be the best city in the world. John decided to share the book *Hear Ye of Boston* by Polly Curren. He made this poster.

Hear Ye of Boston by Polly Curren

Colorful ships sail at sea.

People play guitar music.

Fine old buildings and tall new buildings make the city beautiful.

People ride on white swan boats in the Public Garden.

Think and Discuss

- What did you learn about Boston?
- Why is this a good way to share a book?
- What describing words did John use on his poster?

Share Your Book

Make a Poster

1. First, plan your poster on a separate piece of paper. Where will you put the title and the author's name? Think of the characters, happenings, or information that you could picture. What pictures will show the most about your book? How many pictures will you use?
2. Draw your pictures on the poster.
3. Write a sentence about each picture on the poster.
4. Show your poster.

Other Activities

- Pretend you are a travel agent. Have classmates ask questions about your book and its setting. Try to answer with information from the book.
- Make a class poster. Each student should draw a small picture about a book on the poster. Write the title of the book and the author. Then write a sentence about the book.

 The Book Nook

Time of Wonder *by Robert McClosky* What is it like to spend a summer on an island in Maine? Two sisters share their summer island.	Jane Goodall: Living Chimpstyle *by Mary Fox* Jane Goodall lives in a jungle in Africa. She studies chimpanzees and their way of life.

Mechanics

January shivers,
February shines,
March blows off the winter ice,
April makes the mornings nice,
May is hopscotch lines.

Myra Cohn Livingston
from "Calendar"

Capitalization and Punctuation

Getting Ready Signs help us know what to do. When you write a sentence, you begin the first word with a capital letter as a sign that you have started a new sentence. You use an end mark as a sign that the sentence has ended. In this unit, you will learn other ways in which capital letters and punctuation marks are signs.

Activities

Listening Listen as the poem on the opposite page is read. Where did the reader pause? What punctuation mark was used each time? Which words begin with capital letters? How are these words alike?

Speaking Look at the picture. Say sentences about it. Tell which words need capital letters. Tell which end marks to use. Have someone write the sentences on the board.

1 | Correct Sentences

You know that every sentence begins with a capital letter and ends with an end mark. Study these rules.

1. End a statement with a period.

> Roberto's dad works on a computer.

2. End a question with a question mark.

> Is the computer big?

3. End a command with a period.

> Listen to the computer talk.

4. End an exclamation with an exclamation point.

> It has fifty buttons!

Guided Practice How would you write each sentence correctly?

Example: what is a computer   *What is a computer?*

1. a computer is a machine
2. look at these computer games
3. this game is terrific
4. i have a computer in my classroom
5. do you know how a computer works

Summing up

> ▶ Begin every sentence with a capital letter.
> ▶ End a statement or a command with a period.
> ▶ End a question with a question mark.
> ▶ End an exclamation with an exclamation point.

More Practice Write each sentence correctly.

Example: how are computers useful
How are computers useful?

6. computers remember facts
7. they help space shuttles land
8. they guide airplanes through the sky
9. computers are great machines
10. look around you
11. computers are used everywhere
12. my own computer is fantastic
13. can computers do anything on their own
14. people must give commands to the computer
15. what are the commands called
16. computer commands are called a program
17. i programmed a game into my computer
18. how can computers help children
19. may I use your computer for my math homework
20. watch my computer work
21. it can do math problems quickly
22. some computers do hundreds of problems in one second
23. these answers are all correct
24. please help me program a spelling game
25. i will get my computer book
26. follow the directions

Writing Application: Sentences
Pretend that you have a talking television. What questions could you ask your television? What commands could you give? What would you say about it? Write five sentences, using each kind of sentence.

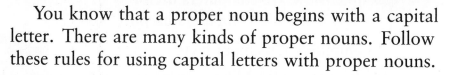

2 | Capitalizing Proper Nouns

You know that a proper noun begins with a capital letter. There are many kinds of proper nouns. Follow these rules for using capital letters with proper nouns.

1. Begin the name of a particular person with a capital letter.

> Steven Jones   Rosa L. Martinez
> Grandmother   Uncle Henry

A family name begins with a capital letter only when it is used in place of a person's name.

WRONG: Today is my Grandmother's birthday.
 RIGHT: I gave Grandmother a present.
 RIGHT: My uncle is taking her to lunch.

2. Begin the name of a pet with a capital letter.

> Ink Spot   Fluffy   Rover

3. Begin the names of days, months, and holidays with a capital letter.

> Tuesday   February   Columbus Day

Guided Practice Which nouns should begin with a capital letter?

Example: Last friday we had company. *Friday*

1. We had a visit from beth.
2. She arrived with aunt helen.
3. They brought their dog named judd.
4. Our family had a labor day cookout.
5. It was a cold day for september.

▶ Begin the name of a particular person, pet, day, month, or holiday with a capital letter.

More Practice Write each sentence correctly.

Example: I was born on flag day.
         I was born on Flag Day.

6. My birthday is in the middle of june.
7. Next tuesday is my birthday party.
8. I showed mom my guest list.
9. I hope grandpa can come to the party.
10. Maybe uncle simon will come with him.
11. I have not seen them since november.
12. They can fly here on sunday.
13. Last saturday I sent out the invitations.
14. My friend amanda helped me write them.
15. She wrote an invitation for charles r. bishop.
16. Did duke chew the invitations?
17. He chewed the invitation for emily thompson.
18. Then he chased muffy under the table.
19. Should I ask nick to bring a game?
20. Will chen have a party this year?
21. He always has a memorial day party.
22. His friend john gave him a parrot.
23. Is keely a good name for a parrot?
24. Are chen and pablo teaching the parrot to talk?

Writing Application: Sentences
Your favorite movie star has invited you to a holiday party. Write five sentences, telling the names of other guests. Name the holiday and the day and month.

3 | Capitalizing Other Proper Nouns

The name of a particular place is a proper noun. Particular places include streets, cities and towns, states, countries, schools, parks, rivers, and lakes. Names of particular places begin with capital letters.

Park Street   Clarke Elementary School
New York City   Whitehall Park
Texas   Red River
Canada   Lake Erie

Begin each important word in a proper noun with a capital letter. Do not begin *of* with a capital letter.

United States of America   Cape of Good Hope

Empire State Building

Central Park

American Museum of Natural History

Guided Practice Which nouns should begin with a capital letter?

Example: Nancy Adams lives on pine street. *Pine Street*

1. Her house is near franklin park.
2. She will travel to new hampshire next month.
3. Her cousin Rita lives in a town called east meadow.
4. Someday Nancy wants to visit the gulf of mexico.
5. Rita goes to prospect elementary school.

▶ Begin the name of a particular place with a capital letter.

▶ Begin each important word in a proper noun with a capital letter.

More Practice Write each sentence correctly.

Example: Many people visit the united states of america.
Many people visit the United States of America.

6. The statue of liberty is a famous sight.
7. The statue came from france long ago.
8. It is on an island in new york.
9. The hudson river flows nearby.
10. I live in new jersey.
11. My town is called west orange.
12. My house is on ridgeview avenue.
13. We have picnics in high point park.
14. We visited the museum of science.
15. I went to gregory school last year.
16. My sisters go to west orange high school.
17. Our neighbors used to live in china.
18. They lived in a city called nanking.
19. They sailed up the yellow river.
20. Julie is from canada.
21. Her family lived in montreal.
22. They liked to shop on brook avenue.

Writing Application: A Description

Pretend that you are taking a boat ride down a river.
Write a description of your ride for your friends.
Name the river and the particular places you see.

4 | Abbreviations

An **abbreviation** is a short way to write a word. Most abbreviations begin with capital letters and end with periods. The days of the week and most months of the year have abbreviations. Study the chart below.

Days of the week	Sunday	Sun.	Thursday	Thurs.
	Monday	Mon.	Friday	Fri.
	Tuesday	Tues.	Saturday	Sat.
	Wednesday	Wed.		
Months of the year	January	Jan.	July	—
	February	Feb.	August	Aug.
	March	Mar.	September	Sept.
	April	Apr.	October	Oct.
	May	—	November	Nov.
	June	—	December	Dec.

Titles are special words used with people's names. Abbreviations are used for most titles. The title *Miss* does not have an abbreviation.

Dr.   Mr.   Miss   Mrs.   Ms.

Guided Practice How would you write each name and abbreviation correctly?

Example: mrs Tina Anderson   *Mrs. Tina Anderson*

1. fri
2. nov
3. mr Lee Chin
4. miss Rosa Santos
5. oct
6. dr Peter Adams

▶ An **abbreviation** is a short way of writing a word.
▶ Most abbreviations begin with capital letters and end with periods.

More Practice

A. Write the correct abbreviation for each day and month.

Example: thursday *Thurs.*

7. monday
8. april
9. december
10. march
11. saturday
12. wednesday

13. september
14. february
15. sunday
16. november
17. tuesday
18. january

Thurs. Aug. 17
- party at Ben's house
- Bring present.

Fri. Aug. 18
- trip to beach with Mom and Dad
- Wear new bathing suit.

B. Write each title and name correctly.

Example: mr Chester chan *Mr. Chester Chan*

19. Mrs Mary Dobek
20. miss pam Lake
21. mr pablo alvez
22. dr Lily Ono
23. mr Steven goldman
24. dr marcos perez
25. Ms laura Rudd

26. mrs Waneta Smith
27. ms sandra potts
28. mrs jill Stevens
29. dr Anna romero
30. mr toshio brook
31. miss Lily Murphy
32. dr patrick Riley

Writing Application: Sentences

Pretend that you are a famous singer. Write five sentences about the other people in your band. What instruments do they play? Give the other band members names and titles.

5 | Book Titles

You know that every book has a title. Begin the first, last, and each important word in a book title with a capital letter. Always underline a book title.

Tammy has the book <u>Bear Mouse</u>.
Our teacher read <u>The Goat in the Rug</u>.

Guided Practice How would you write these book titles?

Example: splash the dolphin   *Splash the Dolphin*

1. four donkeys
2. hungry sharks
3. poppy the panda
4. leo the lop
5. the thanksgiving treasure
6. betsy and the circus

Summing up

▶ Begin the first, last, and each important word in a book title with a capital letter. Underline the title.

More Practice Write these book titles correctly.

Example: the bears upstairs   *The Bears Upstairs*

7. puppy summer
8. freckle juice
9. the long winter
10. henry and ribsy
11. the little red hen
12. snail in the woods

Writing Application: Sentences
Write the titles of several books that you have read. Then write sentences that tell something about them.

Books About Whales

Whale Adventure
Willard Price

Whale of a Rescue
Eleanor Hudson

Whales:
Giants of the Deep
Dorothy H. Patent

6 | Introductory Words

A comma shows a pause. Use a comma after *yes,
no, well,* and order words when they begin a sentence.
Some order words are *first, second, next,* and *finally.*
Do not use a comma after *then.*

Yes, I love to finger paint.   First, I need paper.

Guided Practice Where are commas needed?

Example: Well is the door wet?   *Well, is the door wet?*

1. No it's not painted yet.
2. First the paint spilled.
3. Then the stool fell.
4. Yes hold the stool.
5. Next hand me the paint.
6. Well the can is heavy.

Summing up

▶Use commas after *yes, no, well,* and order words at
the beginning of a sentence. Do not use a comma
after *then.*

More Practice Write each sentence correctly.

Example: First I get a brush.   *First, I get a brush.*

7. Second I mix the paint.
8. Then I paint.
9. Finally I clean up.
10. Yes you can help.
11. Well get another brush.
12. No I don't paint fast.

Writing Application: Instructions
Write five sentences that tell a friend how to make
cheese sandwiches. Use order words.

You know that a comma tells your reader where to pause. A comma also helps to make the meaning of a sentence clear.

Three or more words listed together are called a **series**. Always use commas to separate the words in a series. Read these sentences.

> Betty Ann and Mike have birthdays in May.
> Betty, Ann, and Mike have birthdays in May.

In the first sentence, it is not clear how many children have birthdays. In the second sentence, you can tell that three different children have birthdays. The commas help to make the meaning of the sentence clear. They separate the words *Betty, Ann,* and *Mike.*

WRONG: Mike asked for sneakers toys and a puppy.
RIGHT: Mike asked for sneakers, toys, and a puppy.

Guided Practice Where are commas needed in each sentence?

Example: Cindy Carmen and Rob shopped for presents.
Cindy, Carmen, and Rob shopped for presents.

1. Matt Brian and Cathy came to the party.
2. They brought kites games and puzzles.
3. The room was filled with balloons streamers and signs.
4. The children ate sandwiches salad and fruit.
5. There are more parties in June July and August.
6. One party will have music races and prizes.
7. The prizes will include ribbons toys and books.

More Practice Write each sentence. Put commas where they are needed.

Example: I saw Grandma on Friday Saturday and Sunday.
I saw Grandma on Friday, Saturday, and Sunday.

8. Mom Dad and Jon met me there.
9. Grandma bought me socks pants and gloves.
10. Did Jon like his new mittens boots and hat?
11. Uncle Jack Bob and Emily came over on Sunday.
12. We shopped for carrots radishes and peppers.
13. We also bought apples oranges and pears.
14. Who took the milk eggs and cheese out of the bag?
15. Grandma made noodles fish and salad for dinner.
16. We played games read and talked after dinner.
17. Did Dad Mom and Uncle Jack clear the table?
18. Then we watched football baseball and tennis on TV.
19. I went with Jon Emily and Bob to the park one day.
20. Emily took a ball bats and books with her.
21. Bob helped me with my math reading and spelling.
22. Jon saw rabbits birds and squirrels.
23. Men women and children enjoyed the sunshine.
24. One man sold flowers peanuts and juice.

Writing Application: Creative Writing

Imagine that you were a guest at Gateway Castle. Write five sentences about your visit. Use a series of three or more things in each sentence. You may wish to write about people or animals that you saw.

8 | Quotation Marks

You have read stories in which people talk, or have a conversation, with each other. **Quotation marks** (" ") show you the exact words that each person says.

Sometimes you may want to write a conversation. When you write a conversation, be sure to put quotation marks at the beginning and the end of the exact words someone says.

> Ed said, "Look at my terrarium!"
> Tony asked, "What is a terrarium?"

Guided Practice Where do quotation marks belong in each sentence?

Example: Ed said, A terrarium is a garden in a bottle.
Ed said, "A terrarium is a garden in a bottle."

1. Tony asked, How did you put it together?
2. Ed said, I put soil in the bottle and added plants.
3. Tony asked, How do the plants get water?
4. Ed answered, I spray water from a bottle.
5. Tony exclaimed, Your terrarium is great!

Summing up

▶ Use **quotation marks** (" ") at the beginning and end of a person's exact words.

More Practice Write each sentence. Add quotation marks.

Example: Tara said, Come to the library.
Tara said, "Come to the library."

6. Joy asked, Why do you want to go?
7. Tara answered, The library has some new books.
8. Joy asked, What kind of books does it have?
9. Tara replied, It has books about the old West.
10. Joy exclaimed, I love to read about the West!
11. Tara said, I like to read about the heroes.
12. Joy asked, Who is your favorite?
13. Tara answered, Pecos Bill is my favorite.
14. Joy exclaimed, He wasn't even a real person!
15. Tara asked, Have you ever read about Paul Bunyan?
16. Joy asked, Who is Paul Bunyan?
17. Tara replied, Paul Bunyan was a lumberjack.
18. Joy asked, What does a lumberjack do?
19. Tara answered, A lumberjack cuts down trees.
20. Tara added, Paul Bunyan had an ox named Babe.
21. Joy asked, What was so special about Babe?
22. Tara said, Babe was a very strong blue ox.
23. Tara added, She could carry a forest of logs.
24. Joy asked, Is this a true story?
25. Tara said, You can find out at the library.
26. Joy exclaimed, Let's go now!

Writing Application: Creative Writing
Who is your favorite storybook character? Pretend that you become that character for a day. Write a conversation between you and someone else. Use quotation marks to show what each of you says.

9 | More About Quotation Marks

You have learned that quotation marks set off someone's exact words. Follow these rules when you write a conversation.

1. Use a comma to separate the speaker's exact words from the rest of the sentence.

    Beth said, "Look at my new kite."

2. Begin the first word inside the quotation marks with a capital letter.

    Lin asked, "Will it fly?"

3. Put the end mark inside the quotation mark.

    Alan replied, "I will hold the string."
    Beth asked, "Is the wind strong enough?"

Guided Practice Where does a comma, a capital letter, and an end mark belong in each sentence?

Example: Beth said "let's start running"
Beth said, "Let's start running."

1. Lin said "run down the hill"
2. Alan shouted "you are running the wrong way"
3. Beth asked "will the kite catch in a tree"
4. Alan answered "now you are fine"
5. Lin cried "the kite is in the air"

> ▶ Use a comma to separate the speaker's exact words from the rest of the sentence.
> ▶ Begin a quotation with a capital letter.
> ▶ Put the end mark before the last quotation mark.

More Practice Write each sentence correctly. Add a comma, a capital letter, an end mark, or quotation marks to each sentence.

Example: Mrs. Fox asked, "Did you like the museum"
Mrs. Fox asked, "Did you like the museum?"

  6. Martha said, "the pottery was beautiful."
  7. Barry added, "I loved the bright colors"
  8. Jeff exclaimed, I didn't know what to look at first!
  9. Jessica asked, "Did you see the huge pot"
 10. Carlos said "The bowl was my favorite."
 11. Dana asked, "Where did the bowl come from"
 12. Jeff answered, The sign said it came from China.
 13. Martha said, "the dish is the best."
 14. Jessica added, "It was made in 1790"
 15. Mrs. Fox said, "today we will make pottery."
 16. Jeff asked "how do you make pottery?"
 17. Mrs. Fox asked, "have you ever played with clay?"
 18. Carlos answered "I made a dish for my mother."
 19. Martha asked, "Can I paint my pottery"
 20. Mrs. Fox said, We will all paint the pottery.

Writing Application: Sentences

Pretend that you and a friend are in a room full of stuffed animals. What do you see? Write a conversation between you and your friend.

Building Vocabulary

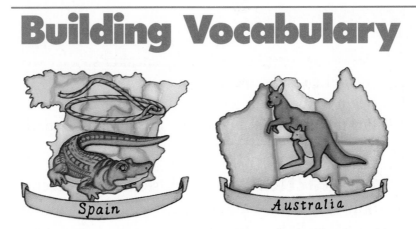

Spain

Australia

Words from Other Languages

The English language is made up of words from many languages. Some words come from languages of Native Americans. Some words come from the different languages the settlers spoke.

Umbrella, for example, is a word from Italy. It means "little shade." The people of Italy use umbrellas to keep the sun off their heads. The people in America use umbrellas to keep off the rain.

These familiar words come from other languages.

Word	Country	Word	Country
kindergarten	Germany	taco	Mexico
alligator	Spain	silk	China
lasso	Spain	kangaroo	Australia
ranch	Spain	raccoon	America
chimpanzee	Africa	moose	America
banjo	Africa	shampoo	India
pizza	Italy	pajamas	India
spaghetti	Italy	tulip	Turkey

People come to the United States from many lands. In time we will add more words to our language.

Practice

A. Write each sentence. Underline the words that come from other languages.

Example: That big moose is hiding behind a rock.
That big <u>moose</u> is hiding behind a rock.

1. An alligator has sharp teeth and strong jaws.
2. Allison will spend the summer on a ranch.
3. One of the strings snapped on my banjo.
4. My mother wore her silk dress to the meeting.
5. Edward's pajamas are blue with green stripes.
6. My sister's shampoo smells good.

B. Complete each sentence with a word from this lesson. Write the sentences. You may use your dictionary to help you.

Example: A ____ is a Mexican food filled with meat.
A taco is a Mexican food filled with meat.

7. I use my ____ when it rains.
8. A food made of thin noodles is called ____.
9. One kind of ape is a ____.
10. A ____ is covered with tomato sauce and cheese.
11. The cowhand threw the ____ around the calf's neck.
12. Before first grade, many children go to ____.
13. A mother ____ carries her baby in a pouch.
14. An animal that has a face like a mask is a ____.
15. A soap used to wash the hair is called ____.
16. A ____ is a colorful flower shaped like a cup.

Writing Application: A Story

Write a story. Use at least five words from the chart on page 278. Then have a friend underline the words you chose.

Grammar-Writing Connection

Combining Sentences: Using Commas in a Series

Writers look for ways to turn short, choppy sentences into longer, smoother sentences. Sometimes you can combine three short sentences to make one longer sentence. The sentences below have the same predicate. The subjects *Pablo, Saul,* and *Sarah* are combined to make a series.

Pablo went to the circus.
Saul went to the circus.
Sarah went to the circus.

Pablo , Saul , and Sarah went to the circus.

Revising Sentences

Make each group of sentences into one sentence. Write the new sentences.

Example: The clowns juggled.
The clowns skipped.
The clowns danced.
The clowns juggled, skipped, and danced.

1. Sarah saw Jessie.
Sarah saw Kimi.
Sarah saw John.

2. The lions played.
The lions jumped.
The lions rolled.

3. Men rode horses.
Women rode horses.
Children rode horses.

4. The crowd laughed.
The crowd cheered.
The crowd clapped.

Creative Writing

The America by James E. Buttersworth
Mystic Seaport, Inc.

How wonderful to sail the sea! James E. Buttersworth painted many pictures of sailing boats. This one shows a boat called *America*. It won a sailing race long ago.

• What makes you feel the wind blowing in this picture?

Activities

1. **Report the race.** Suppose you are watching this sailing race. Write a made-up report of what happens.
2. **Write the ship's log.** Imagine you are the ship's captain. Write your adventures in the ship's record book.
3. **Describe the place.** Where would you most like to sail to? Describe the place and why you would go there.

Check-up: Unit 9

Correct Sentences *(p. 262)* Write each sentence correctly.

1. are masks made of wood or rubber
2. they can be made of many things
3. look at this mask
4. it looks so scary
5. would you like to make a mask

Capitalizing Proper Nouns *(pp. 264, 266)* Write each sentence correctly.

6. Every summer I go to uncle larry's ranch.
7. He lives in idaho.
8. This labor day I watched a horse show.
9. It was held in emerson park.
10. My uncle rode his horse sparky.
11. First prize went to sally j. hayes.

Abbreviations *(p. 268)* Write the abbreviation for each day and month correctly. Write each name correctly.

12. december
13. mr phil johnson
14. wednesday
15. dr alan chi
16. miss marta garcia
17. february
18. ms hilda goodman
19. mrs kim wong

Book Titles *(p. 270)* Write these book titles correctly.

20. the mouse wife
21. the owl and the woodpecker
22. alex and the cat
23. billy gorilla
24. little house in the big woods

Introductory Words *(p. 271)* Write each sentence. Put a comma where it is needed.

25. Yes Ed's snowman is big.
26. First he made the snowman's body.
27. Next he made a face.
28. No the sun didn't melt the snowman.
29. Well he won the contest.

Commas in a Series *(p. 272)* Write each sentence. Put commas where they are needed.

30. Miss Todd Mrs. Chu and Mr. Stone are salespeople.
31. They sell clothes jewelry and shoes.
32. The rings pins and watches cost a lot.
33. Does Miss Todd work on Monday Tuesday and Thursday?
34. Sarah Patrick and Robin bought boots.

Quotation Marks *(p. 274)* Write each sentence. Add quotation marks.

35. Dad asked, Will you win the sack race?
36. Tim answered, I can run faster than Michael.
37. Dad asked, How old is Michael?
38. Tim said, He is three years older than I am.
39. Dad exclaimed, You must be pretty fast!

More About Quotation Marks *(p. 276)* Write each sentence. Add a comma, a capital letter, an end mark, or quotation marks to make it correct.

40. Theresa asked, "Would you like to go to Funland"
41. Jamie replied "I will ask my parents."
42. Theresa said, My favorite part is the Fun House.
43. Jamie said "The strange mirrors make me laugh."
44. Theresa asked, "can we slide down the chute?"

Enrichment

Unit Nine: Capitalization and Punctuation

The Seasons

Create a wall calendar on poster board. Make twelve equal sections. Write the name of a month in each section. Divide months by days of the week. Write in all holidays. Show the first day of the new seasons with a small picture for each one.

Hear! Hear!

Your nature club is going camping. Write a short announcement of the trip. Include the following information: (1) time, date, place; (2) clothes campers should bring; (3) other supplies needed; and (4) the weekend's activities. Use capital letters, periods, and commas correctly. Draw pictures to go with the announcement.

Character Quotations

Think about a book that you have read recently. Write down the title and the author's name on a sheet of paper. Next, think about the main character in the story. What would that person say to make your classmates want to read the book? Think of one good sentence and write it down. Use quotation marks correctly. Then exchange papers with a partner. Ask and answer questions about one another's books.

Extra Practice: Unit 9

1 | Correct Sentences (p. 262)

● Each sentence below is missing a capital letter or an end mark. Write each sentence correctly.

Example: Why do some people use computers
Why do some people use computers?

1. Think about it
2. computers play games.
3. Can they think
4. Wow, this computer sings
5. do you want a computer?
6. i can't wait to get one!

▲ Write each sentence correctly.

Example: a robot is a machine   *A robot is a machine.*

7. it has a computer for a brain
8. how are robots different from other computers
9. many robots have arms or hands
10. tell me what robots can do
11. robots can do simple jobs around the house
12. they do not get tired
13. gee, your robot is so smart

■ Each sentence has the wrong end mark. Write each sentence correctly. Then write *statement, question, exclamation,* or *command* next to each sentence.

Example: will computers be used in the future!
Will computers be used in the future?   question

14. robots could help fight fires?
15. can computers save lives.
16. computers will help doctors save lives!
17. they could even help wipe out some disease?
18. will robots wash windows in tall buildings.
19. look at this new computer?
20. it has so many dials?

Three levels of practice 285

● Write the proper noun that is correct in each pair.

Example: theresa Sanchez
Theresa Sanchez   *Theresa Sanchez*

1. Chirpy
chirpy

2. aunt sue
Aunt Sue

3. Memorial day
Memorial Day

4. Anne
anne

5. october
October

6. lois t. Dodge
Lois T. Dodge

7. sunday
Sunday

8. Bill Howe
Bill howe

9. flag day
Flag Day

▲ Write each sentence correctly.

Example: I am ted a. squire.   *I am Ted A. Squire.*

10. I was named after my uncle theodore.

11. My favorite holiday is thanksgiving.

12. The holiday comes in november.

13. It is always on a thursday.

14. I visit grandfather on that day.

15. Once he invited rona c. fores to dinner.

16. She surprised me with a kitten named rags.

17. My friend ben has a new kitten too.

■ Finish each sentence with a proper noun for the word in ( ). Write the complete sentence.

Example: Every ____ I go on vacation.   (month)
Every May I go on vacation.

18. I usually spend my vacation with ____.   (person)

19. This year ____ came with me.   (pet)

20. On ____ I went to a parade.   (holiday)

21. I saw my friend ____ there.   (person)

22. We decided to go to the park on ____.   (day)

23. One ____ night I had a party.   (day)

24. I invited ____ and ____.   (people)

● Write the proper noun in each pair that is correct.

Example: dade city
Dade City   *Dade City*

1. Africa
africa

2. bear Lake
Bear Lake

3. Winter street
Winter Street

4. Jackson Park
jackson park

5. smithtown
Smithtown

6. California
california

7. Wilson School
wilson school

8. gulf of Mexico
Gulf of Mexico

▲ Write each sentence correctly.

Example: In 1896 utah became a state.
In 1896 Utah became a state.

9. It is part of the united states of america.

10. The green river flows through the state.

11. Its largest city is salt lake city.

12. One of its lakes is lake powell.

13. I visited zion national park once.

14. Peter goes to the brigham young school.

15. Is the school near dexter street?

■ Write a sentence to answer each question.

Example: What park do you go to?   *I go to Rose Park.*

16. What street do you live on?

17. What town or city does your best friend live in?

18. What country would you like to visit?

19. What is the name of your school?

20. What is the name of your favorite state?

21. What lake or river would you like to swim in?

22. What state would you like to live in when you grow up?

4 | Abbreviations (p. 268)

● Write the correct abbreviation in each pair.
Example: Thurs.
       Thurs   *Thurs.*

1. Oct.	**4.** Nov	**7.** Apr.	**10.** Miss
oct.	Nov.	apr.	miss
2. Mr.	**5.** Tues.	**8.** mrs.	**11.** wed
mr.	Tues	Mrs.	Wed.
3. feb	**6.** Dr	**9.** Sun	**12.** Dec.
Feb.	Dr.	Sun.	dec

▲ Write each abbreviation and name correctly.
Example: dr lawrence stone   *Dr. Lawrence Stone*

13. fri	**19.** miss Megan Shaw
14. mar	**20.** sat
15. mrs Carla gomez	**21.** mr paul wilson
16. dr roger wang	**22.** nov
17. wed	**23.** ms mary Rossi
18. aug	**24.** sept

■ Write the answer to each question. Use the abbreviations that you have learned.
Example: Which day starts the school week?   *Mon.*

25. Which month comes after March?
26. Which day ends the school week?
27. In which month is Valentine's Day?
28. Which day comes after Tuesday?
29. What is your teacher's name?
30. What is your doctor's name?
31. In which month is your favorite holiday?
32. Which day comes before Sunday?
33. What was your second-grade teacher's name?
34. What is the first month of the year?

● Copy these sentences. Underline the book titles.
  Example: I read the book The Great Frog Swamp.
           I read the book The Great Frog Swamp.
   1. Gloomy Louie is a book about a sad boy.
   2. I read The Bee Sneeze.
   3. Hurry Home tells about a basketball game.
   4. Would you like to read Skunk Lane?
   5. Who wrote the book Uncle Nikos?
   6. Have you read Bumps in the Night?
   7. Pat likes the book Lester and Mother.

▲ Write each book title correctly.
  Example: the hill and the rock
           The Hill and the Rock
   8. animals sleeping
   9. sun and light
  10. baby dinosaurs
  11. home at last
  12. the velveteen rabbit
  13. a monkey in the family
  14. amanda and the mysterious carpet
  15. the most wonderful egg in the world

■ Write each sentence correctly.
  Example: Robin read humphrey, the dancing Pig.
           Robin read Humphrey, the Dancing Pig.
  16. Who wrote the book hiawatha?
  17. a snake is totally tail was fun to read.
  18. I enjoyed jenny and the cat club.
  19. My favorite book is the red cycle.
  20. Have you read the valentine box?
  21. My teacher read us annie and the wild animals.
  22. Our school library has the night the monster came.

● Write the sentence that is correct in each pair.

Example: Well what time is it?

Well, what time is it?   *Well, what time is it?*

1. Yes, I'm in a hurry.
   Yes I'm in a hurry.

2. No I don't have a watch.
   No, I don't have a watch.

3. Well I've plenty to do.
   Well, I've plenty to do.

4. First, I'll get dressed.
   First I'll get dressed.

5. Second I'll eat.
   Second, I'll eat.

6. Last I'll go to school.
   Last, I'll go to school.

▲ Write these sentences correctly.

Example: Yes the television is broken.
         Yes, the television is broken.

7. No you cannot fix it.

8. Well we should call a repair shop.

9. First get the telephone book.

10. Yes I know the name of the repair shop.

11. Second look up the telephone number.

12. Yes there are five repair shops in town.

13. Next call the repair shop.

14. Finally wait for the repair person.

■ Add a word from the Word Box to each sentence.
Write each sentence correctly.

Example: _____ it is fun to bake bread.
         Yes, it is fun to bake bread.

15. _____ i did not add the flour.

16. _____ how long should the bread bake?

17. _____ place the bread in a pan.

18. _____ put the pan in the oven.

19. _____ check the time.

20. _____ remove the bread carefully.

| First |
| No |
| Well |
| Finally |
| Second |
| Yes |
| Then |

EXTRA PRACTICE: UNIT 9

● Write each sentence. Underline the words in a series.

Example: Kim, Eric, and Carey are on baseball teams.
Kim, Eric, and Carey are on baseball teams.

1. The games are on Sunday, Monday, and Tuesday.
2. They are in the spring, the summer, and the fall.
3. Girls, boys, and coaches meet at the field.
4. Nina, John, and April are on the same team.
5. The ball sails over Ina, Luis, and Bob.
6. Nina runs to first base, second base, and third base.
7. Fans jump, shout, and clap.

▲ Write each sentence correctly.

Example: Amy Kurt and Carlos visited the library.
Amy, Kurt, and Carlos visited the library.

8. They read books newspapers and magazines.
9. Amy found a book about stars planets and the sun.
10. Mercury Venus and Mars are on the cover.
11. Carlos chose books about monkeys goats and bears.
12. Kurt saw Mrs. Taylor Sam and Sal.
13. Sal wrote a report on seals whales and sharks.
14. On Tuesday Thursday and Friday we saw films.

■ Write each sentence, using commas correctly. Write *correct* for sentences that need no commas.

Example: Dale Chico and Nina went shopping.
Dale, Chico, and Nina went shopping.

15. They looked at games toys and clothes.
16. Chico bought a card and gloves for his mother.
17. He tried on shoes coats and belts.
18. Nina saw a puppy and rabbits in the pet store.
19. She bought a collar food and bones for her dog.
20. Kittens fish and birds are Dale's favorite pets.

● Write each sentence. Underline the speaker's words.

Example: Chris said, "The race is starting."
Chris said, "The race is starting."

1. Greg asked, "What kind of race is it?"
2. Chris answered, "It is a wheelchair race."
3. Chris added, "Only wheelchair racers can enter."
4. Greg asked, "Is it hard work?"
5. Chris replied, "They train for many weeks."
6. Greg asked, "How do they move so fast?"
7. Chris said, "The racers spin the wheels around."

▲ Write each sentence. Add quotation marks.

Example: Maria said, I just finished a great book.
Maria said, "I just finished a great book."

8. Lee asked, What kind of book is it?
9. Maria replied, It's a mystery book.
10. Maria added, The detective's name is Starr E. Eyes.
11. Lee asked, May I borrow your book?
12. Maria said, I will bring it to school tomorrow.
13. Maria asked, Do you want to know the ending?
14. Lee exclaimed, You'll spoil all the fun!

■ In each sentence below, quotation marks are in the wrong place. Write each sentence correctly.

Example: "Lou asked, How does a blind person read?"
Lou asked, "How does a blind person read?"

15. "Abbey said, A blind person can use Braille."
16. "Lou asked, "What is Braille?
17. "Abbey said," It's an alphabet made of raised dots.
18. "Lou" asked, What do the dots stand for?
19. "Abbey said, "They are letters and numbers.
20. Lou "said, The library has books written in Braille."

● Write each sentence correctly. Add a comma where it is needed.

Example: Ray asked "Do sharks have teeth?"
Ray asked, "Do sharks have teeth?"

1. Tina said "A shark has several rows of teeth."
2. Leo added "The teeth that fall out grow back."
3. Ray asked "What do sharks eat?"
4. Tina replied "Sharks eat meat and fish."
5. Ray asked "How big are they?"
6. Leo exclaimed "Some sharks are sixty feet long!"

▲ Write each sentence correctly. Add a comma, a capital letter, an end mark, or quotation marks.

Example: Andrew asked, "what is an octopus?"
Andrew asked, "What is an octopus?"

7. Hoshi said, "it is a sea animal."
8. Nicole asked, "What does an octopus look like"
9. Ramona said "It has a soft body with eight arms."
10. Ramona added, The octopus uses its arms to get food.
11. Andrew asked, "what does an octopus eat?"
12. Ramona replied "It eats clams and other fish."

■ Write each sentence correctly. Add a comma, a capital letter, an end mark, and quotation marks.

Example: Liza said look at this picture
Liza said, "Look at this picture."

13. Mario explained it is a fish called an electric eel
14. Jade said its body is long like a snake
15. Ruby asked where does the eel live
16. Mario said some eels live in South America
17. Liza asked why is it called an electric eel
18. Jade replied it gives an electric shock to its enemies

With this typewriter
I am connected
with these words
and these words
with this paper
and this paper with you.

Norman Jordan
from "August 8"

Letters

Getting Ready Everyone loves to get letters! It can be almost as much fun to write them. People write letters to invite others to parties, to thank them for gifts, or to cheer up a sick friend. Can you think of other times when you might send a letter? In this unit, you will read some letters and write one of your own.

Activities

Listening Listen as the poem on the opposite page is read. How does the typewriter connect the writer to the person getting the letter?

Speaking Look at the picture. Imagine that the boy in the picture is writing a letter to your class. Why is he writing? What is he writing? What would you write back?

Composition Skills

Parts of a Letter

After Bill read "The Storm," he wanted to write to the author. Here is the letter Bill wrote.

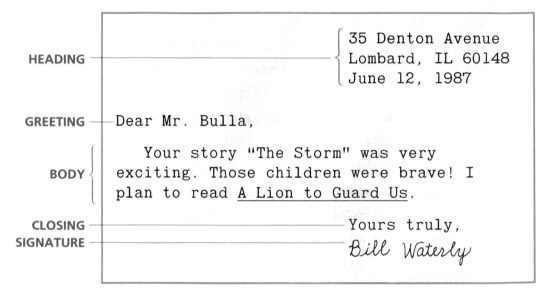

HEADING	35 Denton Avenue Lombard, IL 60148 June 12, 1987
GREETING	Dear Mr. Bulla,
BODY	Your story "The Storm" was very exciting. Those children were brave! I plan to read A Lion to Guard Us.
CLOSING **SIGNATURE**	Yours truly, Bill Waterly

Look at the five parts of the letter above.

1. The **heading** gives the letter writer's address and the date. The street, city, state abbreviation, and month begin with capital letters.
2. The **greeting** says "hello." Begin the first word with a capital letter.
3. The **body** is the main part. It tells the message.
4. The **closing** says "good-by." Begin the first word with a capital letter.
5. The **signature** tells who wrote the letter.

• Which parts line up with each other?

Prewriting Practice

Write the five parts of this letter in the correct order.

Your friend,   Dear Jessie,

32 West Street
Sparta, NJ 07871
March 15, 1987   *Theresa*

   My dad is reading me a book called <u>Swiss Family Robinson</u>. It is about another shipwrecked family. You should read it!

Kinds of Letters

   When you write a letter, remember your purpose. An **invitation** invites someone to something. A **get-well note** is sent to someone who is sick. A **thank-you note** thanks someone for a present or a favor.

   Each kind of letter is shown on this page and the next page. Each kind has all five parts, but the headings are not shown in these examples. Read the letters.

Invitation

Dear Mrs. Bell's class,

   Please come watch our play on May 25 at 2 o'clock in the afternoon. Come to Room 126. We hope you will have fun!

                          Yours truly,
                          Jared

Get-well Note

Dear Rico,

How I wish you had been in school to see our class play! I was a sailor. When are you coming back to school? We miss you. Get well soon.

Your friend,
Willy

Thank-you Note

Dear Mr. Amato,

Thank you for helping us build scenery for our play. After we finished, those boxes really did look like a ship! More than 200 people came to the play. It was a big success!

Sincerely,
Lindsay

• What information is included in each kind of letter?

Prewriting Practice

Write an invitation, a thank-you note, or a get-well note to someone you know. Remember to include all five letter parts.

Using Commas Correctly in Letters

Look at where commas are used in the heading, greeting, and closing of this letter.

932 Cedar Creek Road

between city and state ——→ Cranston, RI 02907

between day and year ——→ April 5, 1987

Dear Brett, ←—— **after the greeting**

We visited Plimouth Plantation today. The houses were like the ones the Pilgrims used, and the people talked and acted the way the Pilgrims did. I'll tell you more when I get home.

after the closing ——→ Your friend,
Ronnie

Practice Copy this letter. Add commas.

1363 Kraft Drive
Seattle WA 98110
April 5 1987

Dear Aunt Louise

Our ocean trip was long, but we had a good time. It was wonderful to see land again! Please join us soon.

Sincerely
Hope

The Writing Process
How to Write a Letter

Step 1: Prewriting

Suki wanted to write a letter to Mrs. Winston, her second-grade teacher. She made a list of ideas.

my new neighbor — Suki had not met her yet.

my vacation in Florida — She would enjoy writing about this.

my math project — The project was not very interesting.

Suki thought that Mrs. Winston would like to hear about her trip. She circled *my vacation in Florida*.

On Your Own

1. **Think and discuss** Think of someone you would like to write to. List things you would like to write about. Use the Ideas page to help you. Discuss your ideas with a partner.

2. **Choose** Ask these questions about each topic.
   Would my reader like to hear about this?
   Would I enjoy writing about this?
   Circle the topic you want to write about.

3. **Explore** What information will you include in your letter? Do one of the activities under "Exploring Your Topic" on the Ideas page.

Ideas for Prewriting

Choosing Your Topic

Topic Ideas

A big storm
A trip
Your class play
A new friend
The town fair
A funny thing that
    happened to you
A special event
A recital
Your team

Letter Starters

Pick three people to write to.

a grandparent   a pen pal
a cousin   a neighbor
a friend   a teacher

What can you write about?
Answer these questions.

Have you done anything new?
Have you made something?
Have you gotten something
    new?

Exploring Your Topic

Draw

Draw pictures about your topic. Here is part of Suki's drawing.

Talk It Out

Have a classmate pretend to be the person you are writing to. Have your classmate ask questions about your topic. Answer the questions.

Step 2: Write a First Draft

Suki began her letter to her second-grade teacher. She knew that she could correct mistakes later. Now she just wanted to get her ideas on paper. Here are the greeting and body of Suki's letter.

Part of Suki's first draft

dear Mrs. Winston

I went to Florida. I did lots of fun things. The beach was beautiful. I found two shells for your shell collection. ~~When can~~ I will give them to you.

Think and Discuss

- Did Suki think about her reader? How?
- Where could she add more details?

On Your Own

1. **Think about purpose and audience** Ask yourself these questions.
   To whom am I writing my letter?
   What will I write about?
   What would interest my reader?

2. **Write** Write your first draft. Think about the person to whom you are writing. Write about something that will interest that person. Write on every other line so that it will be easier to make changes later.

Step 3: Revise

Suki read her first draft. She noticed that most of her sentences began with the word *I*. She changed her last sentence.

Then Suki read her letter to John. She wanted to know if she should make any other changes.

Reading and responding

Suki made more changes in her letter.

Part of Suki's revised draft

dear Mrs. Winston

~~In December I flew to Florida~~
^I went to Florida. I did lots of
and swam fished and sailed
fun things. The beach was beautiful.
a conch and an angel wing
I found^ two shells for your shell
can't wait to
collection. ~~When can~~ I ~~will~~ give

them to you.

Think and Discuss

- Why did Suki change her first two sentences?
- What details did she add?
- Why is her last sentence better?

On Your Own

1. **Think again** Read your letter. Ask yourself these questions.

   > Does my letter sound as though I am talking to my reader?
   >
   > Is my letter interesting? Could I add more details?
   >
   > Is there anything else I would like to say?

2. **Revise** Make changes in your first draft. Add exact words and details to make your letter more interesting. You may want to use words from the thesaurus below or the one beginning on page 414.

3. **Read/Listen/Respond** Read your letter to a classmate or your teacher.

Ask your listener:	As you listen:
"Did I make my letter interesting?" "Could I add details?" "Will the person feel like writing back?"	I must listen carefully. What else would I like to know? Would I want to write back?

4. **Revise** Think about your listener's suggestions. Do you have any more ideas? Make those changes.

Thesaurus

great terrific, fine, wonderful, superb

laugh giggle, chuckle

like appreciate, enjoy, admire

party celebration

thoughtful kind, considerate

trip journey, tour, trek, outing

Step 4: Proofread

Suki proofread her letter. She used a dictionary to check spellings. She used proofreading marks.

Here is part of Suki's letter after proofreading.

Part of Suki's proofread draft

14 francis street

Chicago, IL 60624

~~February~~

~~Febuary~~ 4, 1987

dear Mrs. Winston,

In December I flew to Florida

∧ ~~I went to Florida.~~ I did lots of and swam, fished, and sailed.

~~fun things.~~ The beach was beautiful.

Think and Discuss

- Which spelling did Suki correct?
- Why did she add capital letters?
- Why did she add commas?

On Your Own

1. Proofreading Practice Proofread for a spelling mistake, three missing commas, and a word that needs a capital letter. Write the letter.

dear Jennifer

It's been kwiet since you moved away. Well maybe I'll see you next summer.

Your friend
Julie

Proofreading Marks

- ¶ Indent
- ∧ Add something
- ℰ Take out something
- ≡ Capitalize
- / Make a small letter

2. **Proofreading Application** Proofread your letter. Use the Proofreading Checklist and the Grammar and Spelling Hints. Use a dictionary to check spellings. Make changes with a red pencil.

Proofreading Checklist

Did I

☑ **1.** use commas correctly?

☑ **2.** use capital letters and end marks correctly?

☑ **3.** spell all words correctly?

The Grammar/Spelling Connection

Grammar Hints

Remember these rules from Unit 9.

- Use a comma after *yes*, *no*, and *well* at the beginning of a sentence. (*Yes, I am sleepy.*)
- Use commas to separate words in a series. (*Lara found her sneakers, belt, and gloves.*)

Spelling Hints

- The consonant sound in *jeans* and *page* may be spelled *j* or *g*. (*just, huge*)
- The consonant sounds in both *quit* and *squeeze* may be spelled *qu*. (*quite, square*)

Step 5: Publish

Suki was ready to make a final copy of her letter. She made her own special paper. She copied her letter onto this paper. She included all the changes.

Then Suki addressed an envelope, put a stamp on it, and mailed it to her teacher.

On Your Own

1. **Copy** Copy your letter in your neatest handwriting.
2. **Check** Read your letter again. Be sure you have not left out anything or made any copying mistakes.
3. **Share** Think of a special way to share your letter. You may want to use the Ideas for Sharing box.

Ideas for Sharing

- Make a card for your letter. Decorate the card. Put your letter inside. Mail your card and letter.
- Paste your letter on large paper. Add photos or drawings. Read and show your letter to the class.

Writing Across the Curriculum
Letters

Literature and Creative Writing

In "The Storm," three children are caught in a dangerous storm at sea. Luckily they reach land before their ship sinks.

Have fun using what you have learned about writing a letter. Do one or more of these activities.

> **Remember these things:**
> Include the five parts of a letter.
> For thank-you notes and invitations, make your letter suit your purpose.
> Include interesting details.

1. Write about the storm. Pretend that you are Jemmy. Write a letter to a friend in England. Tell about all the exciting things that happened to you during the storm.

2. Write to an author. Write a thank-you note to the author of your favorite book. Tell why the book is your favorite.

3. The captain writes a letter. Pretend that you are the captain of the *Sea Adventure*. You are in charge of Amanda, Jemmy, and Meg. Write a letter to their father. Explain where you are and how you plan to get the children to him safely.

Health

People enjoy receiving letters. Letters help others feel good about themselves. Letter writing is a nice way to share information.

Choose one or more of the following activities. Follow the five steps for writing a letter.

1. **Send cheer.** Sometimes our friends become ill and cannot leave their homes or hospitals. A cheery letter will bring them news and will help them feel better. Write a letter to a friend. **Extra!** Design special stationery for these letters.

Writing Steps
1. Choose a Topic
2. Write a First Draft
3. Revise
4. Proofread
5. Publish

2. **Invite a special guest.** Veterinarians are animal doctors. Write a letter inviting a veterinarian to talk to your class about caring for pets.

3. **Say thank you.** Look at the school helpers pictured below. Write a thank-you letter to a school helper. You may want to use some of the words in the box.

custodian
crossing guard
librarian
secretary
bus driver

Book Report

Making a Picture Postcard

Tim really liked historical fiction. He decided to share the book *The Long Way to a New Land* by Joan Sandin with his friend Robert by making a picture postcard.

Dear Robert,
 Carl Erik's family sails to America from Sweden. The ship is dark and smelly! It takes a long time to cross the ocean.
 Will they get there safely? Read the book to find out!
          Your friend,
          Tim

Robert Weiss
28 Main Street
Candia, NH
  03040

Think and Discuss

- Who is the main character in this story?
- What is the story about?

Share Your Book

Make a Picture Postcard

1. First, get a piece of heavy paper. Cut it to the size you want your postcard to be.
2. Draw a picture for the story on one side. Write the title and the author's name at the top.
3. On one half of the other side of the card, write a message that tells about the book. Do not give away the ending.
4. Write the name and address of the person to whom you are sending the card. Draw a stamp.

Other Activities

- Write a postcard or letter that your book character might send to you. Have the character tell about events in the book the way he or she saw them.
- Draw a map that shows where your book character lives. If it is a real place, use information from an atlas. If it is a make-believe place, make up a map of your own.

The Book Nook

The Drinking Gourd	The Courage of Sarah Noble
by F. N. Monjo	*by Alice Dalgleish*
A boy helps a black family to escape on the Underground Railroad.	Sarah travels into the wilderness with her father.

Grammar

I am the sister of him
And he is my brother.
He is too little for us
To talk to each other.

Dorothy Aldis, from "Little"

Pronouns

Getting Ready When you speak and write, you use certain words in place of people's names. You use words such as *I, you, it, we, they, me, him, her, us,* or *them*. These words are pronouns. In this unit, you will learn how to use pronouns correctly to make your speaking and writing clear.

Activities

Listening Listen as the poem on the opposite page is read. What pronouns are used? Which person in the picture is speaking?

Speaking Look at the picture. Say sentences that tell about the girl and boy. Use pronouns. Have someone write the sentences on the board and underline the pronouns.

1 | Subject Pronouns

A **pronoun** is a word that can take the place of one or more nouns in a sentence.

NOUNS
<u>Melissa</u> heard the wind.
<u>The wind</u> was howling.
<u>The children</u> stayed home.

PRONOUNS
She heard the wind.
It was howling.
They stayed home.

The pronouns above are subjects. The pronouns *I, you, he, she, it, we,* and *they* are **subject pronouns**. Pronouns can be singular or plural.

Subject Pronouns					
Singular	I	you	he	she	it
Plural	we	you	they		

Guided Practice Find the subject pronouns.

Example: Last night we had a big storm. *we*

1. I could not sleep.
2. She pulled the curtains closed.
3. They read by the fire.
4. We have big puddles in the street.
5. Are you wearing a new raincoat?

▶ A **pronoun** takes the place of one or more nouns.
▶ The pronouns *I, you, he, she, it, we,* and *they* are **subject pronouns**. Pronouns can be singular or plural.

More Practice Write a subject pronoun to replace the underlined word or words in each sentence.

Example: <u>Sam and I</u> went camping.   *We*

  6. <u>The campers</u> sat around the campfire.
  7. <u>The fire</u> felt warm.
  8. <u>Pete</u> played the guitar.
  9. <u>Marsha</u> sang a song.
10. <u>The children</u> joined in.
11. <u>The song</u> was about a boat at sea.
12. <u>Jeff and I</u> liked the song.
13. <u>Mrs. Roy and Dan</u> went sailing.
14. Is <u>Dan</u> a good sailor?
15. <u>Mrs. Roy</u> brought some apples along.
16. <u>The apples</u> were in her backpack.
17. How many sails does <u>the boat</u> have?
18. Can <u>two people</u> handle the sail?
19. <u>The wind</u> filled the sail with air.
20. <u>Dan</u> watched the clouds.
21. <u>Marsha and I</u> waved to the sailors.
22. <u>The sailors</u> had a great afternoon.

Writing Application: Creative Writing

Imagine that you and several friends live on a cloud. Write five sentences that tell about what your day would be like. Use a subject pronoun in each.

2 | Pronouns and Verbs

You know that a pronoun can be the subject of a sentence. Remember that verbs in the present have two forms. The correct form of the verb to use depends on the subject pronoun.

1. Add *s* or *es* to a verb in the present when the subject is *he, she,* or *it.*

   <u>She</u> fixes dinner.   <u>He</u> sets the table.

2. Do not add *s* or *es* to a verb in the present when the subject is *I, you, we,* or *they.*

   <u>I</u> fix dinner.   <u>We</u> set the table.

Guided Practice Choose the correct verb form to complete each sentence.

Example: We (like, likes) eggs for breakfast. *like*

1. You (buy, buys) twelve eggs.
2. I (cracks, crack) six eggs in half.
3. He (adds, add) some milk.
4. She (mix, mixes) the eggs in a bowl.
5. They (pour, pours) the eggs into a pan.

Summing up

▶ Use the form of the verb that goes with the subject pronoun. Add *s* or *es* to a verb in the present when the subject is *he, she,* or *it.*

▶ Do not add *s* or *es* to a verb in the present when the subject is *I, you, we,* or *they.*

More Practice Choose the correct verb form to complete each sentence. Write the sentences.

Example: We (sees, see) some balloons overhead.
We see some balloons overhead.

   6. They (float, floats) over the trees.
   7. You (jumps, jump) for the silver balloon.
   8. It (look, looks) like a cat.
   9. I (takes, take) the balloon with the red string.
   10. She (grab, grabs) for the smallest balloon.
   11. She (toss, tosses) the balloon in the air.
   12. It (break, breaks) with a pop.
   13. We (hears, hear) the loud noise.
   14. You (find, finds) a message inside the balloon.
   15. He (read, reads) the short message.
   16. It (tells, tell) about children in another town.
   17. They (wants, want) a letter in return.
   18. He (search, searches) for a pencil.
   19. I (get, gets) some paper.
   20. She (writes, write) the letter.
   21. We (rush, rushes) to the mailbox.
   22. You (puts, put) the letter in the mailbox.
   23. It (reach, reaches) the children.
   24. We (become, becomes) pen pals.
   25. I (call, calls) my pen pal on the telephone.
   26. She (invite, invites) me to her house.

Writing Application: A Description

You find a tiny key in one of the balloons that you have just bought. The key will unlock a special box. What is inside the box? What will you do with it? Write five sentences that describe what you find inside the box. Use a subject pronoun in each sentence.

3 | Object Pronouns

You know that a subject pronoun can be the subject of a sentence. Other pronouns can follow action verbs and words like *to, for, at, of,* and *with.* These pronouns are called **object pronouns.** *Me, you, him, her, it, us,* and *them* are object pronouns.

NOUNS

Nina painted with <u>Lou</u>.
Ben and I met <u>Nina and Lou</u>.
Ben brought <u>a brush</u>.

PRONOUNS

Nina painted with him.
Ben and I met them.
Ben brought it.

The pronouns *it* and *you* are both subject pronouns and object pronouns. Study the chart.

Object Pronouns					
Singular	me	you	him	her	it
Plural	us	you	them		

Guided Practice Find the object pronouns.

Example: Mrs. Russell told us about the play. *us*

1. Lisa tried out for it.
2. Mrs. Russell gave a part to me.
3. Carl painted the stage with her.
4. Dale and Kristin made a costume for you.
5. Joy watched them.

More Practice

A. Change the underlined word or words in each sentence to a pronoun. Write the new sentences.

Example: Come with <u>Dad and me</u>.   *Come with us.*

   6. You go with <u>Lara</u>.
   7. I invited <u>Bill</u> to the game.
   8. Bill sat with <u>Eva and me</u>.
   9. Did you see <u>the teams</u>?
   10. Ana wore <u>a funny hat</u>.
   11. The hat kept <u>Ana</u> warm.
   12. Dad brought warm cider to <u>Eva and Ana</u>.

B. Write each sentence, using the correct pronoun.

Example: Rita kicked the ball to (they, them).
         Rita kicked the ball to them.

   13. Randy helped (she, her).
   14. We cheered for (they, them).
   15. Dad looked at (I, me) proudly.
   16. It was an exciting game for (he, him).
   17. Randy met (we, us) after the game.
   18. Dad will watch (I, me) tomorrow.

Writing Application: A Letter
Your class is putting on a play. Something funny happens. Write a letter to your friend. Tell what happens. Use an object pronoun in each sentence.

4 | Using *I* and *me*

You often use the pronouns *I* and *me* when you speak and write. Use only the pronoun *I* as the subject of a sentence. Use only the pronoun *me* as an object pronoun.

SUBJECT PRONOUN	OBJECT PRONOUN
I left a message for Nat.	Nat called me right back.

When you talk about another person and yourself, it is polite to name yourself last. Always capitalize the word *I*.

Nat and I helped Mom.	She gave Nat and me some money.

Try this test if you have trouble choosing between *I* and *me*. Say the sentence with only *I* or *me*. Leave out the other noun.

Nat and I went to the store.	I went to the store.
Dad walked with Nat and me .	Dad walked with me .

Guided Practice Choose the correct word or words in ( ) to complete each sentence.

Example: (Nat and I, Nat and me) bought model airplanes.
　　　　Nat and I

1. Dad helped (I, me).
2. He gave (Nat and me, me and Nat) some paint.
3. (I, Me) painted my airplane blue.
4. (Nat and I, I and Nat) worked hard all day.
5. Mom brought sandwiches to (Nat and I, Nat and me).

▶ Use *I* as the subject of a sentence. Use *me* as an object pronoun. Always capitalize the word *I*.

▶ Name yourself last when you talk about another person and yourself.

More Practice Choose the correct word or words in ( ) to complete each sentence. Write the sentences.

(Ann and I, I and Ann) went to the store.
Ann and I went to the store.

6. Mom gave (I, me) a grocery list.
7. (I, Me) left the list on the table.
8. Dana brought the list to (Ann and I, Ann and me).
9. She found the flour for (Ann and I, Ann and me).
10. (Ann and I, Ann and me) stood in line.
11. Dana helped (Ann and me, me and Ann).
12. Mom took the big bag from (me, I).
13. (Me, I) unpacked the groceries.
14. (Dana and I, Dana and me) wanted to bake bread.
15. Ann handed (me and Dana, Dana and me) the flour.
16. The eggs were near (Dana and me, Dana and I).
17. Mom gave (I, me) the salt.
18. (Dana and I, Dana and me) mixed everything together.
19. (I, Me) put the bread in the oven.
20. (Mom and I, I and Mom) watched the bread.
21. Kim asked (Ann and me, Ann and I) for a slice.
22. (Kim and I, I and Kim) tasted the hot bread.

eggs
salt
flour
milk
yeast
peas
corn
grapes
limes
beans
rice
cheese
fish
juice

Writing Application: Writing About Yourself

Write five sentences, telling your class about your favorite hobby. Use *I* or *me* in each sentence.

5 | Possessive Pronouns

You have learned that a noun that shows ownership is a possessive noun. Some pronouns can take the place of possessive nouns. A pronoun that shows ownership is called a **possessive pronoun.**

Amy's radio is broken.   Her radio is broken.

She took it to Al's shop.   She took it to his shop.

Amy has the twins' radio.   Amy has their radio.

Study the chart below.

Possessive Pronouns						
my	your	her	his	its	our	their

Guided Practice

A. Find the possessive pronoun in each of the following sentences.

Example: Two gorillas sit with their trainer. *their*

1. My class watches the gorillas.
2. Their names are Candy and Ralph.
3. Candy wants to shake your hand.

B. Which possessive pronoun would you use in place of the underlined words?

Example: Candy's best friend is Ralph. *Her*

4. Ralph paints a picture on Ralph's paper.
5. The gorillas sit on the gorillas' blanket.
6. Candy pats Candy's kitten.

▶ A **possessive pronoun** shows ownership.
▶ The pronouns *my, your, her, his, its, our,* and *their* are possessive pronouns.

More Practice

A. Write the sentences. Underline the possessive pronoun in each sentence.

Example: Candy names her kitten "Lips."
Candy names her kitten "Lips."

7. Its pink nose reminds Candy of lipstick.
8. Candy puts Lips on her lap.
9. Candy brushes its orange fur.
10. I can't believe my eyes!
11. Ralph uses sign language with his trainer.
12. He makes a sign for food for our teacher.
13. I take a picture with your camera.

B. Write the possessive pronoun that takes the place of the underlined word or words in each sentence.

Example: Candy looks at Jimmy's book. *his*

14. A cat is with <u>a cat's</u> kittens.
15. Candy looks at <u>the book's</u> pictures.
16. Candy makes <u>Candy's</u> sign for "love."
17. The gorillas take naps after <u>the gorillas'</u> lunch.
18. The boys loved <u>the boys'</u> trip.

Writing Application: Creative Writing
Pretend that you have a pet that can talk to you. Write five sentences that tell what you would talk about. Use a possessive pronoun in each sentence.

6 | Contractions

You know that a contraction is a word made by putting two words together. An apostrophe replaces the letter or letters that are left out. Many contractions are made by joining a pronoun and a verb.

TWO WORDS	CONTRACTION
I will clean my room.	I'll clean my room.

Study the chart below.

Common Contractions with Pronouns

Two words	Contraction	Two words	Contraction
I am	I'm	it will	it'll
he is	he's	we will	we'll
she is	she's	they will	they'll
it is	it's	he has	he's
you are	you're	she has	she's
we are	we're	it has	it's
they are	they're	I have	I've
I will	I'll	you have	you've
you will	you'll	we have	we've
he will	he'll	they have	they've
she will	she'll		

Guided Practice What is the contraction for each pair of words?

Example: it is *it's*

1. we are
2. she will
3. it has
4. I am
5. he is
6. you will
7. I have
8. they are

▶ A contraction can be made by joining a pronoun and a verb. Use an apostrophe in place of the letter or letters that are left out.

More Practice

A. Write the contractions for the underlined words.

Example: <u>We will</u> clean the whole house. *We'll*

9. <u>It is</u> such a big job.
10. <u>It will</u> take a long time.
11. <u>We are</u> a good clean-up team.
12. What a mess <u>they have</u> made!
13. <u>She has</u> left her flute on the floor.
14. <u>You are</u> a hard worker.
15. When we finish <u>I am</u> going to take a shower.

B. Write the words that make up each contraction.

Example: <u>You've</u> heard the good news. *You have*

16. <u>We're</u> off to Florida.
17. Soon <u>they'll</u> meet us in Miami.
18. Now <u>he's</u> ready to go!
19. <u>We've</u> put our instruments in the suitcases.
20. <u>She'll</u> bring her flute.
21. <u>I've</u> practiced for many days.
22. Maybe <u>you'll</u> hear us play when we return.

Writing Application: A Story
Write a story. Use contractions in your sentences. Start your story with this sentence.

When Jeff opened his suitcase, out popped—

7 | Using *there*, *their*, and *they're*

The words *there*, *their*, and *they're* sound alike but have different spellings and meanings. Remember that the clues in a sentence can help you decide which word to use.

Word	Meaning	Example
there	at or in that place	They work there.
their	belonging to them	It's their store.
they're	they are (contraction)	They're at work.

Guided Practice
Would you use *there*, *their*, or *they're* to complete each sentence?

Example: They sell magazines in ___ bookstore.   *their*

1. My two favorite books are ___.
2. I think that ___ in the mystery section.
3. They say ___ getting some in next week.
4. Isn't ___ bookstore a great place?
5. We should go ___ again.

Summing up

▶ Use *there* to mean "at or in that place."
▶ Use *their* to mean "belonging to them."
▶ Use *they're* to make the contraction for *they are*.
▶ Use sentence clues to decide which word to use.

More Practice Complete each sentence with *there, their,* or *they're.* Write the sentences.

Example: Ivy and Alex begin ____ paper route early.
Ivy and Alex begin their paper route early.

6. ____ earning money for new bicycles.
7. They pick up ____ newspapers at the corner.
8. The delivery truck waits ____ for them.
9. Mr. Ruso puts the papers in ____ sacks.
10. Then ____ ready to begin.
11. They deliver newspapers to ____ neighbors.
12. ____ route starts at my house.
13. I wait ____ for them every morning.
14. ____ always on time.
15. ____ prepared for anything.
16. Once a dog stood near ____ bikes.
17. Alex waited ____ while Ivy gave the dog a bone.
18. Another time a car broke down near ____ route.
19. Alex rode past ____ on his way home.
20. Two people were trying to start ____ car.
21. They were wearing ____ clown costumes!
22. Alex helped them start ____ car.
23. The other passengers were standing ____ quietly.
24. One clown gave Alex tickets to ____ show.
25. Alex promised to go ____ on Saturday.
26. Will Ivy meet him ____?

Writing Application: Sentences
Think of a place where the people were doing interesting jobs, such as making pizza in a restaurant or feeding animals at a zoo. Write five sentences that describe the job. Use *there, their,* or *they're* in your sentences.

Building Vocabulary

Homophones

You have learned that *to, two,* and *too* and *there, their,* and *they're* sound alike but have different spellings and meanings. Such words are called **homophones**.

You're late for your party!

Did you write the right time on the invitations?

I hear that Maria is already here .

We ate enough food for eight people.

Jenny looks dear in her deer costume.

Greg won one game already.

He chose a pale blue puppet from a pail of prizes.

It's fun to make its feet dance.

Practice

A. Write the homophone for each word.

Example: write *right*

1. hear   **3.** it's   **5.** eight   **7.** right
2. dear   **4.** pail   **6.** your   **8.** one

B. Choose the correct homophone in ( ) to complete each sentence. Write the sentences.

Example: Sarah's dog had (eight, ate) puppies.
Sarah's dog had eight puppies.

9. Is (your, you're) cousin taking a puppy?
10. He is taking the spotted (won, one).
11. (Its, It's) the smallest puppy in the litter.
12. Can you (hear, here) it barking?
13. I think he made the (write, right) choice.

C. Write the answer to each riddle, using a homophone from the Word Box.

here	right	pail	ate	deer	won

Example: Two people ran in the race, but how many came in first? One ____. *One won.*

14. How does Mrs. Moose begin a letter to her cousin? She begins it with "Dear ____."
15. If eight people went out to eat, how many people had dinner? Eight ____.
16. What do you call a bucket that has seen something frightening? The bucket is called a pale ____.
17. What did the teacher say to the students when their letters slanted to the left? Write ____.
18. If you do not listen over there, where should you listen? Hear ____.

Writing Application: A Story

Choose three pairs of homophones from this lesson or other homophones you know. Then write a story. Use a different homophone in each sentence. Have a friend read your story and underline the homophones.

Grammar-Writing Connection

Writing Clearly with Pronouns

You have learned to write as clearly and as smoothly as you can. If you use too many nouns, your writing may be boring and unclear. You can make your writing clearer and more interesting by using pronouns in place of some of the nouns. In the second paragraph below, the pronoun *they* takes the place of *Ann and Lynn,* and the meaning is still clear.

> Ann and Lynn studied the old house. Ann and Lynn saw a cracked window. The girls peeked inside.

> Ann and Lynn studied the old house. They saw a cracked window. The girls peeked inside.

Revising Sentences

In each paragraph, replace at least one noun with a pronoun. Write the new paragraph.

Example: Tommy and Joey lost their new kitten. Tommy and Joey searched outside. The boys found the kitten in the garage.
Tommy and Joey lost their new kitten. They searched outside. The boys found the kitten in the garage.

1. A daisy grew by the fence. The daisy had droopy leaves. It never got enough water.
2. Gina and Ben walked by the daisy. Gina and Ben brought a watering can. The children watered the flower.

Creative Writing

How wonderful it feels to put your books away and run into the autumn sunshine! You can feel the energy of these boys as they play. Winslow Homer understood such fun. His paintings show the quiet beauty of country life.

- How can you tell that this is an early autumn day?
- How did Homer create a feeling of movement?

Activities

1. **Write a letter.** Winslow Homer liked the country better than the city. Do you agree with him? Write a letter to Homer explaining why you agree or disagree.

2. **Write your autumn memories.** Which autumn day have you enjoyed the most? Write down your memories of the day. Explain what made it such a special day for you.

Check-up: Unit 11

Subject Pronouns *(p. 328)* Write a pronoun to replace the underlined word or words in each sentence.

1. <u>Pete</u> sings a song to the crowd.
2. <u>Eva</u> plays the piano by herself.
3. <u>Amy</u> plays the horn.
4. <u>The horn</u> is the loudest instrument in the band.
5. <u>Tyler</u> sings a song with Manuel.
6. <u>The children</u> take a bow.
7. <u>The music</u> is over too soon.
8. <u>Mom and I</u> clap loudly.

Pronouns and Verbs *(p. 330)* Choose the correct verb form to complete each sentence. Write the sentences.

9. You (wash, washes) the fish tank.
10. We (put, puts) the fish tank in the den.
11. It (look, looks) good there.
12. She (fill, fills) the tank with water.
13. They (place, places) the fish in the tank.
14. He (reach, reaches) for the food.
15. I (feed, feeds) the fish.

Object Pronouns *(p. 332)* Write a pronoun to replace the underlined word or words in each sentence.

16. Susan went to the pet store with <u>Mike and me</u>.
17. The pet store owner fed <u>the cats and fish</u>.
18. He handed a tiny kitten to <u>Susan</u>.
19. He handed a spotted rabbit to <u>Mike</u>.
20. Mike petted <u>the rabbit</u>.
21. He bought the rabbit for <u>Susan and me</u>.
22. We always enjoy playing with <u>the animals</u>.

Using *I* and *me* *(p. 334)* Choose the correct word or words in ( ) to complete each sentence. Write the sentences.

23. Dad gave (I, me) a map.
24. (Mario and I, Mario and me) went on a hike.
25. (I and Jim, Jim and I) hiked all day.
26. (I, me) got tired.
27. Then it rained on (Jim and I, Jim and me).
28. Jim gave (I, me) a rain hat.

Possessive Pronouns *(p. 336)* Write the sentences. Underline the possessive pronoun in each sentence.

29. My mother made different sandwiches for everyone.
30. You ate your sandwich very slowly.
31. Molly had a strange look on her face.
32. Matt gave his sandwich to Patty.
33. Molly and Patty gave their sandwiches to Matt.
34. Mom had mixed up our sandwiches!

Contractions *(p. 338)* Write the contraction for each pair of words.

35. I will	**38.** we have	**41.** it is
36. we are	**39.** they have	**42.** she has
37. you will	**40.** he has	**43.** I am

Using *there, their,* and *they're* *(p. 340)* Complete each sentence with *there, their,* or *they're*. Write the sentences.

44. Mr. Kaplan and Cindy are on ____ boat.
45. ____ sailing to Marblehead.
46. I am meeting them ____.
47. On Saturday ____ planning a picnic on the beach.
48. ____ boat is entered in a race on Sunday.

Cumulative Review

Unit 1: The Sentence

Subjects and Predicates in Sentences *(pp. 8, 10)* Write each sentence. Draw a line between the subject and the predicate. If the group of words is not a sentence, write *not a sentence*.

1. Kate wrote a social studies report.
2. It was about George Washington.
3. George Washington was born in 1732.
4. Fought in the war against England.
5. Became the first President of the United States.

Unit 3: Nouns

Common and Proper Nouns *(pp. 58, 60)* Write each noun. Then write *common* or *proper* after each one.

6. August was a busy month.
7. Beth Wright and Carmen Rivera had parties.
8. My family spent a week in New Hampshire.
9. Our town held a fair.
10. Grandpa flew in from San Francisco.

Singular and Plural Nouns *(pp. 64, 66, 68)* Write the plural form of each noun.

11. desk
12. wax
13. porch
14. princess
15. tooth
16. penny
17. camera
18. goose

Possessive Nouns *(pp. 70, 72)* Write each word group, using a possessive noun.

19. a girl kite
20. boys bikes
21. Spencer lunch
22. men belts
23. babies rattles
24. painter ladder

Unit 5: Verbs

Verbs in the Present and Past (*pp. 132, 136*) Write the verbs. Label each one *present* or *past*.

25. Megan loves all kinds of animals.
26. One day Mom surprised Megan with a puppy.
27. My brothers play with the puppy all the time.
28. The puppy chases our kittens under the bed.
29. Once the puppy buried a bone in our neighbor's yard.

Helping Verbs, the Special Verb *be,* **and Irregular Verbs** (*pp. 140, 142, 144*) Write each sentence correctly.

30. The newspaper has (came, come) at six o'clock.
31. A girl (has, have) delivered it.
32. It (was, were) on the front porch.
33. The children (took, taken) the newspaper indoors.
34. The rain (has, have) soaked the front section.

Unit 7: Adjectives and Adverbs

Adjectives (*pp. 198, 200*) Write the adjectives.

35. Kim and two friends took the ferry to Nantucket.
36. They looked at the beautiful ocean along the way.
37. The children rented some bicycles.
38. They rode the bikes around the small island.
39. The tired children slept on the ferry home.

Adverbs (*pp. 206, 208*) Write each adverb.

40. Gina always attends the Thanksgiving parade.
41. Usually Dad goes with her.
42. Gina races ahead with other children.
43. They soon find a good spot.
44. Suddenly the floats appear.

Cumulative Review, continued

Unit 9: Capitalization and Punctuation

Four Kinds of Sentences and Proper Nouns
(pp. 262, 264, 266) Write each sentence correctly.

45. Have you fished in Lake White this summer
46. Is it near bellmore high school?
47. ask Aunt Ruth for directions to the lake.
48. My friend abe katz caught ten fish in two hours!
49. Come with me on Sunday

Abbreviations and Book Titles *(pp. 268, 270)* Write each abbreviation, name, and book title correctly.

50. sept
51. fri
52. mrs lee duffy
53. dr fred kent
54. the biggest nose
55. the turnip

Commas *(pp. 271, 272)* Write each sentence. Put commas where they are needed.

56. Mark Ann and Seth went on a treasure hunt.
57. Well Ann found the red pencil.
58. Seth found the seashell a comb and the soap.
59. Mark found the chalk the button and the pine cone.
60. Yes Mark won first prize.

Quotation Marks *(pp. 274, 276)* Write each sentence. Add capital letters and punctuation where needed.

61. Grandma asked, Did you go to the library?
62. Amanda answered "I found a book about rainbows."
63. Grandma asked, "Do you see the rainbow in the sky"
64. Amanda exclaimed, It is so beautiful!
65. Grandma said, "I saw seven colors in the rainbow"

Unit 11: Pronouns

Subject and Object Pronouns *(pp. 328, 332)* Write a pronoun to replace the underlined word or words.

66. <u>Stacey and Brian</u> went to the Grand Canyon.
67. They rode with <u>Aunt Gert and Uncle Leroy</u>.
68. <u>Aunt Gert</u> drove the car.
69. Brian hiked down the Grand Canyon on <u>a donkey</u>.
70. He waved to <u>Stacey</u> from the bottom.

Pronouns and Verbs *(p. 330)* Write each sentence, using the correct present form of the verb in ( ).

71. I (paint) my room.
72. He (move) the bed.
73. She (clean) the rug.
74. You (hang) a poster.
75. It (look) good.
76. They (finish) the job.

Possessive Pronouns *(p. 336)* Write the sentences. Underline the possessive pronoun in each sentence.

77. My mother has a job.
78. Her office is busy.
79. Our car did not start.
80. Its battery is old.
81. Mom rode with your aunt.
82. Their ride was long.

Contractions *(p. 338)* Write the contractions.

83. it is
84. he has
85. I am
86. it will
87. you are
88. she is

Using *I, me, there, their,* **and** *they're (pp. 334, 340)* Write the correct word or words.

89. Dad and (I, me) chop wood for the fireplace.
90. Ed helps Dad and (I, me).
91. Dad and Ed wear (there, their) hats.
92. (I, Me) bring the wood into the den.

Enrichment

Unit Eleven: Pronouns

TIME MACHINE

Pretend that a time machine takes you to another time and place. You meet and talk with someone from this new setting. Decide on your new time and place. Then draw a cartoon strip about your meeting. Show conversations with balloons. Use the pronouns *I* and *me*.

Good Snacks

You probably like snacks that taste good. Are they good for you? What healthy snacks do you enjoy eating? How about your friends? Write six sentences about healthy snacks that you and your friends enjoy. Begin each sentence with a different pronoun, as in "He likes carrots." Draw a mural or large picture that illustrates these sentences. Write your sentences on the mural.

Garage Sale

You and your friends are having a garage sale. Write an advertisement announcing it. When and where will it be held? What will be for sale? Use pronouns in your ad. Underline each one.

<u>We</u> are having a garage sale.
<u>I</u> am selling <u>my</u> fish tank.

Extra Practice: Unit 11

1 | Subject Pronouns (p. 328)

● Write each sentence. Underline the pronoun.
Example: I looked at the stars.   *I looked at the stars.*
  1. They seemed far away.
  2. I found the Big Dipper.
  3. Where is it?
  4. He looked for the moon.
  5. She pointed to the sky.
  6. Did you see the moon?
  7. We saw the full moon.
  8. It was high overhead.

▲ Write a pronoun to replace the underlined words.
  Example: Many people are on the beach.   *They*
  9. The sun feels very hot.
  10. Sami and Tina collect shells.
  11. Maria goes swimming.
  12. Johnny sits under an umbrella.
  13. Grandma gives us sandwiches.
  14. You and I drink cold milk.
  15. The beach is lots of fun.

■ Change the underlined word or words in each sentence to a subject pronoun. Write the sentences. Then write *plural* if the pronoun is plural.
  Example: Uncle Joe and I walked to the library.
         We walked to the library.   plural
  16. The library is five blocks away.
  17. David was at the library.
  18. David and I waved to each other.
  19. Two children read quietly.
  20. Mrs. Putnam works at the library.
  21. Uncle Joe took out three books.
  22. The books looked interesting.

2 | Pronouns and Verbs (p. 330)

● Write the correct sentence in each pair.
Example: We plays a game.
We play a game.   *We play a game.*

1. It seems easy.
   It seem easy.

2. I tells Bob the rules.
   I tell Bob the rules.

3. He move three spaces.
   He moves three spaces.

4. They spin the arrow.
   They spins the arrow.

5. We watch the board.
   We watches the board.

6. You takes a turn.
   You take a turn.

7. He lose a turn.
   He loses a turn.

8. She wins the game.
   She win the game.

▲ Write each sentence, using the correct verb form.
Example: You (find, finds) a map.   *You find a map.*

9. It (leads, lead) to a surprise.
10. We (follow, follows) the directions.
11. She (rush, rushes) over the hill.
12. He (look, looks) behind the oak tree.
13. They (dashes, dash) into the yard.
14. I (help, helps) with the search.
15. We (sees, see) three tiny kittens by the barn.

■ Complete each sentence with the correct form of the verb in ( ). Write the sentences.
Example: She ___ lettuce. (buy) *She buys lettuce.*

16. He ___ an orange.   (eat)
17. I ___ for the cereal.   (search)
18. She ___ for the milk.   (reach)
19. It ___ from a farm.   (come)
20. You ___ five pounds of potatoes.   (want)
21. He ___ in line.   (stand)
22. They ___ for the groceries.   (pay)

● Write *singular* if the underlined pronoun is singular. Write *plural* if the underlined pronoun is plural.

Example: Mrs. Robins taught <u>us</u> about old coins. *plural*

1. Everyone listened to <u>her</u>.
2. Mrs. Robins handed two silver dollars to <u>me</u>.
3. The government made <u>them</u>.
4. Saul brought in some coins for <u>us</u>.
5. The dates on <u>them</u> were very old.
6. Mrs. Robins asked <u>him</u> about the coin book.
7. Saul showed <u>it</u> to the class.

▲ Change the underlined word or words in each sentence to a pronoun. Write the new sentences.

Example: We collect <u>seashells</u>. *We collect them.*

8. Emilio found a shell for <u>Colleen</u>.
9. Colleen washed <u>the shell</u> in the sink.
10. She told <u>Ray</u> about the pretty colors.
11. Ray showed the shell to <u>Greg</u>.
12. Greg gave a book to <u>the boys</u>.
13. The book helps <u>Greg and me</u>.
14. I put <u>a label</u> on the shell.

■ Write each sentence, using a subject or an object pronoun. Use a different pronoun in each sentence.

Example: Sarah started a stamp collection with ____.
   Sarah started a stamp collection with them.

15. ____ surprised Sarah with an airplane stamp.
16. Peter saved a bird stamp for ____.
17. I gave a Mexican stamp to ____.
18. Today ____ went to Mr. Tello's store.
19. He had some old stamps for ____.
20. Karen liked ____.

● Write the correct sentence in each pair.

Example: Ed and I made masks.
Ed and me made masks.
Ed and I made masks.

1. Me drew the shape.
   I drew the shape.

2. Ed asked I for glue.
   Ed asked me for glue.

3. I used the scissors.
   Me used the scissors.

4. Mom helped me and Ed.
   Mom helped Ed and me.

5. I and Ed worked hard.
   Ed and I worked hard.

6. My mask fit me.
   My mask fit I.

7. Ed and I looked silly.
   Ed and me looked silly.

8. Mom laughed with me.
   Mom laughed with I.

▲ Write each sentence, using the correct word or words.

Example: (David and I, David and me) built a robot.
David and I built a robot.

9. Our friends helped (David and me, me and David).
10. The grocer gave (me, I) some large boxes.
11. (Me, I) put the boxes together.
12. (Carl and I, Carl and me) added arms and legs.
13. Lori handed (I, me) the paint.
14. (I and Robin, Robin and I) painted two eyes.

■ Write each sentence correctly with *I* or *me*.

Example: ____ and Evan own model cars.
Evan and I own model cars.

15. ____ and Evan wanted to race the cars.
16. Everyone watched ____ and Evan.
17. The red car belonged to ____.
18. How excited Evan and ____ were!
19. Sandy cheered for Evan and ____.
20. ____ was the winner of the race!

● Write each sentence. Underline the possessive pronoun.

Example: Is that your kite? *Is that your kite?*

1. My kite is yellow.
2. Has Amanda seen our new train?
3. Its wheels are big and shiny.
4. Mary Beth found her stuffed animal.
5. The boys counted all their blocks.
6. Where are your puzzles?
7. Robert put his puzzles on the shelf.

▲ Change each underlined word or words to a possessive pronoun. Write the new groups of words.

Example: Pedro's and my dog *our dog*

8. Dad's car
9. Mrs. Green's book
10. the giraffe's food
11. the girls' games
12. Lisa's sandwich
13. Rob's and my bike
14. the puppet's face
15. the man's coat
16. Allison and Pete's paint
17. Tony's and my horse

■ Write each sentence. Use a possessive pronoun that goes with the underlined word or words.

Example: Matt and Nina looked out ____ window.
Matt and Nina looked out their window.

18. The big tree had lost ____ leaves.
19. Pedro and I waited inside for ____ ride.
20. Gary took out ____ umbrella.
21. Ann buttoned ____ raincoat.
22. Gary and Ann heard ____ mother at the door.
23. I looked for ____ warm socks.
24. You wore ____ rain hat.
25. The children put on ____ boots.

6 | Contractions (p. 338)

● Write the word in ( ) that is a contraction for each pair of words.

Example: I will   (Ill, I'll)   *I'll*

1. he has   (he's, hes)
2. it is   (its, it's)
3. we have   (weve, we've)
4. she will   (she'll, shel)
5. I am   (Im, I'm)
6. you have   (youve, you've)
7. they will   (they'll, theyll)
8. you are   (your, you're)

▲ Write the contraction for each pair of words below.

Example: she is   *she's*

9. they will	13. I have	17. it is
10. we are	14. they are	18. you will
11. I am	15. he has	19. she has
12. he will	16. we have	20. we will

■ Write each sentence. Replace two words in each sentence with a contraction.

Example: I am in music class.   *I'm in music class.*

21. She is my music teacher.
22. First they will play the violins.
23. He has already learned the new song.
24. She will tap out the beat for us.
25. You are a good singer.
26. We have had enough time to practice.
27. It is lively in the music room.
28. We are excited.
29. Tomorrow we will play for our school.
30. I have invited my family.

Grammar: Pronouns

● Write each sentence. Use the correct word in ( ).

Example: My friends are with (they're, their) parents.
My friends are with their parents.

1. (They're, There) all at the movies.
2. They go (there, their) every Sunday.
3. (There, They're) seeing a funny movie.
4. (There, Their) favorite actors are in it.
5. One Sunday I saw them (there, their).
6. I might go (they're, there) with them next Sunday.

▲ Complete each sentence with *there, their,* or *they're.*
Write the sentences.

Example: Lin and Dan invited ____ friends on a picnic.
Lin and Dan invited their friends on a picnic.

7. ____ bringing plenty of food.
8. Lin and Dan are bringing ____ kites.
9. It will not take long to walk ____.
10. The children will eat ____ lunches quickly.
11. They will swim in the lake ____.
12. Then ____ going to fly the kites.

■ Write each sentence. Write *correct* if the underlined word is correct. If the underlined word is not correct, replace it with *there, their,* or *they're.*

Example: My grandparents are busy in <u>there</u> store.
My grandparents are busy in their store.

13. <u>Their</u> getting ready for a big sale.
14. The story is near <u>their</u> home.
15. I go <u>they're</u> to shop.
16. Do you want to shop <u>there</u> now?
17. <u>There</u> prices are low.
18. I bought a belt and a hat <u>they're</u>.

Many insects have very bright colors. Their enemies can easily see them, but they do not go after them. The bright bands of black and yellow on bees and wasps are "warning" colors that give the message "I sting."

Millicent Selsam and Ronald Goor
from *Backyard Insects*

Research Report

Getting Ready Writing a report is a good way to learn about an interesting subject. A report is based on facts. It is not made up of the writer's own ideas! In this unit, you will write a report. This will be a good chance to find out more about a favorite subject. Start thinking of questions you would like to have answered.

Activities

Listening Listen as the paragraph on the opposite page is read. What information does it give? What other information would you like to know?

Speaking Look at the picture. What do you see? What other information can you learn about bees from the picture? What questions about bees do you have that are not answered in either the paragraph or the picture?

The Grasshopper

By David McCord

Down
a
deep
well
a
grasshopper
fell.
By kicking about
He thought to get out.
  He might have known better,
  For that got him wetter.
To kick round and round
Is the way to get drowned,
  And drowning is what
  I should tell you he got.
But
the
well
had
a
rope
that
dangled
some
hope.

And sure as molasses
On one of his passes
  He found the rope handy
  And up he went, *and he*

it
up
and
it
up
and
it
up
and
it
up
went

And hopped away proper
As any grasshopper.

Questions
1. Why did the grasshopper almost drown? How did he save himself?
2. Several words in the poem **rhyme,** or have the same last sound. One pair of rhyming words is *well* and *fell.* What other words in the poem rhyme?
3. Why do you suppose the poet wrote some of the lines to be read from the bottom up? Do you like it? Why or why not?

How does the Dove help the Ant? How does the Ant show that she is grateful?

The Ant and the Dove

An Aesop fable
retold by Anne Terry White

A thirsty Ant was climbing down a blade of grass that grew beside a spring. She was trying to reach the water so she could take a drink. Unluckily she slipped and fell into the spring.

Now a Dove was sitting on a branch over the water. She saw the Ant fall in and was filled with pity. Quick as a wink she pulled off a leaf and let it fall into the spring.

The little raft settled down on the water right beside the drowning Ant. The Ant climbed on the leaf and was soon safe on shore again.

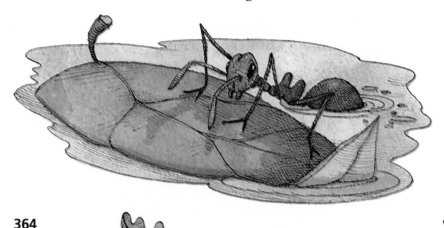

But what did she see? Hidden behind a bush, a hunter was spreading his net. He was going to catch the Dove!

"No!" the grateful Ant said. "You shall not take the bird that saved my life!" And with all her might she bit the hunter on his bare foot.

With a cry the hunter dropped his net, and the Dove flew away to the wood.

One good turn deserves another.

Questions

1. How do the Ant and the Dove help each other?
2. "The Ant and the Dove" is a kind of story called a **fable.** A fable always teaches a lesson. What is the lesson of this fable? How would you put the lesson in your own words?
3. Is a story like "The Ant and the Dove" a good way to teach a lesson? Why or why not?

An ant's body is very different from ours. What body parts does an ant use for seeing, feeling, and smelling?

Ants

By Charles A. Schoenknecht

The busy ant is one of the most interesting of insects. A worker ant is easy to find and fun to study.

Look at an ant, and you will see that its body is made up of three large parts.

Its head, the first part, has two small eyes. Most ants cannot see very well.

The ant has two feelers, called antennae. They are like long poles on top of its head. These are very important, for the ant uses its antennae to feel with and also to smell with.

The ant has no nose. But with its antennae it can smell an enemy or a friend. It can smell its way back to its nest with its antennae.

In the ant's mouth is a tongue, which it uses to clean itself and its sister, too. It also uses its tongue to lick up liquids.

The ant's jaws work sideways like a pair of scissors.

The jaws are large. They are used to carry things, to crush food, to dig and pack soil in the tunnels, and to fight enemies.

The second part of the ant's body, the thorax, is long and slender. The queen ant and males are born with wings at the top of the thorax. Worker ants do not have wings.

Ants have six legs, three on each side of the body. The legs are long, and an ant can run very fast for its size.

In the first pair of legs toward the head there is a notch. Ants clean their antennae by fitting them into this notch. It is called the antennae comb.

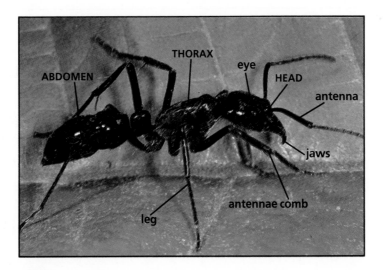

The third part of the ant's body is the abdomen.

The worker ant has two stomachs in its abdomen. One stomach is called the crop. It is a place where most of the food the ant finds is stored. When the ant needs food, it pumps juice from its crop to the true stomach.

The abdomen also has many small holes in it for air to enter. This is the way ants get air. They do not have lungs.

There are thousands of different kinds of ants all over the world. In the United States, there are about 400 different kinds. They live and eat in many different ways. But they are all social insects. They all live together with their own kind.

Questions

1. How does an ant see, feel, and smell?
2. Why do you suppose an ant must clean its antennae?
3. Any type of writing that tells about real people and animals or things that really happened is called **nonfiction**. "Ants" comes from a nonfiction book. In what ways does "Ants" differ from the fable "The Ant and the Dove"?
4. Why do you think it is easier for ants to live in groups rather than by themselves?

RESPONDING TO LITERATURE

The Reading and Writing Connection

Personal Response The three literature selections in this unit are all very different. Which one did you like best? Write a paragraph telling why.

Creative Writing Write a new fable teaching the lesson *Look before you leap*. Use two frogs or other animals as the main characters.

Creative Activities

Draw Pretend that you are an ant. Draw a picture of a school playground from your point of view.

Interview With two other classmates, prepare an interview with the Ant and the Dove. One student should act as a news reporter. The reporter should ask questions that begin with the words *who, what, where, when, how,* or *why*. The Ant and the Dove should answer with details from the fable.

Vocabulary

Many words have more than one meaning. Look up *spring* in a dictionary. What meanings are given? Which meaning is used in "The Ant and the Dove"?

Looking Ahead

Reports A report gives facts about a topic. In this unit, you will look for facts for a report. Look at "Ants" on pages 366–368. What facts are given about an ant's jaws?

Listening/Speaking/Thinking

Listening: For Information

When you listen to find out the time of a meeting, you are listening for information. When you listen for information, listen for answers to the questions *Who? What? Where? When? Why?* and *How?*

Listen as your teacher or a classmate reads the paragraph below from "Ants." Listen to find out the answer to the question *What is an antennae comb?*

> In the first pair of legs toward the head there is a notch. Ants clean their antennae by fitting them into this notch. It is called an antennae comb.

When you listen for information, remember this guide.

Listening Guide

Listen for answers to the questions *Who? What? Where? When? Why?* and *How?*

Practice

Use the Listening Guide as your teacher reads information about ants. Answer these questions.

1. What are worker ants?
2. How do they find their way?
3. What work do these ants do in an ant colony?

Speaking: Having Discussions

People have discussions to share information and ideas, answer questions, or solve problems. To have a good discussion, follow these guides.

Discussion Guides

1. Stick to the topic of the discussion.
2. If you are unsure of anything, ask questions.
3. Share your information with the group.
4. Take turns speaking.

Read the discussion below. Did these students follow the guides?

PEDRO: Let's pick an insect for our report.
LYNN: I think we should choose bees. They—
LEE: *(interrupting)* Yes! Bees might be interesting.
MINDY: We had a hornet's nest in our tree once. It was huge.
PEDRO: Are there any other suggestions?

- Who did not keep to the topic?
- Who forgot to take turns?
- Who kept the discussion moving?

Practice

Divide into small groups. Discuss one of the topics below or your own topic. Follow the Discussion Guides.

1. Places to go for a field trip
2. Ways to improve the playground or schoolyard
3. Limiting time for watching TV

Thinking: Facts and Opinions

A **fact** is something that can be proved true. Which sentences below state facts?

> An ant has six legs.
> An ant's legs look funny.
> The first pair of an ant's legs has little notches.

Sentences 1 and 3 state facts. You can prove that the facts are true by looking at an ant or by checking an encyclopedia or another book.

Sentence 2 gives an **opinion.** It tells only what someone thinks or feels. It cannot be proved true. Do you think an ant's legs look funny? You may, or you may not. Not everyone thinks or feels the same way you do.

Practice

Number your paper from 1 to 8. Decide if each sentence states a fact or an opinion. Write *fact* or *opinion* after the number of the sentence.

1. An ant's body has three separate parts.
2. An ant is an insect.
3. Ants are interesting to watch.
4. Most ants are pests.
5. An ant has two stomachs.
6. Ants can smell their way back to their nests.
7. Grasshoppers are far stranger than ants.
8. Ants have no lungs.

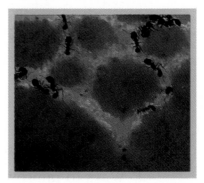

Thinking: Summarizing

You know that a topic sentence states the main idea of a paragraph. A **summary** is very similar. It sums up the main idea and important points of a whole selection in a few sentences.

Reread "Ants" on pages 366–368. What is the main idea of the selection? What are the important points? Read the summary of "Ants" below.

> An ant's body has three main parts. The first part, the head, has eyes, antennae, a tongue, and strong jaws. The second part is the thorax. An ant's legs join its body there. The third part is the abdomen with its two stomachs and many small holes for breathing.

The main idea of "Ants" is that an ant's body has three main parts. The first sentence of the summary states that main idea. The other sentences tell the important points. They briefly tell what the three main parts are.

When you write a summary, ask these questions.

1. What is the main idea of the selection?
2. What are the important points?

Keep your summary short. Write the summary in your own words.

Practice

Turn to pages 364–365. Write a summary of "The Ant and the Dove" in three or four sentences.

Composition Skills

Finding Information

Suppose you are writing a report about insects. Where could you go to find the information? The best place to start is the library.

Nonfiction books have information about insects. How do you find the books you need? Look in the card catalog. It lists books in the library by author, title, and subject. You would look up the subject *Insects* to find titles of books about insects.

Reference books will also give you information about insects. Reference books include dictionaries, encyclopedias, and atlases. Do you know how to pronounce *katydid*? A dictionary will tell you. Do you want to know about the different kinds of ants or about life in an ant colony? You can look up this information in an encyclopedia. You could also use an atlas, or a book of maps, to find the areas where certain kinds of insects lived.

Prewriting Practice

Would you use a dictionary, an encyclopedia, or an atlas to find information about these topics? Write your answers. Some will have more than one answer.

1. Where is Germany?

2. How are stamps made?

3. What does *mango* mean?

4. What is a palomino?

5. How big is Jupiter?

6. Where is Alaska?

7. Who was Mark Twain?

8. How do you say *gnu*?

Taking Notes

A good way to remember information is to take notes. When you take notes, write only enough words to help you remember the important facts.

Patrick wanted to find the answer to the question *Where do ants live?* He found this paragraph.

> Ants do not always live in nests underground. Doorkeeper ants live inside plant stems. Mudball ants build their nests in trees and disguise them with plants. Tailor ants work together to build a nest out of leaves.
>
> Henry Pluckrose

Patrick took these notes to answer his question.

Where do ants live?
- underground
- inside plant stems
- in trees
- in nests of leaves

Prewriting Practice

Take notes about this paragraph. Write facts that answer the question *What kinds of ants are there?*

There are six groups of ants. Army ants are fierce hunters. Harvester ants collect seeds. Slave makers kidnap the eggs of other nests. Both dairy ants and honey ants live on honeydew, a juice which comes from plants. The last group, called fungus growers, grow their own gardens.

Writing Across the Curriculum
Research Report

Literature and Creative Writing

"The Grasshopper," "The Ant and the Dove," and "Ants" are different types of literature. These selections are different, but they all are about insects.

Have fun using what you have learned about writing a report. Do one or more of these activities.

Remember these things:

Take notes to remember facts.

Use your questions as topic sentences.

Use your notes to write supporting details.

1. **Learn about insects.** Write a report about an insect. Explain how it is helpful or harmful.

2. **Can you imagine?** Write a report about an imaginary insect. Describe how it looks, where it lives, and what it eats. Give your insect a name. Draw a picture of the insect.

3. **Find out about scientists.** Scientists who study insects are called **entomologists.** Write a report about these scientists. How do they collect facts about insects? What do they do with the information they collect?

Social Studies

Have you ever wondered what schools were like 200 years ago or how people traveled before there were paved roads? Some people make careers out of researching how people live, work, and play. They may share this information by writing reports.

Choose one or more of the following activities. Follow the five steps for writing a report.

1. **Put out the fire!** Firefighters today race to the scene of a fire in fast trucks. What did firefighters do before there were trucks? Write a report about how the fires were put out.

2. **How have toys changed?** Write a report about toys that children have played with in the past. Draw a picture of one that you would like to have.

3. **What are totem poles?** Native American tribes in the northwest part of the United States and Canada carved totem poles. Find out more about totem poles. What kinds of animals were carved? What did these animals stand for? You may want to use some of the words in the box.

carve	tribe
ancestor	symbol

> **Writing Steps**
> 1. Choose a Topic
> 2. Write a First Draft
> 3. Revise
> 4. Proofread
> 5. Publish

Book Report

Making a Book Jacket

Melissa really liked reading "Ants." She liked nonfiction books. Melissa decided to find a nonfiction book about an interesting animal. She chose *Lucky Porcupine!* by Miriam Schlein. She decided to share the book with her class by making a book jacket. On the outside, she drew a picture of a porcupine. On the inside, she wrote about the book.

Lucky Porcupine!
by Miriam Schlein
    What is that round, fuzzy thing up in the tree? Did you know that porcupines can climb trees? How many quills does a porcupine have? Can a porcupine "shoot" its quills? How did the porcupine get its name?

    The porcupine is a peaceful animal. It does protect itself from its enemies, though. Animals are careful to keep away from the porcupine's quills.
    Anyone who is interested in animal life will learn a lot from this book.

Think and Discuss

• Why is this a good way to share a book?
• What did you learn about the book?
• How did Melissa try to interest others in the book?

Share Your Book

Make a Book Jacket

1. First, get a large sheet of drawing paper. Then fold a flap about four inches wide on each side. Paste a strip of lined paper on each flap.
2. Decide what kind of picture you will draw on the book jacket. Draw the picture with crayons and markers on the side of the paper without the flaps. Print the title of the book and the author's name.
3. On the left flap, print the book title and the author's name again. Below this and on the right flap you have space to tell about the book.
4. Share your book jacket by showing the cover picture and reading the information on the flaps.

Other Activities

- Cut out pictures and words from magazines that could be included in your book. Make a poster.
- Make a scrapbook of facts and pictures about your book. Use your book jacket as the cover.

 The Book Nook

Corn Is Maize *by Aliki* This book tells how corn grows and how Native Americans made it a part of their lives.	Dinosaurs of North America *by Helen R. Sattler* This book gives facts about the giant reptiles that lived in North America long ago.

Student's Resource Book

Study Skills Lessons

1 Alphabetical Order

Words listed in the same order as the letters of the alphabet are in **alphabetical order**. This order helps you find words easily. For example, words in a dictionary are in alphabetical order.

These rules will help you place words in alphabetical order.

1. Look at the first letter of each word. Decide which of those letters comes first in the alphabet.

apple   cart   guide

2. When the first letter is the same, use the second letter of each word.

fall   field   float   fruit

3. When the first two letters are the same, use the third letter of each word.

package   page   paint   palace   parade

Practice

Write each group of words in alphabetical order.

1. donkey, goat, bear
2. gate, pony, garden
3. rain, ride, rest
4. dancer, doctor, dentist
5. long, lovely, lost
6. belt, bee, bench
7. fish, fox, fly, frog
8. shell, share, ship, shoe

2 Finding Words in a Dictionary

A dictionary gives the meanings of hundreds of words. The words are listed in alphabetical order. To find a word, think, *Where in the alphabet would the word come?*

a b c d e f g	h i j k l m n o p q	r s t u v w x y z
beginning	**middle**	**end**

Then look in that part of your dictionary. *Collie* would be at the beginning, with the other *c* words.

The words in large, dark type on each dictionary page are called **entry words**. The first letter or two of all entry words on the page are usually the same.

---

collar • colonist

collar *noun* **1.** The part of a garment that fits around the neck. **2.** A neck band for an animal. ◊ *verb* To catch and hold by the collar; capture.
col•lar (kŏl′ər) *noun, plural* collars *verb* **collared, collaring**

collarbone *noun* A bone that links the breastbone and shoulder.
col•lar•bone (kŏl′ər bōn′) ◊ *noun, plural* **collarbones**

---

colonial *adjective* **1.** Of or relating to a colony. **2.** Of or relating to the 13 original colonies that became the United States.
co•lo•ni•al (kə lō′ nē əl) ◊ *adjective*

colonist *noun* A person who lives in a colony.
col•o•nist (kŏl′ə nĭst) ◊ *noun, plural* **colonists**

At the top of each dictionary page are **guide words.** The first guide word is the first entry word on the page. The next guide word is the last entry word. Each other entry word on the page comes between the guide words in alphabetical order. When you look up a word, find the guide words that are closest to the word you want.

Entry words usually are listed in simple forms, without endings such as *-ing* or *-s.*

TO FIND: **tossing**   LOOK FOR: **toss**
            shoes   **shoe**

Practice

A. Use the sample dictionary page to answer these questions.
   1. What are the first and last entry words on the page?
   2. What is the second entry word on the page?
   3. If you wanted to find the meaning for *collaring,* under what word would you look?

B. Study each set of guide words and the entry word. Write *before* if the entry word comes before the guide words. Write *after* if it comes after them.
   4. **beauty • beehive** bird   6. **party • passing** park
   5. **little • lizard**   log   7. **daisy • danger** dad

C. Write the entry word in each group that is on the same page as the pair of guide words.
   8. **dive • do**   dizzy   draw   deaf
   9. **club • coach**   crayon   chin   clue
   10. **mole • monkey**   music   meet   Monday
   11. **topcoat • tot**   tool   total   torch

3 Choosing the Correct Definition

A dictionary tells you the **definitions** of words. A definition is the meaning of a word. If there is more than one definition for a word, a dark number shows where each new definition begins.

definition   example sentence

gentle *adjective* **1.** Mild and soft: *A gentle breeze rustled the leaves.* **2.** Kindly and thoughtful: *You have a gentle nature.* **3.** Easily managed;
synonym ——→ tame: *That is a gentle pony.*
gen•tle (jĕn′tl) ◊ *adjective* **gentler, gentlest**

Sometimes a single word is used as a definition. That word is called a **synonym**. A synonym has almost the same meaning as the entry word.

An **example sentence** may follow the definition. That sentence helps you better understand the meaning of a word. It shows you how the word can be used.

Which is the correct definition for *gentle* as it is used in this sentence?

Her pet raccoon seemed quite *gentle*.

To help you decide, follow these steps.

1. Read each of the definitions for the word.
2. Reread the sentence.
3. Choose the definition that makes the most sense in the sentence.

The third definition, "easily managed; tame," makes the most sense.

Sometimes you will see two dictionary words that are spelled alike. However, they have very different meanings. To show that each word is a separate entry, a little raised number follows the word.

In the part of a dictionary shown below, how many entries are there for the word *squash*? Remember that an entry word appears in large, dark type. You can see that there are two entries for *squash*—*squash*[1] and *squash*[2].

squash[1] *noun* A fleshy fruit that is related to the pumpkins and the gourds and is eaten as a vegetable.
squash[1] (skwŏsh) ◇ *noun, plural* squashes *or* squash
squash[2] *verb* To press or be pressed into a flat mess or pulp; crush.
◇ *noun* A game played in a walled court. The players hit a hard rubber ball with a racket.
squash[2] (skwŏsh) ◇ *verb* squashed, squashing
◇ *noun*

Which is the correct meaning for *squash* as it is used in this sentence?

Apples rolled into the street and were *squashed* by cars.

To help you decide which word to choose, follow these steps.

1. Read the definitions after each entry word.
2. Reread the sentence.
3. Choose the definition that makes the most sense in the sentence.

Squash[2] makes the most sense. The apples were "pressed flat" by cars.

Practice

A. Read each of these entry words and definitions. Then write the answers to the questions.

> **soil**[1] *noun* **1.** The top layer of the earth in which plant life can grow. **2.** Land; country: *The settlers landed on foreign soil.*
> **soil**[1] (soil) ◇ *noun, plural* **soils**
> **soil**[2] *verb* To make or become dirty.
> **soil**[2] (soil) ◇ *verb* **soiled, soiling**
> **solve** *verb* To find an answer to.
> **solve** (sŏlv) ◇ *verb* **solved, solving**
> **soon** *adverb* **1.** Before long: *We'll soon know if we passed the test.* **2.** Early: *We arrived at the party too soon.* **3.** Quickly: *We have to finish this job as soon as possible.*
> **soon** (so͞on) ◇ *adverb* **sooner, soonest**

1. Which entry word means "to find an answer to"?
2. What synonyms does *soon* have?
3. What is the first definition of *soon*?
4. What is the third example sentence for *soon*?
5. Which entry for *soil* means "to make or become dirty"?
6. How many definitions does the first entry of *soil* have?

B. Which entry word for *soil* is being used in each sentence below? Write the entry word and the raised number after it.

7. Soon footprints will *soil* the clean floor.
8. Cover the potatoes with rich, dark *soil*.
9. The Hobbs left foreign *soil* and returned home.
10. Worms wiggle their way through the *soil*.

4 Using the Library

The library is filled with books. It is arranged so that you can find books easily. There are places for fiction books, nonfiction books, and reference books.

Stories that are made up by the authors are called **fiction** books. These books are arranged in alphabetical order by the last names of the authors.

Nonfiction books contain facts. These books tell about real people, animals, places, and events. Nonfiction books are grouped by subject. The subjects are given numbers.

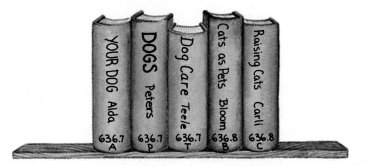

You use **reference** books to find information. They are kept in a separate part of the library.

REFERENCE BOOK	DESCRIPTION
atlas	a book of maps
dictionary	a book having word meanings
encyclopedia	a set of books with facts on a wide range of topics

If you need help, ask the librarian. The librarian also checks out any books you want.

Practice

A. In which part of the library would you find each book? Write *fiction, nonfiction,* or *reference.*

1. *Winnie-the-Pooh,* by A. A. Milne, tells about a talking bear and his friends.
2. The *World Book Encyclopedia* contains facts about many subjects.
3. *Department Store,* by Gail Gibbons, tells what goes on in a real department store.
4. In *A Toad for Tuesday,* by Russell Erikson, Warton the Toad sets out to his aunt's house.
5. *Maps of North America* has maps of many places.
6. *Intermediate Dictionary* is for student use.
7. *Blueberries for Sal,* by Robert McCloskey, tells the story of a girl who mistakes a bear for her mother.
8. *Rabbits, All About Them,* by Alvin and Virginia Silverstein, gives facts about rabbits.
9. *The Riddle Monster,* by Lisl Weil, is about a prince who meets a horrible monster.

B. Number your paper 10 to 13. Write each fiction title and author in Sentences 1–9. Then draw a line under the word that helps you find the book on the library shelf.

C. Look at these nonfiction books. Under what subject would you find each one?

14. *This Is a Leaf*
15. *The Land and People of South Africa*
16. *The Great Cities: London*
17. *How to Identify Minerals*
18. *Exploring the Sun*

5 Using a Table of Contents

A table of contents tells what is in a book. It is at the front, after the title page. The **table of contents** lists the chapters, or parts, of the book. It also tells the page on which each chapter begins. Here is part of the table of contents from *The Friendly Dolphins,* a nonfiction book by Patricia Lauber.

<table>
<tr><td colspan="3" align="center">CONTENTS</td></tr>
<tr><td>1.</td><td>A Friend in the Sea</td><td>2</td></tr>
<tr><td>2.</td><td>Mammals in the Sea</td><td>14</td></tr>
<tr><td>3.</td><td>Dolphin Life</td><td>28</td></tr>
<tr><td>4.</td><td>Baby Dolphins</td><td>38</td></tr>
<tr><td>5.</td><td>Play and Intelligence</td><td>48</td></tr>
</table>

The table of contents in a nonfiction book tells what kind of information is in the book. The chapter titles give the main subjects, or topics.

Practice

Use the table of contents to answer the questions.
1. How many chapters are shown for *The Friendly Dolphins?*
2. What is the title of the first chapter?
3. On what page does the chapter about baby dolphins begin?
4. To learn how dolphins play, on what page should you begin reading?
5. Which chapter will tell you about mammals in the sea?

6 Using an Index

At the back of a nonfiction book, you often find an index. An **index** lists all the subjects, or **topics,** in alphabetical order. It helps you find information in the book. The numbers next to a topic show on what page or pages you can find facts about that topic.

Here is part of the index from the book *The Friendly Dolphins*.

```
                              INDEX
pages ─────────────────────┐
topic ───▶ adaptation, 36–37        blue whale, 19
           animal intelligence,     breathing, 16, 17,
              55                        32, 44
           baleen, 17–18            cold-blooded
           bats, 67                    animals, 34
           birth, 40–42             friendship among
           blubber, 34–37             dolphins, 41, 58
```

An index lists every page on which a topic is found. A dash (–) often appears between two page numbers. This means that the topic is discussed on each of those pages and all the pages in between.

Practice

Write the answers to these questions.

1. Where is an index found?
2. In *The Friendly Dolphins*, on what page can you find facts about the blue whale?
3. On what pages can you read about dolphin friendship?
4. Of these topics, which are listed in the index?

   bats   fins   breathing   brain   blubber

7 Using an Encyclopedia

An **encyclopedia** is a set of useful reference books. It tells about famous people, places, things, and events. These facts are found in pieces of writing called **articles**.

Encyclopedia articles are arranged in alphabetical order. They are put into books called **volumes**. Each volume is labeled with one or more letters. The letters tell you the beginning letters of the articles found in that volume.

To find information in an encyclopedia, you must first think of a key word. The key word should name a subject that you can find in the encyclopedia.

QUESTION: How many islands make up the state
of Hawaii?
KEY WORD: *HAWAII*

Practice

In which volume of the pictured encyclopedia would you find an answer to each question? Write the number and the letters of the volume that you would choose.

1. How soon can baby elephants walk?
2. How is glass made?
3. What did Betsy Ross do that made her famous?

8 Reading a Map

A **map** is a simple drawing of all or part of the earth. It shows how the area might look from the air.

Only the important details are shown. The names of places and things are often included.

Here is a map of the United States. Also shown are parts of two other countries, Canada and Mexico. Broken lines show the **borders,** or the places where the countries meet.

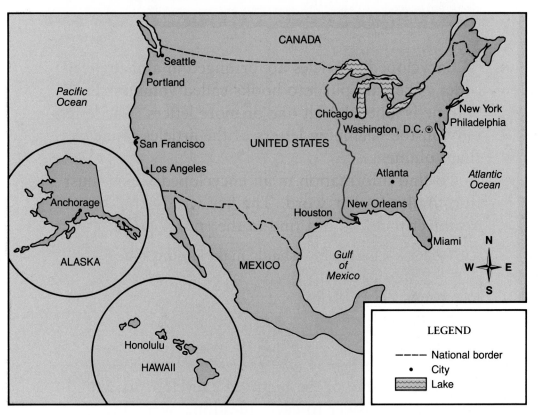

Small pictures, or **symbols,** stand for the things shown on a map. A map key, or **legend,** explains what each symbol means. For example, a black dot on this map stands for a city. Can you find the city of Houston? New York?

Another special symbol, the **compass rose,** shows directions on a map. This symbol points toward the north (**N**), east (**E**), south (**S**), and west (**W**).

How do you figure out which way you are going on a map? You simply find the part of the compass rose that points in the same direction. For example, if you flew from Houston to Miami, you would be flying east.

Practice

A. Use the map to answer these questions.
   1. Which symbol stands for lakes?
   2. Which color stands for the places on the map that are water?
   3. Which country lies to the north of the United States?
   4. Which country lies to the south of the United States?
   5. A river flows south through the United States. Into what body of water does it flow?
   6. Which ocean lies to the west of the United States?
   7. What are the names of two cities on the map?
   8. Find the city of Portland on the map. Which city lies to the north of it?
   9. Which city is next to a large lake?
   10. Which ocean is east of Miami?

B. Draw a map of one of these places or another of your own choosing. Make up your own symbols to show the interesting things that are there. Include a map legend too.

| school | your bedroom | park |
| playground | your neighborhood | your yard |

9 Test-taking Tips

You must take many kinds of tests every year at school. How can you do your best on each one of them? Just follow these tips.

How to Take a Test

Get Ready!
1. Study ahead of time for the test.
2. Bring a pencil and an eraser.
3. Write your name on the test.

Get Set!
1. Read or listen to the directions carefully.
2. Be sure that you understand what the test directions tell you to do.
3. Ask questions if you do not understand.
4. Know how to show your answer.
   Are you to underline it? circle it?
5. Know where to put your answer.
   Sometimes you must write it on the test. At other times, you must mark an answer sheet.

Go!
1. Do the easy items first.
2. If you are not sure of an answer, skip that item. You can go back to it later.
3. Go back to the hard items. Cross out the answer choices that you know are wrong. Then study the choices that are left. Make a good guess.
4. Do not spend too much time on any one question.
5. Check your answers.

Grammar and Usage Guide

Capitalization and Punctuation

Abbreviations

	An abbreviation is a short way to write a word. Most abbreviations begin with a capital letter and end with a period.
Titles	Mr. Juan Albino Ms. Leslie Clark Mrs. Frances Wong Dr. Janice Dodds **Note:** *Miss* **is not an abbreviation and does not end with a period.**
Days of the week	Sun. *(Sunday)* Thurs. *(Thursday)* Mon. *(Monday)* Fri. *(Friday)* Tues. *(Tuesday)* Sat. *(Saturday)* Wed. *(Wednesday)*
Months of the year	Jan. *(January)* Sept. *(September)* Feb. *(February)* Oct. *(October)* Mar. *(March)* Nov. *(November)* Apr. *(April)* Dec. *(December)* Aug. *(August)* **Note:** *May, June,* **and** *July* **are not abbreviated.**

Quotations

Quotation marks with commas and end marks	*Quotation marks* (" ") **set off someone's exact words from the rest of the sentence. The first word of a quotation begins with a capital letter. Use a comma to separate the quotation from the rest of the sentence. Put the end mark before the last quotation mark.** Linda said, "We don't know where Donald went."

Capitalization

Rules for capitalization	**Every sentence begins with a capital letter.** What a pretty color the roses are!
	The pronoun _I_ is always a capital letter. What should I do next?
	Begin each important word in the names of particular persons, places, or things (proper nouns) with a capital letter. George Herman Ruth New Jersey Liberty Bell
	Titles or their abbreviations when used with a person's name begin with a capital letter. Doctor Lin Mrs. Garcia
	Begin the names of days, months, and holidays with a capital letter. Labor Day is on the first Monday in September.
	The first and last words and all important words in the titles of books begin with a capital letter. Titles of books are underlined. The Hill and the Rock The Bashful Tiger

Punctuation

End marks	**A _period (.)_ ends a statement or a command. A _question mark (?)_ follows a question. An _exclamation point (!)_ follows an exclamation.** The scissors are on my desk. (_statement_) Look up the spelling of that word. (_command_) How is the word spelled? (_question_) This is your best poem so far! (_exclamation_)
Apostrophe	**Add an apostrophe (') and _s_ to a singular noun to make it show ownership.** doctor's father's grandmother's family's

Apostrophe (continued)	**For a plural noun that ends in _s_, add just an apostrophe to show ownership.** sisters' families' Smiths' hound dogs'
	Use an apostrophe in contractions in place of missing letters. can't _(cannot)_ we're _(we are)_ I'm _(I am)_
Comma	**Use commas to separate a series of three or more words.** Rob bought apples, peaches, and grapes.
	Use commas after _yes, no, well_, and order words when they begin a sentence. First, set the table. No, it is too early.
	Use a comma to separate the month and the day from the year. I was born on June 17, 1951.
	Use a comma between the names of a city and a state. Chicago, Illinois Miami, Florida
	Use a comma after the greeting and after the closing in a letter. Dear Uncle Rudolph, Your nephew,

Usage

Problem Words

Words	Rules	Examples
its	_Its_ is a possessive pronoun.	The dog wagged its tail.
it's	_It's_ is a contraction of _it is._	It's cold today.

Problem Words continued

Words	Rules	Examples
their	*Their* means "belonging to them."	Their coats are on the bed.
there	*There* means "at or in that place."	Is Carlos there?
they're	*They're* means "they are" (contraction).	They're going to the store.
two	*Two* is a number.	I bought two shirts.
to	*To* means "toward."	A cat ran to the tree.
too	*Too* means "also" or "more than enough."	Can we go too? I ate too many peas.
your	*Your* is a possessive pronoun.	Are these your glasses?
you're	*You're* means "you are" (contraction).	You're late again!

Adjective and Adverb Usage

Comparing	To compare two people, places, or things, add *-er* to most adjectives. This plant is taller than the other one.
	To compare three or more people, places, or things, add *-est* to most adjectives. This plant is the tallest of the three.

Pronoun Usage

I, me	Use *I* as the subject of a sentence. Use *me* as an object pronoun. Name yourself last when you talk about another person and yourself. Beth and I will leave for school soon. Give the papers to Ron and me.

Subject and object pronouns	**Use a subject pronoun as the subject of a sentence.** He wrote many works for the piano.
	Use an object pronoun after an action verb and after words like *to* and *for*. Let's share these bananas with her.
Possessive pronouns	**Use possessive pronouns to show ownership.** My dog is in the yard.

Verb Usage

Agreement: verbs in the present	**Add *s* to a verb in the present when the noun or pronoun in the subject is singular.** The child plays with the toy.
	Do not add *s* to a verb in the present when the noun or pronoun is plural. Some children run to the swings.
The verb *be*	**Use *am, is,* and *are* to show present time.** We are going on a picnic.
	Use *was* and *were* to show past time. The line was long. We were tired.
Helping verbs	**Use *has* with a singular noun in the subject and with *he, she,* or *it*. Use *have* with plural nouns and with *I, you, we,* or *they*.** Kip has phoned. I have taken a message.
Irregular verbs	**Some verbs have one special spelling to show past time. They have another spelling when used with *has, have,* or *had*.** Lisa ate the salad. Tim has eaten the fruit. My brother ran quickly. I have run a mile.

Spelling Guide

Words Often Misspelled

above	cough	half	o'clock	thought
again	could	have	of	through
already	country	head	often	to
answer	daily	heard	ought	toe
any	daughter	heart	pear	too
are	dead	heavy	people	touch
bear	death	helpful	picnic	traveling
beautiful	do	I	pink	trouble
been	does	island	pretty	two
believe	doesn't	judge	rebuild	until
beyond	dollar	July	roar	unusual
blue	done	June	rolling	voice
both	door	key	rough	want
bought	double	large	rule	warm
boxing	dying	laugh	said	was
bread	early	let's	school	wash
break	electric	libraries	sew	watch
breakfast	enough	listen	some	weigh
breath	eye	live	son	what
brother	falling	lose	spread	where
brought	feet	love	straight	who
buy	fought	lying	sure	woman
caught	friend	many	taught	won
ceiling	from	message	tear	wonderful
certain	front	money	teeth	won't
chief	ghost	move	their	word
children	give	neighbor	there	work
choice	glove	noise	they	worried
color	gone	no one	they're	you
comb	great	none	think	young
come	guess	nothing	though	your

Spelling Guidelines

1. The short vowel sound in a word is usually spelled with just one letter: **a, e, i, o,** or **u.**

last	best	lot
flag	left	pop
sand	chip	club
send	bit	luck

2. Long vowel sounds may be spelled vowel-consonant-**e**.

same	**mine**	**note**
made	**smile**	**home**

3. The long **a** sound may be spelled **ai** or **ay**. The long **e** sound may be spelled **ee** or **ea**.

paint	hay	sneak
chain	seem	treat
tray	feel	real

4. The long **o** sound may be spelled **o, oa,** or **ow**. The long **i** sound may be spelled **i, ie,** or **igh**.

sold	own	tie
coach	blow	bright
soap	kind	tight

5. The vowel sound in **town** or **found** may be spelled **ow** or **ou**.

now	**how**	**loud**
crowd	mouth	count

6. The vowel sound in **draw** or **walk** may be spelled **aw** or **a** before **l**.

straw	saw	small
crawl	talk	call

7. The letters **wr, kn,** and **tch** sometimes spell one consonant sound.	**wr**ap **wr**ong	**kn**ow **kn**ee	scra**tch** pi**tch**
8. The vowel + r sounds in **harm, corn,** or **near** may be spelled **ar, or,** or **ear**.	sm**ar**t h**ar**m M**ar**ch	st**or**m f**or**ty sp**or**t	y**ear** cl**ear** f**ear**
9. The vowel + r sounds in **clerk, dirt,** or **burn** may be spelled **er, ir,** or **ur**.	s**er**ve h**er**d n**er**ve	th**ir**sty sh**ir**t b**ir**d	n**ur**se ch**ur**ch h**ur**t
10. The vowel sound in **joy** or **oil** may be spelled **oy** or **oi**.	t**oy** b**oy**	p**oi**nt j**oi**n	c**oi**n br**oi**l
11. The consonant sound in **jeans** or **page** may be spelled **j** or **g**.	**j**ust **j**ump	**g**ym **g**entle	sta**g**e hu**g**e
12. The sound of the vowel + r in **chair** or **care** may be spelled **air** or **are**.	h**air** f**air** **air**	st**air** p**air** sc**are**	b**are** r**are** d**are**
13. Two words that sound alike but have different spellings and meanings are called **homophones**.	knew new	our hour	pale pail

14. When a word ends with **e**, drop the **e** before adding **-ed** or **-ing**. When a word ends with one vowel followed by one consonant, double the consonant.

car**ed**	chas**ed**	trip**ping**
wav**ing**	jok**ing**	pat**ted**
lik**ing**	step**ping**	tap**ping**
bak**ed**	dot**ted**	grin**ned**

15. The vowel sound in **spoon** or **chew** may be spelled **oo** or **ew**.

r**oo**t	t**oo**th	fl**ew**
ball**oo**n	st**ew**	dr**ew**

16. A **prefix** is a word part added to the beginning of a word. A **suffix** is a word part added at the end of a word.

return	thank**ful**	slow**ly**
rejoin	use**ful**	teach**er**
uncommon	sad**ly**	help**er**

17. When a word ends with a consonant and **y**, change the **y** to **i** and add **-es** or **-ed**.

stor**ies**	pupp**ies**	hurr**ied**
cherr**ies**	bab**ies**	dr**ied**
famil**ies**	cr**ied**	stud**ied**

18. The spelling of the final **er** or **le** in a two-syllable word must be remembered.

und**er**	matt**er**	unc**le**
summ**er**	gent**le**	hand**le**
lett**er**	app**le**	ab**le**

19. The consonant sound in **cent** or **space** may be spelled **c** or **s**.

ni**ce**	pri**ce**	ba**se**
city	**c**enter	ca**se**

A Thesaurus for Writing

How to Use This Thesaurus

Your Thesaurus for Writing can help you improve your writing. Suppose that you write this sentence:

Friday was warm, but today is damp and cold.

You notice that *cold* is not a very interesting word. To find a better word, just look up *cold* in the alphabetical listing.

main entry word ———→ part of speech
cold *adj*. without heat.
meaning ———
sample sentence ———→ Keep milk *cold*, or it will spoil.
chilly unpleasantly cool. The fire warmed the *chilly* room.
synonyms ———
frosty very cold. On *frosty* mornings, we wear mittens.
antonyms ———
antonyms: hot, warm *adj*.

Under the **main entry** for *cold,* you find two synonyms—two words that are close in meaning to *cold.* The words are *chilly* and *frosty.* Study the definition and the sample sentence for each synonym.

Now you know which word to use for *cold*:

Friday was warm, but today is damp and chilly.

The main entry also lists antonyms—words that have the opposite meaning.

Cross-references help you find words too. This example tells you to find *chilly* under *cold.*

cross-reference entry → **chilly** See *cold.*

A

active *adj.* moving about; busy.
He needed a rest after his
active day.
energetic full of strength and
pep. My *energetic* sister can
exercise for hours.
lively full of life and cheer. The
lively music kept us dancing.
antonyms: lazy, slow

admire See *like.*

alarm See *frighten.*

amusing See *funny, interesting.*

appreciate See *like.*

appropriate See *good.*

aqua See *blue.*

aroma See *smell.*

assemble See *gather.*

attempt See *try.*

B

bake See *cook.*

beige See *brown.*

big *adj.* of great size. It is easy
to get lost in a *big* city.
large bigger than average. The
large yard gave the children
plenty of room to play.
enormous very big. Look at that
enormous elephant!

huge giant-sized. It took days to
climb the *huge* mountain.
tremendous great in size or
amount. A *tremendous* wind
blew the roof off.
antonyms: little, small, tiny

bind See *fasten.*

bitter See *sour.*

blend See *mix.*

blue *adj.* having the color of a
clear sky. On a sunny day, the
blue boat matched the sky.
navy of a very dark blue. The
police wore *navy* uniforms.
aqua of a greenish-blue color.
Closer to shore, the water has
a lovely *aqua* color.

bold See *brave.*

boost See *lift.*

brave *adj.* having or showing
courage. The *brave* woman
risked her life to help us.
bold willing to take chances.
The *bold* man spoke out
against the cruel leader.
daring brave and adventurous.
The *daring* explorers set off
into the unknown jungle.
antonyms: cowardly, nervous

broil See *cook.*

brown *adj.* of the color of wood
or soil. The leaves on the
ground had all turned *brown.*

➡

A THESAURUS FOR WRITING

A THESAURUS FOR WRITING

brown (continued)

tan of a yellowish brown. The fawn was *tan* with white spots.

beige of a pale brown. The *beige* cottages blended in with the sandy beach.

build See *make*.

C

calm See *quiet*.

capture See *catch*.

carrot See *orange*.

catch *v.* to get hold of something that is moving. I reached out to *catch* the ball.

capture to take by force. They *captured* and jailed the thief.

trap to catch by closing off any way of escaping. He *trapped* the air inside the balloon.

antonyms: free *v.*, release *v.*

celebration See *party*.

cheerful See *happy*.

chilly See *cold*.

chuckle See *laugh*.

close See *fasten*.

cold *adj.* without heat. Keep milk *cold*, or it will spoil.

chilly unpleasantly cool. The fire warmed the *chilly* room.

frosty very cold. On *frosty* mornings, we wear mittens.

antonyms: hot, warm *adj.*

collect See *get*.

compile See *gather*.

complete See *end*.

connect See *join*.

considerate See *thoughtful*.

cook *v.* to prepare food for eating by using heat. For dinner we *cooked* corn in boiling water.

bake to cook in an oven with steady, dry heat. The bread turned golden brown as it *baked* in the oven.

fry to cook in hot oil or fat. The chicken sizzled as it *fried* in the open pan.

broil to cook under or over heat. Dad *broiled* the chicken on the charcoal grill.

create See *make*.

D

danger *n.* the chance of harm. The pioneers feared the *dangers* of the wild forest and the harsh winters.

hazard something that may cause injury or harm. An old electric cord can be a fire *hazard*.

risk the chance of trouble. If you visit Gloria, you take the *risk* of catching the measles.
antonyms: protection, safeguard *n.*

daring See *brave*.

decent See *good*.

delicate See *soft*.

E

eager See *excited*.

end *v.* to bring to a close. The president *ended* the meeting.
finish to reach the end of. He *finished* the book.
stop to cut off an action. The fence *stopped* me from going farther.
complete to make or do entirely. I *completed* the work in a day.
quit to give up. If you *quit* trying, you will never win.
antonyms: begin, continue, start

energetic See *active*.

enjoy See *like*.

enormous See *big*.

entertaining See *interesting*.

enthusiastic See *excited*.

excited *adj.* stirred up. *Excited* teen-agers waved to the rock star.

eager filled with desire. The *eager* crowd pressed toward the theater entrance.
enthusiastic showing strong interest and liking. The *enthusiastic* listeners clapped.
antonyms: bored *adj.*, uninterested

exclaim See *say*.

experiment See *try*.

F

facts See *information*.

fascinating See *interesting*.

fasten *v.* to attach firmly. She *fastened* the tag to her shirt.
tie to fasten with a rope, string, or similar material. She *tied* back her hair with a ribbon.
bind to hold together. Birds *bind* their nests with mud.
close to shut. The lid of the trunk would not *close*.
seal to close tightly with glue, wax, or other hardening material. He *sealed* the letter so that no one would read it.
antonyms: loosen, open *v.*

finally See *last*.

fine See *good, great, nice*.

finish See *end*.

A THESAURUS FOR WRITING

A THESAURUS FOR WRITING

fluffy See *soft.*

form See *make.*

fresh See *new.*

frighten *v.* to make or become afraid. The thunder and lightning *frightened* us.
scare to startle or shock. A door slammed, *scaring* the sleeping cat.
alarm to make suddenly very worried. News of the accident *alarmed* the family.
terrify to frighten greatly. The spreading forest fire *terrified* the animals.
antonyms: calm *v.,* soothe

frosty See *cold.*

fry See *cook.*

funny *adj.* causing smiles or laughter. The *funny* clowns delighted the children.
amusing funny in a light, pleasant way. She smiled at the *amusing* bumper sticker.
silly not showing good sense; foolish. We tried not to laugh at his *silly* answer.
antonym: serious

G

gather *v.* to bring together in one place. He *gathered* a bunch of dandelions.

compile to put together into a single list or collection. They *compiled* cards to make a set.
assemble to put together the parts of. The directions told how to *assemble* the parts.
See also *get.*
antonyms: divide, scatter

gaze See *look.*

get *v.* to go after; fetch. I will *get* the broom from the closet.
collect to get payment of. "Did you *collect* the money that he owes you?" Frank asked.
See also *gather.*

giggle See *laugh.*

glad See *happy.*

glance See *look.*

gloomy See *sad.*

gold See *yellow.*

good *adj.* right, or as it ought to be. A rainy day is a *good* time for doing chores.
fine very good; excellent. The teacher gave her a high grade for her *fine* work.
proper following social rules. It is *proper* to say thank you for a gift.
appropriate suitable. The shoes looked great, but they were not *appropriate* for hiking.

decent honest and thoughtful. Returning the lost ring was a *decent* thing to do.
antonyms: bad, rude, unsuitable

great *adj.* important; outstanding. The statue in the park honored a *great* leader.
terrific very good; very pleasing. I was thrilled with my *terrific* new radio.
fine enjoyable. *Fine* weather helped make the picnic a success.
wonderful marvelous. I thanked them again and again for the *wonderful* gift.
superb grand; splendid. It was worth climbing the mountain to enjoy the *superb* view.
antonyms: awful, terrible

green *adj.* having the color of grass. Some kinds of apples are still *green* when they are ripe.
olive of a dull yellowish green. The *olive* tent blended in with the surrounding bushes.
jade having a deep green color named for a stone that is used for jewelry. Rubber plants have shiny *jade* leaves.

H

happen *v.* to come into being. When did the earthquake *happen*?

take place to come about. The wedding will *take place* on board the ship.
occur to come to pass. How did the accident *occur*?

happy *adj.* very satisfied. I was *happy* to hear the good news.
glad pleased. "I would be *glad* to help," said Vic.
cheerful merry; lively. The *cheerful* song helps him forget his worries.
joyful showing, feeling, or causing great happiness. The puppy galloped toward its owner with a *joyful* bark.
jolly full of fun. The *jolly* waitress liked making us laugh.
antonyms: gloomy, miserable

hazard See *danger*.

hot *adj.* having flavorings that make the mouth feel warm. Use only a little of that *hot* mustard.
spicy tasting of pleasant, strong flavorings. I like chili and other *spicy* food.
sharp having a biting taste. *Sharp* cheese adds some life to plain crackers.
tangy pleasantly sharp in taste or smell. I like the *tangy* smell of freshly picked apples.
antonyms: mild, smooth

huge See *big*.

hurry See *run*.

I

information *n*. part or all of what is known about something. Do you have any *information* about the accident?
news information about recent events. The latest *news* is reported every hour.
facts information known to be true. The science book had many *facts* about the planets.
knowledge understanding. Her *knowledge* of French made her trip to France more interesting.

interesting *adj*. getting and holding attention. The *interesting* display brought many visitors to the museum.
amusing interesting in a light and pleasant way. Solving the clever puzzle was an *amusing* way to pass the time.
entertaining fun to watch, listen to, or take part in. The movie's music and dancing were *entertaining*.
fascinating very interesting. She could not put down the *fascinating* mystery story.
antonyms: boring, dull *adj*.

J

jade See *green*.

jog See *run*.

join *v*. to bring or come together. Let's *join* hands in a circle.
connect to serve as a way of joining things. A wire *connects* the brakes with the wheel.
unite to join in action for a certain purpose. Neighbors from near and far *united* to repair the flood damage.
antonyms: divide, part *v*., separate *v*.

jolly See *happy*.

journey See *trip*.

joyful See *happy*.

K

kind See *thoughtful*.

knowledge See *information*.

L

large See *big*.

last *adv*. at the end. Dessert is usually served *last*.
finally at the end of a series. *Finally*, after the glue dries, paint the model airplane.
antonym: first *adv*.

laugh *n.* a sound that shows amusement. His clever jokes won many *laughs*.

giggle a short, nervous laugh. We hid our *giggles* when the waiter dropped the tray.

chuckle a quiet laugh. Ed let out a *chuckle* as he read the joke.

antonyms: cry *n.*, sob *n.*, wail *n.*

lay See *put*.

lemon See *yellow*.

lift *v.* to pick up. I tried hard to *lift* the heavy box.

boost to give an upward shove or push. *Boost* me into the tree, please.

raise to move to a higher place. She *raised* the bucket from the bottom of the well.

antonyms: drop *v.*, lower *v.*

like *v.* to be fond of. He *likes* to hike in the mountains.

appreciate to know the worth or quality of. She *appreciated* the careful drawings.

enjoy to get joy or pleasure from. We *enjoyed* the lovely weather.

admire to look at with great pleasure. Everyone *admired* her beautiful hair.

antonyms: dislike *v.*, hate *v.*

lively See *active*.

look *v.* to use one's eyes. I *looked* for my friend in the crowd.

see to view. Did you *see* the parade?

glance to look quickly. He *glanced* at me as he ran by.

gaze to look steadily and long. For hours we sat *gazing* at the beautiful view.

stare to look at steadily with wide, unblinking eyes. She *stared* in wonder at the huge pumpkin.

loud *adj.* having a high volume of sound. The window slammed shut with a *loud* bang.

noisy making or filled with loud sounds. They had to shout to be heard in the *noisy* factory.

roaring making a loud, deep sound. The car's *roaring* engine drowned out the radio.

antonyms: quiet *adj.*, soft

M

make *v.* to produce. My mother bought meat to *make* stew.

build to make by putting together materials or parts. Barn swallows use mud and straw to *build* their nests.

form to shape. He *formed* a bowl from the clay.

➡

A THESAURUS FOR WRITING

make (continued)
create to bring into being. She *created* a design with leaves.

march See *walk*.

mend See *repair*.

mix *v.* to combine. *Mix* the peanuts and raisins in a bowl.
blend to combine completely. To make the color orange, *blend* red and yellow together.
stir to mix by using repeated circular motions. *Stir* the soup to be sure that it heats evenly.
antonyms: divide *v.*, separate *v.*

modern See *new*.

N

navy See *blue*.

new *adj.* having just come into being. We started a *new* school year last week.
fresh just made, grown, or gathered. I love eating *fresh* vegetables from my garden.
modern up-to-date. The office replaced the old typewriters with a more *modern* kind.
antonyms: old, outdated, stale *v.*

news See *information*.

nice *adj.* kind and thoughtful. It is a comfort to have *nice* people living next door.

pleasant giving enjoyment. Her friend's *pleasant* company helped the time pass quickly.
fine honest and good. He hoped that his children would grow up to be *fine* men and women.
antonyms: bad, disagreeable

noisy See *loud*.

O

occur See *happen*.

odd See *strange*.

odor See *smell*.

olive See *green*.

orange *adj.* of a reddish yellow color. The *orange* curtains made the room look like a brilliant sunset.
peach of a yellowish pink color named for the fruit. Her *peach* dress matched the glow in her cheeks.
carrot of a bright orange color named for the vegetable. He had freckles and *carrot* hair.

outing See *trip*.

P

party *n.* a gathering of people for pleasure and fun. All of her friends came to her birthday *party*.

celebration a party or other gathering for a special occasion. The *celebration* for the town's hundredth anniversary lasted a week.

patch See *repair*.

peaceful See *quiet*.

peach See *orange*.

peculiar See *strange*.

place See *put*.

pleasant See *nice*.

pleased See *proud*.

proper See *good*.

proud *adj.* feeling good about oneself. Kim was *proud* that she had won the prize.
pleased feeling enjoyment. I am *pleased* that you like my hat and scarf.
satisfied feeling that one's needs have been met. Jeff had hoped to win, but he was *satisfied* to come in second.
antonyms: ashamed, disappointed *adj.*

put *v.* to cause to be in a certain place. *Put* some salt in the soup.
place to put in a certain position or order. I *placed* the index cards in alphabetical order.

lay to put down in a flat or resting position. He *laid* his coat on the bed.
set to put on a surface. Please *set* that box on the table.

Q

quiet *adj.* having very little noise and activity. The busy street grew *quiet* after rush hour.
calm having only smooth, gentle noise and activity. As the wind died down, the water grew *calm*.
silent completely without sound. She listened for footsteps, but the night was *silent*.
peaceful quiet in a pleasant, relaxing way. In the *peaceful* meadow, the only sound was the bubbling brook.
still without any motion. Please remain *still* until I snap your picture.
antonyms: disturbing *adj.*, noisy, restless

quit See *end*.

R

race See *run*.

raise See *lift*.

rare See *unusual*.

recover See *save*.

red *adj.* having the color of strawberries. Stop signs are usually painted *red.*

scarlet of a bright red. The ambulance flashed its *scarlet* light.

ruby of a deep red. Cherries are ripe when they turn *ruby.*

repair *v.* to fix something that is damaged. Do you think that the shop can *repair* our TV?

mend to repair a tear, hole, or crack. Please *mend* the hole in my shirt.

patch to repair by covering with a piece of material. We *patched* the hole in the roof with tar paper.

antonyms: break *v.,* tear *v.*

rescue See *save.*

risk See *danger.*

roaring See *loud.*

ruby See *red.*

run *v.* to move quickly on foot. I *ran* inside to answer the phone.

race to rush at top speed. As the bus pulled away, she *raced* to catch it.

hurry to act or move quickly. *Hurry,* or we will be late.

jog to run at a slow, steady speed. He *jogs* around the block for exercise.

S

sad *adj.* feeling or causing sorrow. The teacher's illness was *sad* news for the class.

unhappy without joy or pleasure. She tried to forget the *unhappy* summer.

gloomy mildly sad. Losing made the team feel *gloomy.*

antonyms: cheerful, glad

sample See *try.*

satisfied See *proud.*

save *v.* to keep from danger or harm. The canned food *saved* them from going hungry.

rescue to remove from a dangerous place. I *rescued* my cat from the tree.

recover to get something back; to regain. The police *recovered* the lost child and took him home.

antonyms: endanger, lose

say *v.* to make known or put across in words. What did your brother *say* in the letter?

speak to say with the voice; talk. The teacher *spoke* into the microphone.

tell to describe. Teresa *told* us what happened at the party.

state to say in a very clear, exact way. The rule *states* that dogs are not allowed.

exclaim to cry out or say suddenly. "That's mine!" *exclaimed* the child.

scare See *frighten.*

scarlet See *red.*

scent See *smell.*

seal See *fasten.*

see See *look.*

set See *put.*

sharp See *hot.*

silent See *quiet.*

silly See *funny.*

smell *n.* what the nose senses. The *smell* of smoke warns us of fire.
scent a light smell. The woman had left, but the *scent* of her perfume remained.
odor a strong smell. The *odor* of moth balls clung to the coat.
aroma a pleasant smell. The *aroma* of Aunt Carrie's cooking made us all hungry.

soft *adj.* not hard or firm. The *soft* cheese spread smoothly.
delicate very easily broken or torn. A slight tug will snap the *delicate* chain.
tender easily bruised or hurt. Her *tender* hands were blistered from pulling weeds.

fluffy light and airy. A puff of wind scattered the *fluffy* feathers.
antonyms: solid, sturdy, tough

sour *adj.* having an acid taste. The lemon juice was too *sour* to drink.
tart sharp in taste. I like *tart* apples better than sweet ones.
bitter having a strong, unpleasant taste. He hated to take the *bitter* medicine.
antonym: sweet

speak See *say.*

spicy See *hot.*

spin See *twist.*

stare See *look.*

state See *say.*

still See *quiet.*

stir See *mix.*

stop See *end.*

strange *adj.* not ordinary. The *strange* look on her face made me wonder what happened.
odd somewhat out of the ordinary. He had an *odd* habit of carrying an umbrella even on sunny days.
weird strange in a frightening way. A *weird* noise made us jump out of our chairs.

➡

strange (continued)

peculiar puzzling or suspicious. It seemed *peculiar* that he should be digging in his garden in mid-winter.

antonyms: familiar, normal

stride See *walk*.

superb See *great*.

T

take place See *happen*.

tan See *brown*.

tangy See *hot*.

tart See *sour*.

tell See *say*.

tender See *soft*.

terrific See *great*.

terrify See *frighten*.

test See *try*.

thoughtful *adj.* caring about the feelings of others. How *thoughtful* of you to remember my birthday!

kind showing goodness, generosity, or sympathy. It was *kind* to share your lunch.

considerate helpful. Because my arms were full, a *considerate* girl held the door for me.

antonyms: mean, rude, selfish

tie See *fasten*.

tour See *trip*.

trap See *catch*.

trek See *trip*.

tremendous See *big*.

trip *n.* a period of time spent going from one place to another. When are you leaving for your *trip* to Canada?

journey a long trip. It took the pioneers months to make the *journey* across the plains.

tour a trip for the purpose of seeing interesting places and sights. The *tour* included visits to museums and theaters.

trek a slow, hard journey. After their *trek* through the desert, the soldiers were tired and ragged.

outing a short outdoor trip for pleasure. We are going to the park for a family *outing*.

try *v.* to put to use for the purpose of judging. If you like apples, *try* these.

test to use in order to discover any problems. *Test* the brakes and the horn to be sure that they work.

sample to test by trying a small part. Before you serve a dish to your guests, *sample* it.

experiment to do a number of tests to find out or prove something. She *experimented* to find out which colors looked best in her design.

attempt to make an effort. After checking the airplane carefully, the pilot *attempted* to fly.

turn See *twist*.

twirl See *twist*.

twist *v.* to move in a winding path. The road *twisted* through the mountains.

turn to move around a center. *Turn* the cap to the right to open it.

twirl to cause to move quickly around a center. The cowhand *twirled* the lasso and then threw it.

spin to move very quickly and continuously around a center. The ice skater *spun* like a top on one foot.

U

unhappy See *sad*.

unique See *unusual*.

unite See *join*.

unusual *adj.* not ordinary. It was *unusual* for my quiet brother to shout.

rare almost never seen or found. The *rare* penny was worth thousands of dollars.

unique being the only one of its kind. Most dancers dressed alike, but Anne's costume was *unique*.

antonyms: normal, ordinary, regular

W

walk *v.* to move or travel on foot. When my bike broke, I had to *walk* home.

march to walk to an even beat. The soldiers *marched* in the parade.

stride to walk with long steps. Sure of his answer, John *strode* to the chalkboard.

weird See *strange*.

wonderful See *great*.

Y

yellow *adj.* having the color of the sun. *Yellow* dandelions dotted the lawn.

gold having a deep yellow color. Wheat turns *gold* when it is ripe.

lemon having a bright yellow color named for the fruit. The *lemon* walls seemed to fill the room with sunshine.

Index

Numbers in **bold type** indicate pages where skills are taught.

INDEX

INDEX

INDEX

(Acknowledgments continued.)

"The Storm," abridged from *A Lion to Guard Us* by Clyde Robert Bulla (Thomas Y. Crowell); additional excerpt on p. 306. Text copyright © 1981 by Clyde Robert Bulla. Reprinted by permission of Harper & Row, Publishers, Inc., and Bill Berger Associates as agents for Clyde Robert Bulla.

"Vern," from *Bronzeville Boys and Girls* by Gwendolyn Brooks. Copyright © 1956 by Gwendolyn Brooks Blakely. Reprinted by permission of Harper & Row, Publishers, Inc.

"When the day is cloudy . . ." from *The Religion of the Crow Indians* by Robert H. Lowie. Copyright © 1971 by Robert H. Lowie. Courtesy, American Museum of Natural History.

Brief Quotations

from "Where Have You Been Dear?" in *Dogs & Dragons, Trees & Dreams: A Collection of Poems* by Karla Kuskin. Copyright © 1962 by Karla Kuskin. Reprinted by permission of Harper & Row, Publishers, Inc. (p. x)

from *My Friend Charlie* (excerpt) by James Flora, copyright © 1964 by James Flora. Reprinted by permission of Harcourt Brace Jovanovich, Inc. (p. 28)

from "The Crane Maiden" by Miyoki Matsutani. Copyright © 1968 Parents Magazine Press. (p. 168)

from *Farmer Boy* by Laura Ingalls Wilder. Text copyright 1933 by Laura Ingalls Wilder. Copyright renewed 1961 by Roger L. MacBride. Reprinted by permission of Harper & Row, Publishers, Inc. (p. 245)

from "Calendar" in *A Song I Sang to You* by Myra Cohn Livingston. Copyright 1984, 1969, 1967, 1965, 1959, 1958 by Myra Cohn Livingston. Reprinted by permission of Marian Reiner for the author. (p. 260)

from "August 8" in *Destination Ashes* by Norman Jordan. Copyright © 1970 by Norman Jordan. Reprinted by permission of the author. (p. 294)

from "Little" by Dorothy Aldis, reprinted by permission of G. P. Putnam's Sons from *Everything and Anything* by Dorothy Aldis, copyright 1925–1927, copyright renewed 1953–1955 by Dorothy Aldis. (p. 326)

from "Insects with Warning Colors," adapted with permission of Four Winds Press, an imprint of Macmillan Publishing Company from *Backyard Insects* by Millicent E. Selsam and Ronald Goor. Copyright © 1981 by Millicent E. Selsam and Ronald Goor. (p. 360)

from *Ants* by Henry Pluckrose, copyright © 1981. Reprinted by permission of Aladdin Books Ltd., London. (p. 375)

Dictionary entries from *Houghton Mifflin Intermediate Dictionary*. Adapted and reprinted by permission from Houghton Mifflin Company, © 1986 by Houghton Mifflin Company. (pp. 392, 394, 395, and 396)

from *The Friendly Dolphins* by Patricia Lauber. Copyright © 1963 by Random House, Inc. Reprinted with permission of Random House, Inc. (pp. 399, 400)

Grateful acknowledgment is given to Tamar Dor-Ner, Sally Haskell, Billy Johnson, Chris Harbert, and Thea Gelbspan for permission to adapt and reprint original material as student writing models in the Writing Process lessons.

The publisher has made every effort to locate each owner of the copyrighted material reprinted here. Any information enabling the publisher to rectify or credit any reference is welcome.

Credits

Series design concept and cover design by Ligature, Inc.
Front cover and title page photograph: Craig Aurness/Woodfin Camp & Assoc.
Back cover and page 390: Ralph Brunke

Illustrations

Anthony Accardo: 38, 241
Mary Jane Begin: 2, 5–7, 130, 131, 136, 138, 139, 211, 264, 272, 276
Boston Graphics/Paul Foti: 402
Marc Brown: 170, 172–174, 181, 182, 192
Susannah Brown: 103, 104, 106

Christine Czernota: 44, 46, 47, 49, 116, 118–119, 121, 184, 186–187, 189, 248, 250–251, 253, 314, 316–317, 319, 378, 380–381, 383

Thomas Di Grazia: 30, 31, 33, 52

Bonnie Gee: 30–35, 40, 43, 54, 176, 194

Leigh Grant: 58, 62–65, 68–70, 72, 134, 147, 198, 206, 328, 330, 341

Deirdre Newman Griffin: 60, 200, 204, 208, 268–270, 332

Judith Griffith: 94–105, 109, 113, 124, 126, 232–238, 240, 244, 247, 256

Ellen Harris: 262, 265

Marilyn Janovitz: 8, 12, 14, 74, 140, 148, 150, 212, 274, 278, 338, 342

Meg Kelleher: 397, 401

Dave Kelley: 258

Carol Schwartz: 45, 55, 117, 127, 185, 195, 249, 259, 315, 325, 379, 389

Collette Slade: 296–306, 322, 324

Mark Tetreault: 275

Pat Wong: 20, 21, 82, 156, 157, 222, 284, 352

Lane Yerkes: 362–369, 376, 386

Hand marbleized English Cockerell paper from Andrews/Nelson/Whitehead Corporation, Long Island City, New York: 16, 17, 76, 77, 152, 153, 170–175, 214, 215, 280, 281, 344, 345

Photographs

0–1 Nancy Sheehan.   3 Dr. E.R. Degginger.   9 Robert V. Eckert/The Picture Cube.   11 (top) Michal Heron.   11 (bottom) Southern Stock Photos.   28–29 Christina Tomson/Woodfin Camp & Assoc.   53 (left) Pam Hasegawa/Taurus Photos.   53 (right) Ellis Herwig/Stock Boston.   56–57 Frank Whitney/The Image Bank.   59 Sheryl McNee/Tom Stack & Assoc.   61 Michal Heron.   92–93 Mike Mazzaschi/Stock Boston.   110 (top) The Stock Market.   110 (bottom) M.P.L. Fogden/Bruce Coleman Inc.   128–129 Animals Animals/Stephen Dalton.   133 Breck P. Kent.   143 Gerald Corsi/Tom Stack & Assoc.   145 NASA.   168–169 Claire and George Louden.   178 Dean Abramson/Stock Boston.   193 Henry Kaiser/Leo deWys Inc.   196–197 Dr. E.R. Degginger.   201 New York Zoological Society.   203 Youngblood.   209 Greg Johnston 1985/ Southern Stock Photos.   230–231 Earth Scenes/Michael Habicht.   257 Courtesy of the New York Historical Society, New York.   260–261 David Muench Photography.   263 Seth Goltzer/The Stock Market.   266 (left) Lisa Podgur/Index Stock.   266 (middle) Jon Goell/The Picture Cube.   266 (right) Michael Tamberrino/The Stock Market.   267 Luis Villota/The Stock Market.   294–295 James L. Ballard.   323 (top left) Michal Heron.   323 (top right) Bohdan Hrynewych/Stock Boston.   323 (bottom) Lou Jones. 326–327 Nancy Brown/The Image Bank.   329 Bob Daemmrich.   337 Dr. Ronald H. Cohn, The Gorilla Foundation.   360–361 John Shaw/Tom Stack & Assoc.   366 George D. Dodge & Dale R. Thompson/Tom Stack & Assoc.   367 George D. Dodge/Bruce Coleman Inc.   371 Animals Animals/Carson Baldwin.   372 S.L. Craig/Bruce Coleman Inc.   374 Kjell B. Sandved/Bruce Coleman Inc.   387 Earth Scenes/E.R. Degginger.

Charlie Hogg: 44, 47, 50, 51, 115, 116, 119, 122, 123, 184, 187, 190, 191, 248, 251, 254, 255, 314, 317, 320, 321, 378, 381, 384, 385

Fine Art

17 *Sunday Afternoon on The Island of La Grande Jatte,* by Georges Seurat, 1884–86, oil on canvas, 207.6 × 308 cm, Hellen Birch Bartlett Memorial Collection. © The Art Institute of Chicago. All rights reserved.   77 *A Holiday,* by Edward Henry Potthast, 1915, oil on canvas, 30½ × 40½ inches, Friends of American Art. © The Art Institute of Chicago. All rights reserved.   153 *Balloon,* by Grandma Moses. © 1987, Grandma Moses Properties Co., New York. (Anna Mary Robertson Moses, born in 1860, first began painting when she was very old. She became known all over the world as "Grandma Moses.")   193 (left) *The Rattlesnake,* by Frederic Remington, bronze, 1905, Amon Carter Museum.   215 *Faraway,* by Andrew Wyeth. Private Collection.   281 *The America,* by James E. Buttersworth, Mary Anne Stets Photo. Mystic Seaport Inc., Mystic, CT.   345 *Snap the Whip,* by Winslow Homer, The Metropolitan Museum of Art, Gift of Christian A. Zabriske, 1950.